Western Europe and South-East Asia

Co-operation or Competition?

Edited by

Giuseppe Schiavone

M
MACMILLAN

First published 1989

Published by
THE MACMILLAN PRESS LTD
Houndmills, Basingstoke, Hampshire RG21 2XS
and London
Companies and representatives
throughout the world

Printed in the People's Republic of China

British Library Cataloguing in Publication Data
Western Europe and South-East Asia:
co-operation or competition?
1. Western Europe. Economic relations with
South-east Asia 2. South-east Asia.
Economic relations with Western Europe
I. Schiavone, Giuseppe
337.4059
ISBN 0–333–46703–5

WESTERN EUROPE AND SOUTH-EAST ASIA

Also by Giuseppe Schiavone and published by Macmillan

INTERNATIONAL ORGANISATIONS: A Dictionary and Directory
THE INSTITUTIONS OF COMECON
EAST–WEST RELATIONS: Prospects for the 1980s (*editor*)

Contents

List of the Contributors

Florian Alburo, School of Economics, University of the Philippines and National Economic and Development Authority (NEDA), Manila

Mohamed Ariff, University of Malaya, Kuala Lumpur

Franco A. Casadio, Libera Università Internazionale degli Studi Sociali (LUISS) and Italian Society for International Organization (SIOI), Rome

Edward K.Y. Chen, Centre of Asian Studies, University of Hong Kong

W. Colozo, National Economic and Development Authority (NEDA), Manila

Luigi Vittorio Ferraris, Ambassador of Italy, Rome

Noboru Hamaguchi, School of Social Sciences, Waseda University, Tokyo

Rolf J. Langhammer, The Kiel Institute of World Economics, Kiel

Lau Teik Soon, Department of Political Science, National University of Singapore, and Member of Parliament, Republic of Singapore

Andreas Lukas, Chamber of Commerce, Augsburg

Elfriede Regelsberger, Institute for European Policy, Bonn

Kamal Salih, Malaysian Institute of Economic Research, Kuala Lumpur

Giuseppe Schiavone, Institute of European Studies 'Alcide De Gasperi', Rome, and University of Catania

Djisman S. Simandjuntak, Centre for Strategic and International Studies, Jakarta

Kusuma Snitwongse, Institute of Security and International Studies, Bangkok

Vincenzo Tornetta, Ambassador of Italy, Rome

Rolando Valiani, President, EFIM Holding Group, Rome

Phan Wannamethee, Ambassador of Thailand and former Secretary-General of ASEAN, Bangkok

Foreword

The Institute of European Studies 'Alcide De Gasperi', founded in Rome in 1956 by De Gasperi himself, is a research and teaching institution devoted to the promotion and advancement of studies on multilateral co-operation and integration in Western Europe.

In addition to its academic programme, operated within the framework of the Postgraduate School of European Studies, the Institute has been undertaking and promoting research on the basic political and economic issues of the East-West relationship[1] and on the external relations of the European Community (EC) with a special emphasis on the dialogue with other regional inter-governmental institutions.

An economic and commercial co-operation agreement for a renewable five-year period was signed by the EC with the member countries of the Association of South-East Asian Nations (ASEAN) in March 1980, thus paving the way for the development – on several planes – of stronger ties between Western Europe and South-East Asia. The agreement between the EC and ASEAN represents, to my knowledge, the first example of an institutionalised link connecting two regional groupings made up, respectively, of highly industrialised and developing countries. Other co-operation agreements have subsequently been concluded by the EC or are under negotiation.

The failure of repeated efforts to launch North-South negotiations at the global level within the United Nations' framework enhances the significance of inter-regional agreements as possible models for co-operative relations between countries at varying levels of development.

Moreover, the strategic location of ASEAN member countries in the Pacific Basin could provide the EC with an easier access to a new development centre for the world economy, should ASEAN decide to take an active role in the formation of a Pacific community. In fact, it has become increasingly fashionable over the past decade to stress the growing economic and technological dynamism of the Asia-Pacific region in contrast with the steady decline of Europe. Be all that as it may, the relationship between the EC and ASEAN appears to be of considerable importance not only for the organisations themselves and their member countries but for major economic powers bordering the Pacific.

With a view to providing a forum where experts and scholars from the EC and ASEAN countries could exchange ideas and develop scenarios based on a realistic appraisal of the opportunities for, and obstacles to, more effective ties between the two groupings, the Institute of European Studies – in association with the Institute of South-East Asian Studies (ISEAS) of Singapore – convened an international Conference in Rome.

The Conference, held on 11–13 December 1986, was made possible by a substantial grant from the Italian National Research Council (CNR) and by other contributions, notably from the Commission of the EC, the Directorate-General for Economic Affairs of the Italian Ministry of Foreign Affairs, and the Information Directorate of NATO. The participants were academics and experts from West European and South-east Asian countries; they were joined by scholars from China, Hong Kong, Japan and the USA.

The Conference works were divided into the following sessions: (1) Global Security, Regional Decision-making and Systems of Alliances; (2) The EC-ASEAN Inter-dependence in a Global Perspective; (3) Major Opportunities for EC-ASEAN Economic Co-operation; (4) Current Economic Trends and their Implications for EC and ASEAN External Relations; and (5) EC-ASEAN Interaction, Competition and Collaboration in a Multilateral Framework. Most of the papers presented at the Conference are now collected in this volume bringing viewpoints from Europe and Asia to highlight areas of convergence as well as differences against the background of today's volatile world economic and financial problems.

The papers deal with the political, economic and security factors affecting the EC-ASEAN relationship within the framework of regional and global trends. The problems and prospects of security in both Western Europe and South-East Asia are dealt with in the first part of the book which also examines the main aspects of the EC-ASEAN interdependence. The interplay of common and conflicting interests of the two organisations assumes particular relevance with regard to economic issues, chiefly trade, industrial co-operation and foreign investment.

The second half of the book focuses on the external relations of each group with major partners such as China, Japan and the United States. Despite remarkable dissimilarities with respect to their goals, functions and powers and the difficulty of generating a wider basis of consensus among the member countries on issues affecting the respective regions, the EC and ASEAN have succeeded, at least in a number of instances, in adopting a joint approach to key questions within the framework of the United Nations, international conferences and other multilateral fora. Although the possibilities of effectively asserting an alternative opinion in front of global or regional super-powers should not be overestimated, the fact remains that the EC and ASEAN appear basically able to convert common interests into a satisfactory geostrategic partnership. Unfortunately, the members of each organisation are frequently divided among themselves and reluctant to assume the full burden of responsibility at regional level. The decision-making processes which impinge on regional economic and political co-operation are far from perfect, especially as far as ASEAN is concerned. On the other hand, it should be stressed that the sophistication of the institutional and decision-making mechanisms cannot by itself replace the persistent lack of the political will to advance co-operation.

The papers explore postures and strategies of both the EC and ASEAN and put their relationship in the appropriate contexts, be they subregional, regional or global. In fact, the purpose behind this collection of conference papers is not so much to give a detailed account of the several areas of EC-ASEAN co-operation but to identify and assess the interests which shape the attitudes of the two organisations concerning mutual relations and their efforts to undertake concerted actions on the world scene. The interaction between politics and economics may often be a cause of friction and a deeper knowledge of each other's perceptions or strategy over basic international issues appears a prerequisite for effective movement towards consensus.

Since one of the most disturbing trends of the 1980s has been the weakening of confidence in multilateral co-operation, a more sustained co-operation between the EC and ASEAN during the final years of the current decade and beyond could provide substantial and much-needed support and, hopefully, a general sense of direction for international efforts at creating a more stable and equitable world.

In conclusion, I would like to express my thanks to all those responsible for the planning and organisation of the Conference, especially to Professors K.S. Sandhu and Hans Christoph Rieger on the side of ISEAS. I very much hope that the efforts of these people and of all others participating in the Conference will contribute to bring about a better understanding of the many opportunities for fruitful co-operation between Western Europe and South-East Asia in the coming 'age of the Pacific'.

EDOARDO MARTINO
President
Institute of European Studies
'Alcide De Gasperi'

Note

1. See G. Schiavone (ed), *East-West Relations: Prospects for the 1980s* (London: Macmillan, 1982), a collection of papers presented at an international conference convened by our Institute in Rome in 1980.

1 Western Europe and South-East Asia: Partners in a Pacific Age?

Giuseppe Schiavone

1. It has been a fashionable view among observers of international affairs during the past two decades that the rich resource endowments, impressive economic growth and development ambitions of Asian-Pacific countries would bring about a radical transformation in the global balance of power with the establishment of the Pacific region as the focal point of the world economy. Visions of a 'Pacific age' or 'Pacific century' have been variously articulated by scholars and experts as well as by political and business leaders.[1] Furthermore, several attempts have been made to translate the somewhat vague aspiration to a 'Pacific Community' into a blueprint for collective and pragmatic action. In fact, the growing recognition of a substantial interest in developing regional co-operation has originated a number of proposals intended to build a stronger relationship among Asian-Pacific countries and eventually to set up a framework for permanent inter-governmental co-operation in economic, political and security matters.[2]

It appears to be of paramount importance for Western Europe and especially the European Community (EC) to address the central fact of the rising importance of the Pacific Basin, finding ways to participate in the gradually expanding trade and investment opportunities through closer ties with key countries or groups of countries in the region. In particular, the East Asian portion of the Pacific Rim has shown an exceptional dynamism, characterised by spectacular growth rates and increasing economic interdependence, and would offer the EC outstanding opportunities to benefit from the incoming Pacific century.

As a matter of fact, several approaches to the Asia-Pacific region seem to be open to the EC. The more general pan-Pacific approach – yet to be effectively undertaken – should be directed toward bodies concerned with the economic and social development of the Pacific region as a whole, at both the intergovernmental and the non-governmental levels. It is worth stressing that private-sector groups have been particularly active over the past twenty years in encouraging economic and business co-operation throughout the region.

The second kind of approach – which has been under way since the mid-1970s – is based on the setting up of institutional links with sub-regional groupings, first and foremost among these being the Association of South-East Asian Nations (ASEAN).

The third kind of approach would involve the establishment of direct co-operation links between the EC on one side and a single Asian–Pacific country on the other side, as has notably been the case with China since the second half of the 1970s.

2. The picture of the Pacific Rim that emerges from basic political and economic data is that of a highly complex and varied region.

The concepts and proposals which have been developed so far identify potential participants in Pacific co-operation initiatives on the basis not only of geographical criteria but of political and economic considerations. The 'core' of the Pacific Basin is often meant to include North America (Canada and the United States), Japan, the six members (Brunei, Indonesia, Malaysia, the Philippines, Singapore, Thailand) of ASEAN, Australia and New Zealand. The non-ASEAN newly industrialising countries (NICs) – or, more precisely, newly industrialising economies (NIEs) – of Asia (Hong Kong, South Korea and Taiwan) should also be counted as part of the 'core'; obviously, the inclusion of Taiwan – whose government has been long since 'de-recognised' by most of the world's countries – would raise delicate problems of a political nature. The problems would be all the more serious since the prospective participation of China in any long-term co-operation effort involving Pacific Basin economies is deemed essential.[3]

Besides the 'core' countries and China, a broader geopolitical and economic concept of Pacific Basin interdependencies may embrace part of Latin America, especially countries whose trade and investment links with Japan and South-East Asia have shown a remarkable increase over the past few years. This might involve not only countries actually bordering the Pacific (such as Mexico, Peru and Chile), but also countries, notably Brazil, facing the Atlantic but with growing ties to development trends in the Pacific Basin.

The small island-states of the South Pacific, which gained independence during the past three decades, have special relationships notably with Australia and New Zealand. The importance of Australia's role in maintaining balance in the Pacific between the West and the Soviet Union need not be stressed. The establishment in 1986 of diplomatic relations between the Soviets and Vanuatu (formerly the Franco-British condominium of the New Hebrides) and the conclusion in 1985 of a fishing agreement between the Soviet Union and Kiribati (formerly the Gilbert Islands) have brought an element of uncertainty to the South Pacific environment.[4] The Soviet Union's deal with Kiribati was terminated after only one year, but a new fishing agreement was concluded with Vanuatu in early 1987. The situation may be further complicated by the continued unrest and demands for independence in New Caledonia and the growing opposition to French nuclear testing in the South Pacific.[5]

The non-ASEAN nations of South-East Asia, that is Burma and the countries of Indochina (Kampuchea, Laos and Vietnam), may also be viewed, from a geographical standpoint, as potential participants in a Pacific Basin integration scheme. However, the countries of Indochina – and, above all, Vietnam – are generally perceived by neighbours as a major threat to the area's political stability and security, not to mention the difficulties of establishing a meaningful multilateral co-operation with centrally-planned economies.

The last, but by no means the least, problem arises with regard to the Soviet Union. Beyond doubt an 'Asian-Pacific country', according to the definition used by Gorbachev in his major policy speech in Vladivostok in July 1986, the Soviet Union would radically alter through its participation all of the co-operation patterns which have been envisaged thus far by scholars and experts. On the other hand, the growing Soviet interest in multilateral co-operation and intergovernmental economic organisations, at both global and regional levels, should be carefully considered in any assessment of the pros and cons of a possible involvement of the Soviet Union in attempts to foster international co-operation in the Pacific Basin. It is well known that the Kremlin's 'new political thinking' assigns a lower priority to the military expansion of Soviet interests in the Third World and clearly prefers non-military means, such as trade and industrial co-operation, to further its aims and spread influence. This seems to be the case particularly of the Asia-Pacific area where, besides expanding relations with key regional actors, China and Japan, the Soviet Union would welcome the establishment of a permanent co-operation link with ASEAN, as a 'dialogue partner' – on an equal footing with Australia, Canada, the EC, Japan, New Zealand and the United States.

The technological dynamism, growing industrial and manufacturing base and exporting power of Pacific Basin countries are often contrasted with the perceived inability of Western Europe to adjust effectively to changing conditions in the world marketplace and to re-emerge swiftly from political and economic crises.

According to conventional wisdom, Western Europe is the region which stands to lose the most from the steady ascent of Asian-Pacific economies. The complexities of the economic and political commitments of the West European countries hinder more often than not the adoption of co-ordinated responses to the new structural and technological challenges emerging at the dawn of the twenty-first century.

The boldest experiment in economic integration undertaken so far, the European Community,[6] despite undeniable achievements spanning a thirty-year period, still appears unharmonious and unfinished. Considerable strains remain on the way to the creation of a single internal European market by 1992 and doubts arise on the Community's overall willingness to remove the rigidities which retard its economic performance. The ongoing round of multilateral trade talks will be an important opportunity to test the ability of the EC to liberalise both within and outside its market.

The inadequate commitment of the Twelve to overcoming national segmentation in favor of consistent long-term liberalisation and development strategies hampers adjustment to difficulties both within the EC and *vis-à-vis* non-member countries. The cumbersome decision-making process, based on the lowest common denominator of national interests, does not provide the EC with enough flexibility in international negotiations.

At a decisive moment in its fortunes, the EC finds itself confronted with a fresh Soviet approach to East-West relations, on both the military and economic planes, and with the objective necessity to co-operate with the United States and Japan with a view to reshaping the world's economic and monetary order.

3. Unlike Europe and Latin America, serious efforts at regional co-operation and consultation in the Asia-Pacific region have been few and far between. All the existing intergovernmental organis-

ations possess a rather loose character, ASEAN being the only notable exception. The six ASEAN countries constitute one of the most dynamic and fastest growing areas in the world and could act as a catalyst – on both the conceptual and the policy levels – in any attempt to draft co-operation schemes for the Pacific Basin.[7]

Although ASEAN's goals – according to the 1967 Bangkok Declaration – primarily lie in the economic, social, cultural and technical fields, a major effort has been made, since the late 1970s, toward a co-ordination of the member countries' foreign policies, especially on highly sensitive regional security issues. Activities at the intergovernmental level with a view to building a firm foundation for regional co-operation are complemented by several initiatives undertaken by the private sector which is playing an increasingly active role in each member country. The generally favourable business climate and free enterprise orientation prevailing in most member countries make it easier for the private sector to become involved in a wide range of co-operative activities in industrial development and trade within a formal ASEAN mechanism which is both flexible and pragmatic.

The gradual shift of the world's economic and political centre of gravity from the Atlantic to the Pacific calls not only for an intensification of co-operation among Asian-Pacific countries in dealing with major trade and development problems but for fresh and far-reaching political initiatives. Any initiative, however, has to confront itself with the widely different characteristics of the countries involved.

Unlike other regions which are made up of countries at roughly comparable levels of development (all developing countries either in Latin America or Africa, practically all developed countries in Europe), the Asia-Pacific region comprises two economic superpowers (the United States and Japan), three highly-industrialised nations (Australia, Canada, and New Zealand), a number of NICs (such as Hong Kong, South Korea, Singapore and Taiwan), and several developing countries at varying stages of industrialisation. Moreover, the whole gamut of economic systems is represented, from free market and *laissez-faire* to highly centralised planning. From a political standpoint, the region offers a no less articulate picture, its systems ranging from Western-style liberal democracies to rigid Marxist-Leninist régimes with a rich variety of shades in between. Indeed, the Asia-Pacific region is a microcosm presenting the many facets of political and socio-economic development.

The dramatic political, economic, social and cultural disparities which are typical of the Asia-Pacific region are reflected in the varied and sometimes split loyalties of its countries *vis-à-vis* international organisations.

The heterogeneity and the vastness of the area involved have made it impossible so far to establish a mechanism for permanent political co-operation on a region-wide scale as has been the case, notably, with the Organisation of American States (OAS) and the Organisation of African Unity (OAU) in their respective areas.

At one end of the spectrum there are three intergovernmental bodies whose membership embraces practically all the countries of the region: the Economic and Social Commission for Asia and the Pacific (ESCAP) which operates within the United Nations system; the Asian Development Bank (AsDB) which also includes over a dozen countries outside the region; and the Colombo Plan for Co-operative Economic and Social Development in Asia and the Pacific.[8]

All three organisations, within their respective terms of reference, aim to foster economic growth and social progress by assisting member countries in the co-ordination of economic policies and the promotion of investment and technological development.

At the subregional level, economic co-operation for development is carried out within a small number of intergovernmental bodies responsible for South-East Asia (as is the case of ASEAN), South Asia (the South Asian Association for Regional Co-operation – SAARC) and the South Pacific (the South Pacific Bureau for Economic Co-operation – SPEC).

At the other end of the spectrum there are intergovernmental economic organisations located outside the region which, however, number several countries of the Asia-Pacific among their members. The Paris-based Organisation for Economic Co-operation and Development (OECD) comprises Australia, Canada, Japan, New Zealand and the United States, while the Moscow-based Council for Mutual Economic Assistance (CMEA or Comecon) includes Mongolia and Vietnam as full members and other socialist countries of Asia as observers. The Asian-Pacific countries also play a role in most commodity-based international organisations.[9]

Within the framework of the Uruguay Round of Multilateral Trade Negotiations (MTNs), a significant effort for achieving a reform of agricultural trade is being carried out by the Cairns Group which comprises among its members both developed and developing countries of the Asia-Pacific region.

Most developing nations of the Asia-Pacific participate in a number of Third World groupings, notably the Non-aligned Movement and the Group of 77.[10] The Moslem countries of the region are among the members of the Organisation of the Islamic Conference (OIC). In several cases, the Asian-Pacific countries have actively contributed to shape the positions of the various groupings, avoiding divisive political disputes and moderating attacks against Western powers, especially the United States.

Besides intergovernmental institutions, a significant number of non-governmental organisations (NGOs) are actively involved in initiatives intended to foster regional co-operation and consultation on trade and investment issues. In particular, private business organisations have been addressing an ever-increasing range of regional issues and problems within the context of international markets and trade flows. Among non-governmental fora, an outstanding role has been played by the various sessions held by the Pacific Economic Co-operation Conference (PECC) since 1980.[11]

4. As regards co-operation in the field of security, mention should first be made of ANZUS, the 1951 tripartite treaty, signed by Australia, New Zealand and the United States, whose recent vicissitudes have commanded considerable attention;[12] each party agrees to 'act to meet the common danger' in case of aggression by means of armed attack on any of the other parties in the Pacific. The 1971 Five-Power Defence Arrangement (FPDA) is designed to protect Malaysia and Singapore in the event of an armed attack or threat of attack and provides for military co-operation and regular joint exercises among Australia, Malaysia, New Zealand, Singapore and the United Kingdom.

The 1954 Manila Pact, originally signed by Australia, France, New Zealand, Pakistan, the Philippines, Thailand, the United Kingdom and the United States, is still in force notwithstanding the withdrawal of France and Pakistan in the early 1970s and the dissolution, in 1977, of the institutional mechanism set up to implement the Pact, that is the South-East Asia Treaty Organisation (SEATO). Each party is bound to act in case of armed aggression and to enter into consultations if any other threat is posed to the territory, sovereignty or political independence of any party.

Over the past decades, both the United States and the Soviet Union have built a network of bilateral security and co-operation treaties and military-aid agreements with their respective allies in the region.[13] Besides the superpowers, China and Japan are likely to fulfill a role of growing significance in shaping the future security pattern for the Asia-Pacific. The steady improvement in the Sino-Soviet relationship is removing a major cause of tension, while the gradual increase in Japan's military spending may eventually translate into a shift, in regional defence responsibilities, from the United States to Japan itself.

The very fact that both superpowers have borders on the Pacific gives possible schemes of co-operation in the area a peculiar character, although the degree of involvement in regional issues is far greater in the case of the United States than in that of the Soviet Union. In fact, only recently has the Soviet Union been raising its profile in the region, a policy authoritatively reaffirmed by Gorbachev's speech in Vladivostok.

The speech underscored the Soviet Union's new foreign policy objectives in the Asia-Pacific region and called for a *rapprochement* with China and *détente* with Japan with a view, *inter alia*, to securing an Asia-Pacific nuclear-free peace zone. A proposal was put forward by Gorbachev for an Asia-Pacific version of the Helsinki Conference on Security and Co-operation in Europe (CSCE).[14]

The United States' growing ties with the Pacific Basin countries are reflected by a variety of indicators confirming both political and empirical evidence. The Asia-Pacific region is becoming more and more crucial to US economic and security interests, while the US West Coast has gradually increased its relative weight *vis-à-vis* the East Coast on several planes such as population, industrial locations and manufacturing power in key branches, and foreign trade flows.

The share of Pacific countries in US foreign trade has been showing a remarkable rise over the past twenty years while the share of Western European countries has been steadily declining. Given the current growth rates and economic potential of many Asian countries, the next decade could well see the Pacific Basin overtake Western Europe in economic influence. The relative loss of importance of Western Europe in US eyes affects not only transatlantic commercial and economic issues but the political relationship as well.

The continuing differences with its transatlantic partners on arms control and nuclear strategy and other West-West controversies resulting in increased European criticism of the volatility and discontinuity of US policies, as well as the gradual fading of communism as a political threat to the stability of Western European democracies are among the many factors which could lead the United States to diminish its commitment to Western Europe and to give a high priority to its Asian-Pacific interests. Although this should not necessarily materialise – at least in the near future – in a formal disengagement on the part of the United States, there seems to be little doubt that the post-World War II geopolitical order in both halves of Europe is being called into question. In particular, the agreement on the elimination of Intermediate-range Nuclear Forces (INF), reached at the Washington summit of December 1987, may have far-reaching implications for the American-European security ties, whilst enhancing Soviet superiority in non-nuclear forces *vis-à-vis* Western Europe. The Soviet Union itself is strained by its heavy commitments in an increasingly restive Eastern Europe which no longer appears a bulwark for the protection of Soviet security interests. The development of special inter-German relations may further complicate the picture for both superpowers.

However, the Soviet Union's primary security concerns may gradually shift from the European theatre to the regions adjacent to its Eastern borders – that is China and North-East Asia. Moreover, Soviet strategic involvement in South-East Asia, not long ago considered an area of secondary interest to the Soviet Union, has been rapidly expanding since the late 1970s. In the Asia-Pacific, the Soviet Union may well be preparing to confront the longer-term 'prospect of a US-Japan-China-ASEAN-ANZUS grouping, which will have parallel interests in containing the Indochina-Soviet bloc'.[15]

From a strictly economic standpoint, it should be noted that the Eastern regions of the Soviet Union participate, albeit modestly, in Pacific regional trade and that closer co-operation links and contacts are being developed with other Pacific powers, notably Japan, with a view to setting up joint ventures in the Soviet Far East.[16]

The countries of Eastern Europe may also play a role in Soviet strategy toward the Asia-Pacific region, above all within the context of the renewed Sino-Soviet dialogue.[17] Government and party links with China have been restored by all East European countries – with the obvious exception of Romania which had never severed ties with Beijing – and trade and economic relations are steadily improving.

5. The shift of the balance of global economic power in the direction of the Asia-Pacific region could be strengthened by the growing trend to concentrate on regional approaches to trade liberalisation, industrial co-operation and human resources development.

The crisis of the efforts to establish guidelines for a globally valid trade policy in the context of the North-South dialogue enhances the importance of regional co-operation in the Asia-Pacific. Whatever the outcome of the Uruguay Round of multilateral trade talks, the decline of the 'classical' order of international trade as enshrined in the basic rules of the General Agreement on Tariffs and Trade (GATT) now seems to be a widely accepted fact. The imposing proportion of 'managed' trade and the widespread use of non-tariff barriers (NTBs) have made the process of multilateral decision-making envisioned by GATT largely ineffective. Trade problems are further complicated by the persistent disarray of international co-operation in monetary matters.

The fundamental issues involved in the North-South dialogue (such as aid, minerals and energy trade, direct foreign investment and capital movements, technology transfer, food security) could be effectively approached on a regional scale by Asian-Pacific countries, thereby providing, in the longer run, a fresh impulse for relaunching broader negotiations between developed and developing nations. The establishment of some sort of free-trading area in the Pacific Basin – almost inevitably involving the United States and Japan – could be helpful in overcoming protectionist tendencies in the industrialised countries, strengthening the already favourable investment and development climate of the region and offering a permanent framework for comprehensive negotiations at the regional level on a non-discriminatory basis.

Within this context, the ASEAN countries – both severally and collectively – could exercise a much-needed stimulating and stabilising influence since it seems unlikely for a major power (either the United States or Japan) to assume the leadership in a Pacific-wide economic co-operation organisation.

The ASEAN countries themselves appear keen on avoiding an increased dependency *vis-à-vis* major Pacific partners, above all the United States and Japan, and would favour an outward-looking approach, including links with non-regional countries and organisations. This does not imply, of course, an unwillingness on the ASEAN side to strengthen regional ties, for which there are ample opportunities, but rather a broader and more articulated vision of the Association's role and long-term objectives.[18]

On the political and security plane, the establishment of a Zone of Peace, Freedom and Neutrality (ZOPFAN) in South-East Asia has long been one of the main objectives of ASEAN. Among the prerequisites of ZOPFAN – according to official declarations at the

Manila ASEAN Summit of December 1987 – there is the creation in the region of a nuclear-weapon-free zone (NWFZ) with the consequent prohibition on all participating countries to possess, deploy or manufacture nuclear weapons.[19] Plans for a South-East Asian NWFZ have been influenced to a certain extent by the precedent of the nuclear-free zone set up in the South Pacific and would complement the operation of such a zone.[20]

From other standpoints, however, the South-East Asian NWFZ would impose significant restrictions on the policy of deterrence carried out by the United States in the region. The ASEAN countries for their part are fully aware of the potential dangers of a reduced US military-security involvement in South-East Asia for the strategic balance of the region, should the Kampuchean conflict remain unsolved and the Soviet presence in Vietnamese bases at Danang and Cam Ranh Bay continue. Moreover, the build up of the Soviet Pacific Fleet is perceived as a threatening trend which alters the naval balance.[21] In this context, the case has been made for ASEAN countries to develop an appropriate naval capability, either individually or collectively.

6. Notwithstanding the importance of the evolution of the two super powers' military projection capabilities in the region and, more generally, in the Pacific Basin, it is the economic aspect of co-operation that appears to take pride of place in ASEAN's present and future concerns. Within this context, the EC may fulfill a role of the utmost significance both for itself and South-East Asia.

It would seem almost commonplace to stress the importance of ASEAN for the EC as a gateway to the economies of the Pacific Rim. This will be even more significant if substantive progress is made towards regional trade liberalisation around the Pacific.

Despite its loose institutional mechanism and the rather modest results achieved so far in fostering political cohesiveness and economic integration, the Association stands out as the most vocal and assertive intergovernmental grouping in the Pacific Basin and a key partner for initiatives in both regional and extra-regional co-operation. Two of the major economic powers in the world, the United States and Japan, are actively involved in Pacific Basin co-operation projects and the EC cannot afford to be left aside.

The EC-ASEAN economic and commercial co-operation agreement, concluded in 1980 and subsequently renewed, represented for both groupings a historically important move toward the development of a meaningful long-term relationship at the inter-institutional level. The measurable economic benefits of the EC-ASEAN agreement are still far from impressive but nevertheless, firm foundations have been laid for continued dialogue between developed and developing areas of the world which were previously unacquainted with each other's real concerns.

Although there is no question about their overall commitment to Western security objectives, the ASEAN countries may be more concerned by unfavorable economic trends, such as those affecting the prices of commodities, than by the geopolitical designs of the Soviet Union in South-East Asia and the Pacific Basin at large.[22]

The EC appears well fitted to meet at least some of the demands of ASEAN with regard to the expansion and diversification of commercial ties and the promotion of joint undertakings in the industrial sector. However, the EC members (with few exceptions) tend to give priority for their investments to areas other than ASEAN and when operating in ASEAN countries generally focus on services, notably banking and finance, rather than manufacturing. As for the intensification of trade, far too little attention has been paid on the EC side to the involvement of the private sector in interchanging views with the ASEAN counterpart on specific issues.

On the whole, the EC does not seem to recognise the challenges and opportunities offered by a greater flow of goods and services, technology and investment toward ASEAN countries both as a much-needed improvement in the relationship between the two groupings and as a means to secure a strong European presence in the fast-growing area of the Asia-Pacific.

Although the EC is increasingly perceived throughout the world as a tightly-knit economic unit, the Twelve continue in many cases to pursue short-term national advantages in a protectionist context, instead of joining efforts to secure technological competitiveness and play an adequate role in shaping, together with the economic powers of the Pacific Basin, a new order in international relations. At issue for the EC is not only how to create the single internal market by 1992 (along with reducing the soaring costs of farm policies, establishing future financing on a sound basis, and devising new instruments to aid poorer members) but how to effect the reconciliation of essential national interests with the broader European cause on a world scale.

Both the EC and ASEAN have yet to fully realise their respective potentials for integration, the former through the establishment of a single market and effective foreign policy co-ordination, and the latter through the creation of a trade area incorporating mechanisms for the gradual reduction of internal and external trade restrictions. The development of an effective EC-ASEAN partnership in the coming 'age of the Pacific' would probably be expedited by a stronger commitment by both organisations to the fulfillment of their long-term aims, overcoming internal stagnation and reinforcing external projection.

The prospect of continuing short-sighted protectionism on the part of the EC threatens the development of sound relations with ASEAN whose member countries need not only an inflow of European investment for the diversification of the manufacturing base but also a wider access for their products to the EC markets.

An extensive interaction of the two groupings would yield substantial benefits taking full advantage of the potential which exists beyond today's trade and economic disputes. Should competition instead of co-operation prevail, the EC would risk exclusion from an area of unprecedented prosperity and ASEAN would probably remain confined to playing a fairly limited role, both politically and economically, in a region dominated by the two Pacific economic superpowers.

7. The prospects for a stronger and more diversified partnership between the EC and ASEAN must finally be considered against the background of the changing balance of power across the Pacific. Although changes are mostly measured in economic and financial terms, wide-ranging political questions gradually emerge concerning the role that Japan and – to a lesser degree – East Asian NICs should perform in the global adjustment process which has been carried out thus far by essentially Western-dominated institutions and informal processes of negotiation.

It is not only a matter of achieving the full integration into the international economy of the new Asian-Pacific powers but of involving these powers in the international political dialogue especially regarding issues of paramount importance to the region. This is not to ignore the fact that trade problems remain a major foreign-relations concern for several Pacific Basin countries.[23] The acceleration of trade frictions, the growing number of bilateral and regional preferential arrangements and the continuation of highly restrictive farm policies are among the factors worrying Asian exporters and policy-makers. The United States–Canada free-trade agreement which could be extended to include countries in Central and South

America, the expected completion of the single European market by 1992 and the impending Australia–New Zealand free-trade pact are perceived by East Asian nations as a major threat to multilateral trade as envisaged by GATT rules.[24]

As a matter of fact, the gradual emergence of powerful trading blocs and the subsequent division of the world into new spheres of economic influence might tempt Japan into forming some new kind of 'Co-prosperity Zone' comprising East and South-East Asian countries and eventually stretching to South Asia. Japan appears no longer satisfied with being considered in international circles an 'honorary Westerner' and is more and more willing to assert its Asian identity.[25]

Proposals for the setting up of a 'Pacific OECD' have been put forth from time to time by Japanese officials and were relaunched by former Prime Minister Yasuhiro Nakasone at the Osaka General Meeting of PECC held in May 1988.[26] Whatever the outcome of these proposals, it is important to stress Japan's readiness to act as a speaker for Asia's NICs as well as developing countries in international fora. As regards NICs, they can no longer be dismissed as a disruptive element on the world marketplace to be dealt with essentially by forcing substantial exchange-rate adjustments and a wider opening of markets.[27] Japan has emphasised, *inter alia*, the need to bring the NICs into the international debate on global surpluses and deficits. With respect to developing countries – in Asia and elsewhere – Japan is carrying out an expansion of its overseas assistance and is improving it both qualitatively and quantitatively.

Within the OECD framework, current trade imbalances between member countries – and, above all, between the United States and Japan – cause frictions which are far greater than NIC-related pressures.[28] However, the recent decline of Japan's current-account surpluses and the prospects for a stabilised dollar and stronger growth on the part of some of the United States' trading partners are gradually lessening tensions and raising hopes that the United States will begin running a trade surplus some time in the 1990s.

In any case, Japan's new role on the world political stage and the East Asian NICs' – including some ASEAN countries' – economic coming of age are major factors to be reckoned with in any EC future strategy *vis-à-vis* the Asia-Pacific region. This is all the more relevant since EC policymakers do not seem to have given adequate consideration to the external trade and investment dimension of the unified European market.[29]

Although trade matters remain central to the dialogue between the EC and Japan, the need for broader and more effective co-ordination on international political issues – such as arms control negotiation, the resolution of regional conflicts and East–West relations – is being felt by Japanese policymakers, increasingly aware of the relative decline of the United States' role on the political and economic scene.

The European response cannot be confined to strengthening tariff and non-tariff barriers, without any attempt at achieving more balanced patterns of interdependence. Increased protectionist pressures on the part of the EC – and, for that matter, of the United States – would probably hasten the establishment of a defensive economic alliance between Japan and its Asian neighbours. This would also involve closer ties between Japan and ASEAN, an organisation whose eventual extension to the whole of South-East Asia should not be ruled out.[30]

Notes

1. As a journal wittily put it, 'pundits have been forecasting the dawn of the Pacific age for so long that most people have turned over and gone back to sleep' (*The Economist*, 21 July 1984, p. 13). For a general introduction see Staffan Burenstam Linder, *The Pacific Century. Economic and Political Consequences of Asian-Pacific Dynamism* (Stanford, CA: Stanford University Press, 1986).
2. For an overall view see M.W. Oborne and N. Fourt, *Pacific Basin Economic Co-operation* (Paris: OECD Development Centre Studies, 1983); E. Fontela and O. Hieronymi (eds), 'The Expansion of the Pacific Basin', *Annals of International Studies*, vol. 14, 1985 (Geneva: Association des Anciens Etudiants de l'Institut Universitaire de Hautes Etudes Internationales, 1985). An analysis of concepts and goals of economic co-operation in the Pacific is to be found in: W. Kraus and W. Lütkenhorst, *The Economic Development of the Pacific Basin* (London: C. Hurst & Co., 1986) pp. 92–114. For a Chinese perspective see Zhu Chun, 'Growing Role of the Asia-Pacific Region in the World Strategic Pattern', *International Strategic Studies*, Beijing Institute for International Strategic Studies, no. 2, 1987, pp. 1–10; Zhan Yunling, 'The Shift in the Center of Gravity of World's Economy', *West European Studies*, Institute of West European Studies, Chinese Academy of Social Sciences, no. 1, August 1986, pp. 51–65.
3. It should be stressed, however, that both China and Taiwan (the latter under the name of Taipei, China) participate as full members in the

Asian Development Bank; they also attend meetings of the Pacific Economic Co-operation Conference (PECC) as Standing Committee members. Moreover, indirect trade and investment links between the two countries are steadily growing.

4. Partly to counter Soviet moves to build up a stronger presence by means of fishing and trade deals, Japan is steadily increasing its economic assistance to the small nations of the South Pacific.
5. The *coup d'état* in Fiji in May 1987 – the first military putsch against a democratically elected government in the South Pacific – and the subsequent events, including another *coup* in September 1987, are one more example of instability in a once tranquil region. Racial tensions are the root cause of the Fijian events which have no direct connection with wider geopolitical issues, including Soviet and Libyan involvement in the region.
6. The paramount importance of the EC experience for all other regional groupings is stressed by one of the leading Japanese scholars proposing Pacific co-operation schemes who points out that 'if there were no European Community, we would have no need to consider Pacific economic integration either'. See K. Kojima, *Economic Co-operation in a Pacific Community* (Tokyo: Japan Institute of International Affairs, 1980) p. 10.
7. C.E. Morrison, 'American Interests in the Concept of a Pacific Basin Community', in J. Crawford and G. Seow (eds), *Pacific Economic Co-operation: Suggestions for Action* (London, 1981) p. 114 ff.; L.B. Krause, 'The Pacific Economy in an Interdependent World: A New Institution for the Pacific Basin', in J. Crawford and G. Seow (eds), op. cit., p. 128 ff.; K.S. Sandhu, 'The Pacific Basin Concept: A View from ASEAN', in J. Crawford and G. Seow (eds), op. cit., p. 176 ff.; K.D. Jackson, Sukhumband Paribatra and J. Soedjati Djiwandono (eds), *ASEAN in Regional and Global Context* (University of California, Berkeley: Institute of East Asian Studies, 1987). See also R.L. Downen and B.J. Dickson (eds), *The Emerging Pacific Community: A Regional Perspective* (Boulder and London: Westview Press, 1984).
8. For an account of the origin, structure and activities of the main intergovernmental organisations in the Asia-Pacific region see the relevant entries in: G. Schiavone, *International Organisations. A Dictionary and Directory*, 2nd edn. (London: Macmillan, 1986).
9. In particular, Indonesia has been a member of the Organisation of the Petroleum Exporting Countries (OPEC) since 1962.
10. For a survey of ASEAN's contributions to Third World efforts for a New International Economic Order (NIEO) see J. Saravanamuttu, 'ASEAN Postures and Performance in North-South Negotiations', in Pushpa Thambipillai and J. Saravanamuttu, *ASEAN Negotiations. Two Insights* (Singapore: Institute of Southeast Asian Studies, 1985) pp. 29–55.
11. The PECC, which had its origin in the Canberra Seminar in 1980, is a private body comprising academics, businessmen and government officials, all participating in a private capacity. For an updated survey see: Kumao Kaneko, 'A New Pacific Initiative: Strengthening the PECC

Process', *Japan Review of International Affairs*, vol. 2, no. 1 (Spring/Summer 1988) pp. 67–90.

12. J. Bercovitch (ed), *ANZUS in Crisis. Alliance Management in International Relations* (London: Macmillan, 1987).
13. For an updated list of the agreements see *Far Eastern Economic Review, Asia 1988 Yearbook*, pp. 14–16. Both super powers seem to be increasing the conventional and nuclear capabilities to face perceived threats from the other side. See also 'East Asian Security', *The Economist*, December 26, 1987, pp. 57–63.
14. According to Gorbachev, the proposed conference should be open to the participation of all countries with an interest in the Pacific and could take place in Hiroshima, Japan. The establishment of a comprehensive system of security in the Asia-Pacific region obviously implies substantial improvements in the Soviet Union's bilateral relations with China and Japan and the resolution of conflicts in Afghanistan and Kampuchea. The Soviet leader also envisaged a conference of the communist parties of the Asia-Pacific. For an assessment of the importance of the Vladivostok address for Soviet policy in East Asia see R.C. Horn, 'Soviet Policy in East Asia', *Current History*, October 1987, p. 321 ff.; R. Nations, 'Moscow's New Tack', *Far Eastern Economic Review*, 14 August 1986, pp. 30–34.
15. P. Dibb, 'The Interests of the Soviet Union in South-east Asia and the South-west Pacific: Implications for Regional Security', Strategic and Defence Studies Centre, Australian National University, Conference Paper, July 1982, p. 32. See also M. Leifer, *Conflict and Regional Order in South-east Asia*, Adelphi Papers, no. 162 (London: International Institute for Strategic Studies, 1980); F.A. Mediansky, 'Soviet Strategic Interests in South-east Asia', *South-east Asian Affairs 1984* (Singapore: Institute of South-east Asian Studies, 1984) pp. 33–47; R.S. Cline, J.A. Miller, and R.E. Kanet (eds), *Asia in Soviet Global Strategy* (Boulder and London: Westview Press, 1987); H. Kimura, 'Soviet Focus on the Pacific', *Problems of Communism*, May–June 1987, pp. 1–16; M. Kaser, 'Reform in the USSR and China', *The Pacific Review*, vol. 1, no. 1, 1988, pp. 38–49.
16. Despite the huge economic potential of the Soviet Far East, especially with regard to oil, gas and natural resources, the region's share in Soviet total production has recently shown a downward trend. As for the prospects of Soviet-Japanese cooperation for the accelerated development of the Soviet Far East, it should be noted that the failure of the two countries to sign a peace treaty after World War II may still prevent, to a certain extent, the strengthening of economic ties.
17. However, the restoration of 'normal' relations with the USSR was subject, according to the Chinese, to the elimination of three 'obstacles', that is the end of the Soviet-backed Vietnamese occupation of Kampuchea, the withdrawal of Soviet forces from Afghanistan, and the reduction of Soviet troops on the Sino-Soviet border and in Mongolia. According to some Chinese analysts, a meaningful Sino-Soviet relationship could develop within a transnational economic co-operation scheme involving

North-East China, Outer Mongolia, the Soviet Far East, Japan and the Korean peninsula. See L. do Rosario, 'Recovering Lost Time. The Growth of Sino-Soviet Trade has Resumed in Earnest', *Far Eastern Economic Review*, January 1, 1987, pp. 46–7.

18. For a discussion of the prospects of ASEAN integration see H.C. Rieger, *ASEAN Co-operation and Intra-ASEAN Trade*, Research Notes and Discussions Paper, no. 57 (Singapore: Institute of South-East Asian Studies, 1985); H.C. Rieger, 'ASEAN: A Free Trade Area or a Customs Union', *Far Eastern Economic Review*, May 1, 1986, pp. 58–60; *ASEAN: The Tasks Ahead*, Report of a Colloquium on ASEAN Economic Co-operation (Singapore: Institute of South-East Asian Studies, 1987).
19. M. Vatikiotis, 'Zone of Discord', *Far Eastern Economic Review*, January 14, 1988, pp. 12–13.
20. The Treaty establishing a South Pacific nuclear-free zone (SPNFZ) was signed within the framework of the South Pacific Forum (SPF) and forbids production, testing, basing and use of nuclear weapons in the region. Freedom of passage of nuclear-powered or nuclear-armed ships within the area is guaranteed by the treaty, each contracting party retaining the right to allow or deny access of such ships to its ports.
21. R.H. Solomon and Masataka Kosaka (eds), *The Soviet Far East Military Buildup. Nuclear Dilemmas and Asian Security* (Dover, Mass.: Auburn House, 1986).
22. In this connection, it has been stressed that military friends can be economic enemies and *vice versa*.
23. The recent merger in Australia of the Department of Foreign Affairs with the Department of Trade reflects, *inter alia*, the need to expand more actively Australia's presence in foreign markets.
24. Art. XXIV of GATT recognises the desirability of increasing trade through the setting up of customs unions and free trade areas, provided that these groupings are intended to facilitate trade between the constituent territories and not to raise barriers *vis-à-vis* third countries. Actually, the trade-creating and trade-diverting effects of the various regional arrangements submitted to GATT have never been clearly assessed. The provisions of art. XXIV are among those proposed for review and possible amendment during the current round of MTNs.
25. Japan has recently been raising its diplomatic profile mostly with regard to international economic and financial issues but also in the discussions leading up to the INF treaty which includes Soviet SS–20 missiles located in Asia, thereby reducing the threat to Japan itself and to China.
26. 'Pacific Boosterism', *Far Eastern Economic Review*, 9 June 1988, p. 34.
27. In early 1988 the United States has decided to phase out Singapore and three other East Asian NICs out of the Generalised System of Preferences (GSP) causing widespread dissatisfaction on the ASEAN side. For its part, the EC has planned the removal of duty-free trade concessions to South Korea.
28. In 1987, Japan, Taiwan and South Korea had a combined current-account surplus of about $110 billion; of these Japan alone accounted for

$82 billion. At the end of 1987, Japan's trade surplus with the United States amounted to $58 billion.

29. Two recent studies devoted by the EC to the manifold implications of '1992' pay little attention to the external policy aspects. See the 'Cecchini Report' (*The European Challenge 1992* by Paolo Cecchini, published in early 1988 by Wildwood House) and the work appeared in the issue of March 1988 of *European Economy*, the EC Commission's journal.
30. Vietnam's aspirations to join ASEAN are well known, while Burma, already in Ne Win's times, had expressed some interest in attending ASEAN meetings as an observer. The case of Papua-New Guinea – apparently a prospective member – is entirely different owing to the South Pacific affiliations of that country. The prospective ASEAN membership of a truly independent and neutralised Cambodia should also be considered.

2 The Importance of the EC for South-East Asia: The ASEAN Perspective

Phan Wannamethee

The purpose of this paper is to present an overview of ASEAN perceptions concerning the importance of the EC to ASEAN. It is not intended to provide details of every topic to be discussed separately in the agenda of this Conference. Its contents are largely drawn from official ASEAN sources, thus reflecting to a certain extent the views of ASEAN officials and policymakers.

INTRODUCTION

European countries have had a long historical relationship with ASEAN countries and were economically dominant in this part of the world in the pre-war years. The relationship between the EC and ASEAN as regional groupings was initiated in 1972 when ASEAN was still in its formative years – five years after its inception in 1967. This initial contact, in the form of a Special Co-ordinating Committee of ASEAN Nations (SCCAN) consisting of the Ministers of Trade, and the Brussels Committee (ABC) with the EC Commission, focussed on access to the EC market. However, even in the early years of this relationship, ASEAN recognised the importance of the EC as a prospective market for its primary and manufactured products and as a potential source of direct investment for its industrialisation. Hence, access to the market and investment were then, as they are now, the major topics of ASEAN-EC discussion and will probably continue to be so in the future.

ASEAN officials and policymakers also saw in the EC a major power with great economic capabilities and age-old wisdom in international affairs. The EC would therefore perform an influential and meaningful role at the global level as much as that played by the two other superpowers, the US and the USSR. ASEAN regarded the EC as a significant political group to be reckoned with by the world. As a matter of fact, the ASEAN Treaty of Amity and Co-operation 1976 was inspired, as far as political co-operation was concerned, by the Luxembourg Report of 27 October 1970. ASEAN had considered since its early days the significance of the EC as a political partner which was later reflected in the ASEAN-EC Ministerial Meetings.

It should be recalled that the first five years of ASEAN were a crucial period in its development. There was then the possibility that ASEAN would succumb to the same fate as its predecessor, the defunct ASA (Association of South-east Asia). Having survived that period, ASEAN then began to take root in solid ground. After the Bali Summit in 1976, a watershed in ASEAN development, one was assured that ASEAN was here to stay. ASEAN was then little known in Europe and was looked upon with skeptical eyes. The meetings between ASEAN Heads of Government and the Prime Ministers of Japan, Australia and New Zealand in 1977 augmented the status of ASEAN as a regional grouping to be reckoned with. The realisation of ASEAN aspirations for recognition came when the dialogue between ASEAN and the EC, hitherto limited to ASEAN's relationship with the EC Commission, was upgraded to ministerial level in 1978. The conclusion of the ASEAN-EC Co-operation Agreement in 1980, the first ever concluded by ASEAN with any dialogue partner, put the final touch to ASEAN aspirations. It conferred tremendous prestige on ASEAN in the form of recognition by the EC as a viable and cohesive regional group.

ASEAN recognises that the EC is a pioneer in regional co-operation. The EC has also stated that it wants to foster regional co-operation in other parts of the world. It has indicated its willingness to assist ASEAN regional development programmes which would strengthen regional co-operation within ASEAN. Co-operation with the EC has therefore also helped to foster intra-ASEAN co-operation.

ASEAN experiences with the EC which developed before its co-operation with other dialogue partners gave self-confidence to the ASEAN countries and impressed upon them the fact that solidarity and concerted action – speaking with one voice – would strengthen their position and carry weight in their negotiations with their dialogue partners. In other words, it stimulated ASEAN to strengthen its own solidarity for its own benefit as well.

THE EC AS A PARTNER IN INTERNATIONAL POLITICS

The political dimension of ASEAN-EC relations was initiated at the first ASEAN-EC Ministerial Meeting in Brussels in 1978. Herr Hans-Dietrich Genscher, Foreign Minister of the Federal Republic of Germany, the then President of the EC Council, pointed out that the EC saw this meeting as an event of great political significance and was willing to support the political aims of the ASEAN nations and continuing political dialogue between the member states of the two organisations.[1] At this meeting, the ASEAN ministers recognised the role played by the EC as a factor of economic and political stability and as an element of balance in international relations. The EC ministers on the other hand recognised ASEAN as a factor of stability and balance which contributed to the maintenance of peace in South-East Asia.[2]

Since the first meeting, two major political events have taken place: the Vietnamese invasion of Kampuchea in December 1978, which has threatened the stability of the ASEAN region, and the Soviet military intervention in Afghanistan a year later which has been viewed with great concern by EC countries. These two events have brought the political co-operation between the two groups much closer in their diplomatic undertakings to resolve the problems. Hence, when the ASEAN and EC ministers met at their second meeting in Kuala Lumpur in March 1980, the issues of Kampuchea and Afghanistan received great attention. The ministers issued a separate Joint Statement on political issues, an unprecedented practice which has never been repeated since, deploring the armed interventions against Kampuchea and Afghanistan by Vietnam and the Soviet Union respectively. They called for the establishment of an independent and neutral Kampuchea with a genuinely representative government free of all foreign military presence. They appealed to all states to respect the sovereignty, territorial integrity, political independence, and non-aligned character of Afghanistan.[3]

The Kampuchea and Afghanistan issues have become dominant subjects of political discussions at every successive Ministerial Meeting as well as at the annual Post-ASEAN Ministerial Conference. Apart from these two issues, the ministers have also discussed extensively various international political issues of common interest, covering a wide range of subjects including East-West relations, the Middle East, South Africa and international terrorism.[4]

Needless to say, ASEAN has received full support from the EC *en bloc* on the Kampuchean issue which is of great importance to ASEAN. As Sir Geoffrey Howe, the British Foreign Secretary, President of the EC Council, said during the sixth ASEAN-EC Ministerial Meeting: 'The Twelve stand four-square behind ASEAN in seeking the withdrawal of Vietnamese forces and the re-establishment of Kampuchea as a neutral non-aligned and independent State.'[5]

The political understanding reached between the EC and ASEAN on political issues and the mutual confidence that has been built up has laid a strong foundation for closer co-operation in the economic area. After five meetings of Foreign Ministers, the first ASEAN-EC Economic Ministers' Meeting was held in Bangkok in October 1985. This was the first Economic Ministers' meeting the EC has ever held with any other grouping of countries and signified the growing convergence of views and interests between the EC and ASEAN.

THE EC AS AN IMPORTANT TRADING PARTNER OF ASEAN

The European Community is the world's largest trading entity. It is the third largest trading partner of ASEAN after Japan and the United States. The EC is and will continue to be an important market for ASEAN, contributing to the development of ASEAN economies. Trade relations between ASEAN and the EC can be summarily characterised as follows:

First, the original pattern of trade between ASEAN and the EC corresponded to a certain extent to that of North-South relations. This implied that ASEAN countries would supply primary products to the EC and import machinery and consumer goods from the EC. As ASEAN has stepped up its programme of industrialisation and has shifted from substitute-oriented industries to export-oriented industries, the composition of ASEAN exports to the EC has changed significantly. ASEAN exports have been more oriented to manufactured goods. Agricultural products and raw materials which formed 73.9 per cent of the exports in 1973 was reduced to 52.8 per cent by 1980 and 50.8 per cent by 1984. On the other hand exports of manufactured goods rose from 23.5 per cent in 1973 to 35.7 per cent in 1980 and 45.8 per cent in 1984.[6]

Secondly, ASEAN may view the EC as its major trading partner, but the same is not true from the EC's own perception. ASEAN trade with the EC amounts to about 11 per cent of ASEAN trade whilst EC trade with ASEAN accounts for as little as 2 per cent of its total. The EC takes in only 14 per cent of total ASEAN exports representing only 3 per cent of its total imports, which is considerably less than Japan's import from ASEAN accounting for about 14.7 per cent of Japan's global imports. Compared with other developing countries, ASEAN is still a smaller partner of the EC than the African-Caribbean-Pacific (ACP) countries. In 1984, the ASEAN share was 2.5 per cent of EC imports and 2.8 per cent of EC exports while the share of ACP countries was 6.5 per cent and 4.7 per cent and that of Latin America 6.3 per cent and 3.8 per cent respectively.

Thirdly, on the brighter side often quoted by EC officials, a steady growth has been achieved in ASEAN-EC trade since the signing of the Co-operation Agreement in 1980. Between 1980 and 1984, EC exports to ASEAN increased by 84 per cent from 5369 MECU to 9886 MECU and its imports from ASEAN expanded by 41 per cent from 6857 MECU to 9662 MECU with the total trade rising by 60 per cent from 12 226 MECU to 19 548 MECU.[8] However, such growth of trade has been in favour of the EC. ASEAN has consistently suffered a trade deficit with the Community since 1981. The deficit varied from 606 MECU in 1981 to 1368 MECU in 1982, 1349 MECU in 1983 and 224 MECU in 1984.[9]

The first six months of 1986 witnessed the decline of ASEAN exports by about 20 per cent. However, an EC Commissioner, Mr Cheysson has consoled ASEAN by suggesting that this is not alarming in nature; it is rather the conjuncture of the fall in raw material prices, the fall in value of the American dollar and the continuation of the fall in purchasing power.[10]

In view of the small share that ASEAN has in total EC trade, its professed desire is to explore increasing access to the EC market. The ASEAN-EC Co-operation Agreement of 1980 has provided some leeway to the increasing access to the EC market. It contains major provisions on trade. First, it provides for ASEAN countries to receive Most-Favoured-Nation (MFN) treatment under GATT. Second, the parties undertook to promote the development and diversification of their reciprocal exchanges at the highest possible level, and third, it recognised the need to study ways and means to overcome trade barriers, and to cooperate in the solution of commercial problems of common interest.[11]

Of particular interest to ASEAN in this area is the EC's Generalised System of Preferences (GSP). This scheme is intended to improve access to Community markets for finished and semi-finished products of developing countries such as ASEAN countries. ASEAN has consistently acknowledged and recognised the role of the GSP as an effective instrument in expanding EC-ASEAN trade relations. The five ASEAN countries taken together have been among the leading beneficiaries of the system, accounting for 42 per cent of all Community imports under GSP in 1983.[12] The GSP is particularly important to ASEAN as it constitutes the only form of preferential access to the EC market. Hence, one of the important issues currently being discussed between ASEAN and the EC Commission is that of improvement of the GSP. Such improvement, as requested by ASEAN, should include wider product coverage, higher tariff concessions, an increase in import quotas and ceilings and acceptance of the ASEAN rules of origin.[13]

Trade in primary commodities is the major concern of ASEAN. At present ASEAN countries have been hard hit by the depressed price of commodities which is seriously affecting their economies. The commodity issues are global in nature and long-term solutions depend on international arrangements. In this respect, ASEAN looks to the EC, a major consumer of primary commodities, to play a positive role in the efforts to restructure the world economic order, particularly for primary commodities, to ensure a stable market and fair prices.

In addition, there are other aspects where the EC could contribute to the alleviation of ASEAN difficulties.

First, the EC, with its advanced technology, can collaborate with ASEAN on research and development in resource-based industries through technology transfer and marketing in the fields of forestry, rubber and tin and also in increasing productivity and ensuring the security of future supplies in as efficient a manner as possible.

Secondly, the EC should relax its Common Agricultural Policy (CAP) which has restricted the import of ASEAN commodities and deprived developing countries – except, of course, the ACP countries – of markets. The commodity in point is sugar for which ASEAN urges the EC to substantially reduce its sugar subsidies and allow access to its market.[14]

It is almost impossible at present for the EC to modify its CAP as requested by ASEAN. However, the EC has all the potential to collaborate with ASEAN on research and development and transfer of technology in the area of primary commodities.

THE EC ROLE IN INTERNATIONAL ECONOMIC ISSUES

The world economic situation has great impact on the economies of the developed and developing countries alike. ASEAN recognises that the EC as an important and influential economic bloc would be in a position to contribute significantly to the world economic order. As a group, the EC has economic power that can hold the balance with other economic powers, notably the US and Japan. It has close economic co-operation with other European economic groupings – EFTA and the Nordic Council – and close contact with the Socialist bloc of Comecon. At the same time, the EC is the largest investor in the developing world, and a significant importer of both manufactured and primary commodity products from developing countries.

ASEAN, on the other hand, represents a middle-income, market economy and a Western-oriented group within developing countries. Both groups share a common view in many areas of international economic issues, although their interest and approach to the problems may not necessarily be the same. Hence it is desirable that there should be close co-operation, consultation, collaboration and, wherever possible, concerted action between the two groups. For ASEAN, this would strengthen its position in international fora and for the EC, ASEAN as a moderate group of the so called South may serve as a bridge in the North-South dialogue.

ASEAN has consistently pursued the matter with the EC. In principle, ASEAN and the EC have reached convergent views on the following matters:

- co-operation in the search for solutions to international economic, trade and financial problems
- joint efforts at the international level to deal with major economic issues
- co-operation in international fora on the establishment of a new international economic order
- the need to maintain liberal and open trading conditions and the liberalisation of international trade
- the need to resist protectionism and the need for commitment to standstill and roll-back measures as well as for continuing to implement the work programme of GATT
- the need for equitable remuneration and stable international prices for commodities in the world market
- collaboration both in the appropriate international fora and on a

bilateral basis to contribute towards sustained international economic recovery, in particular in the developing countries.[15]

Two main features, among others, to which ASEAN attaches great importance, are protectionism and commodity issues. ASEAN is now suffering from the rising threat of protectionism which adversely affects its exports. The EC often claims that it is the most open trading entity in the world. To a certain extent this is relatively true, with the exception of a few 'sensitive' manufacturing items and agricultural products, in comparison with Japan and the US. Hence, ASEAN welcomes the opportunity of gaining the support of and collaborating with the EC to resist protectionism in all forms, particularly for the realisation of standstill and roll-back measures to overcome protectionism as pledged by industrialised nations at their summit meetings.

On commodity issues which are global in nature and can effectively be resolved in the long term through international arrangements, the EC as an important consumer can play a positive role in international fora in achieving the desired effect. In this respect, ASEAN seeks the support of the EC in the various elements of the United Nations Conference on Trade and Development (UNCTAD) Integrated Programme for Commodities (IPC) and in using its good offices to urge other major countries to ratify the agreement to establish the Common Fund. ASEAN has also requested the EC to implement the Stabilisation of Export Scheme (STABEX) on a global basis and to support ASEAN on various issues including tin, rubber, sugar and others.[16]

The EC has so far made its commitments for closer co-operation necessary for achieving the objectives of the IPC, the establishment of individual commodity agreement and the value of the Common Fund. But on the STABEX which is the mechanism of the Lomé Convention, it is unlikely that the EC would endorse this Scheme either on a global basis or bilaterally with ASEAN.

THE EC AS A POTENTIAL INVESTOR

Trade and investment are equally important to ASEAN in its relations with the EC. For the realisation of its industrialisation programme, ASEAN needs direct foreign investment which would bring capital, know-how and transfer of technology from the industrialised countries. In spite of its historical and traditional economic ties with ASEAN, the EC is relatively under-represented in investment in ASEAN countries, except in Singapore, trailing behind Japan which is the biggest single source of foreign investment in ASEAN (Japan, EC and the USA accounted for 28.3 per cent, 21.5 per cent and 15.8 per cent respectively of total foreign investment in ASEAN in 1983.)[17]

The Co-operation Agreement provides for an undertaking by the parties to it to improve the investment climate, and to encourage the extension of investment. ASEAN and EC ministers recognise that increased European investment in the ASEAN region would be a key element in a long-term strategy to strengthen economic links between the two regions.

Efforts have actually been made by the European Community with a view to promoting investment in ASEAN. In order to bring together representatives of the business community of the two regions, four successive conferences on Industrial Co-operation have been organised. The first and second conferences held in Brussels and Jakarta in 1977 and 1979 covered a large number of industrial sectors. Since then the conferences have been organised on a sectoral basis. The Kuala Lumpur Conference in 1983 concentrated on machine tools, agricultural machinery and processing machinery, while the sectoral conference in Manila in 1985 centered on the food and agricultural sector. The conference held in Bangkok in 1987 focussed on agro-based industries such as aquaculture and dairy products.

The ASEAN-EC Ministerial Meeting on economic matters in Bangkok in 1985 gave new impetus to EC investment when the ministers decided to set up a high level working party including representatives of business circles, particularly banks, to examine investment conditions in the two regions, with a view to identifying any difficulties and to studying ways and means of facilitating European investment in the ASEAN countries, especially by small and medium-sized enterprises.

The findings by the High-Level Working Party (HLWP) as contained in its *Report* which was submitted to the Sixth ASEAN-EC Ministerial Meeting in Jakarta, October 1986, are very interesting and worth summing up here.[18]

First, it appears that direct investment by Europeans in the ASEAN countries represents only a small proportion of the total direct investment abroad. Amongst all the European member states, even more markedly than amongst Japanese or American counterparts, European companies tend to prefer investments in the industrialised West. Intra-Community investments have been boosted just as much as intra-Community trade and it seems probable that with the inclusion of Spain and Portugal in the Community, a new stimulus will be given to direct investment in Western Europe itself.

Secondly, EC investors have accorded relatively low priority to developing countries as a whole. Although European investment in ASEAN would appear to have grown substantially during the past decade, Asia generally and ASEAN in particular are not particularly significant for investment by European countries except Britain. West Germany's investment in Latin America, for example, is ten times more important than its investment in ASEAN. In the case of France and Italy, the differences are even greater.

Thirdly, the *Report* listed various factors considered as impediments to European investment in ASEAN which include, among other things:

the current limitation of the ASEAN internal market since ASEAN is not a single market but six separate national markets
the content, the complexity and diversity of investment regulations and incentives, and the wide margin of discretion in applying regulations
the lack of adequate protection given to intellectual property rights
the lack of information about investment opportunities.

Fourthly, the HLWP made recommendations for possible European initiatives under three main subjects: improvement of information channels, financial issues and training schemes.

On the improvement of information about investment opportunities, it is recommended that the European Community strengthen existing channels for the provision of pre-investment advice and information to firms considering investing in the ASEAN countries which include greater co-operation between its European Chamber of Commerce and ASEAN, the establishment of an ASEAN Investment Data Bank and the establishment of Joint Investment Committees in the capital of each ASEAN country. Encouragement of co-operation is also needed between representatives of the European institutions including the European Investment Bank (EIB) and ASEAN with a view to increasing the volume of intelligence on investment opportunities. Likewise Community funds should be available to increase investment promotion efforts by the ASEAN countries in the European Community.

On financial issues, while the ASEAN side felt strongly the need for official financial assistance to counteract the relative weakness of European investment, the European side argued that lack of finance was not an important deterrent against direct investment and that good projects would always attract good finance. Both sides agreed that the officially financed bilateral aid and public development financial institutions active in the region would be called up to accord high priority to ASEAN. Recommendations on this question also include accession by both sides to the Convention establishing the International Centre for the Settlement of Investment Disputes and that bilateral investment protection agreements should respect the principle of non-discrimination and fair and equitable treatment.

On the training scheme, HLWP recommended the possibility of an increase in the number of students from the ASEAN region at European universities, the expansion of existing opportunities at European business schools and technical colleges, more training schemes offered by banks, extension of the recently established EC-ASEAN two way business executive training scheme and more sponsorship, by the Community and national governments, of experts who would provide training and education in the region itself.

The *Report* of HLWP has received the endorsement of the Commission. The European Commissioner, Mr Claude Cheysson, came out strongly in favour of the recommendations contained in the *Report*.[19] The EC-ASEAN Ministerial Meeting has agreed to examine recommendations and in particular to improve the information and services available to European businessmen interested in investing in the ASEAN region and to encourage representatives of financial institutions in Europe including the EIB to co-operate together in order to promote a more effective European investment effort. The ministers have also endorsed the recommendation for the creation in each ASEAN capital of a Joint Investment Committee.[20]

The possible implementation by the Community of the HLWP recommendation as well as the proposed involvement of EIB would be a considerable improvement for the promotion of European investments in ASEAN. By the same token, efforts have to be made by ASEAN to rectify the impediments and to create a climate more favourable in attracting European investments. Nevertheless, as stated in the *Report*, the reasons for the comparative weakness of

European investment in the region are deep-seated and there is a need for all concerned to take strong action to improve the situation. In fact, in spite of the efforts of the Community and national governments, much would depend on the willingness of the private sector, *i.e.* the investors, who, as the *Report* has rightly suggested, are strongly influenced by their assessment of the general economic vitality and prospects, and political stability of countries or regions in which they may wish to invest.

HUMAN RESOURCE DEVELOPMENT

The development of human resources is a major instrument for regional and national economic development and social progress. Human resource development (HRD) as defined by ASEAN involves the development and utilisation of manpower which is best achieved through training, education, research, information and scholastic exchanges with a view to improving employment and income and supporting expanded economic activity. This also includes those activities designed to enhance knowledge, skills and technology transfer.[21]

ASEAN has already launched its regional HRD programmes with the assistance of the Japanese Government. Five ASEAN HRD Centres and projects have been established in five member countries, *i.e.* the Centre for Vocational Extension Services Training in Indonesia, the Centre for Instructors and Advanced Skills Training in Malaysia, the Centre for Rural Development Programme through the Strengthening of Agro-Industrial Livelihood Activities in the Philippines, the Productivity Development Project in Singapore and the Training Centre for Primary Health Care in Thailand.

It should be mentioned also that ASEAN has experienced HRD co-operation under the ASEAN-Pacific HRD programme, now in abeyance, under which over twenty HRD immediate projects were undertaken by ASEAN in co-operation with its dialogue partners.

The EC possesses great potential and ASEAN welcomes a fresh initiative on HRD co-operation within the framework of the ASEAN-EC Co-operation Agreement as decided by the ASEAN-EC Economic Ministers in 1985.

The ASEAN standpoint in respect of ASEAN-EC co-operation is that the HRD programme should be considered in the context of ASEAN objectives in industrial growth and economic progress. Such a programme should include as a matter of priority entrepreneurial skills development, technical and managerial skills development, increased technology and scientific skills relating to new technology, and the promotion of human resources development in the service sector. Moreover, it should assist and facilitate the capability of ASEAN human resource in the fields of policy formulation, planning and development.

The ASEAN-EC Expert Group on Human Resource Development has discussed the principles and operational guidelines of ASEAN-EC HRD co-operation. The Expert Group recognises the dynamic nature of the HRD co-operation and the need to refine, improve and supplement current HRD activities. In this respect the Expert Group recommended new areas for consideration to develop a more comprehensive HRD programme, such as

- entrepreneurial skills development for small and medium-sized enterprises
- development of technical and managerial skills in private and public enterprises
- development of technological and scientific skills relating to new technologies
- development of skills for rural development.[22]

The initial steps taken by the Expert Group augur well for more positive and fruitful HRD co-operation between ASEAN and the EC. Amongst the new initiatives on HRD co-operation as agreed upon at the seventh ASEAN-EC JCC Meeting, Jakarta, 30 April–2 May 1987, was the setting up of the ASEAN-EC Management Centre.

SCIENCE AND TECHNOLOGY[23]

Recognising the importance of science and technology for economic development, ASEAN started its regional co-operation in this field as early as 1970. The ASEAN Committee on Science and Technology (COST) was established for this purpose.

The objectives of the ASEAN programme in science and technology are directed towards intensifying technological and manpower development and promoting the transfer of technology and the effective and efficient use of national resources. An ASEAN Plan of

Action on Science and Technology was designed in 1980 guided by the principle of an overall ASEAN framework to bring social, economic and cultural benefits to the co-operating parties. The areas identified for co-operation are: (1) Food and Agricultural Development (2) Energy and Natural Resources (3) Manufacturing Industries, Transportation and Communications (4) Health and Social Development (5) Development of Science and Technology Infrastructure and (6) Environment.

In view of the international character of science and technology, ASEAN welcomes the co-operation with dialogue partners as well as regional and international bodies in order to sustain continuing development of science and technology in ASEAN.

The Co-operation Agreement with the EC provides for the encouragement of technological and scientific programmes in the context of economic co-operation. The co-operation would be in the area of energy, environment management and development of science and technology infrastructure.

The ASEAN-EC Ministerial Meeting on Economic Matters in 1985 gave an impetus to the strengthening of the co-operation in this field. The EC's proposed programmes include the linking of research activities in existing institutes in the two regions with a view to exchanging research information and research personnel, sharing facilities and co-operating on research projects; the setting up of networks of linked research institutes, continuing direct support of regional research projects including a network of research institutes in the field of bio-technology. On energy, the EC proposed the creation of an ASEAN-EC Centre for Energy Management, Training and Research which would facilitate improved information, training and exchange of experts and joint research on energy management. The opening of the ASEAN-EC Energy Management, Research and Training Centre located in Jakarta, Indonesia, was announced for July 1987. On environment, an ASEAN-EC project on Urban Air Monitoring through the creation of networks was proposed which covered different actions including training, technical assistance and the collection and treatment of data.

The current ASEAN point of view on the priorities of co-operation is that priorities should be given to biotechnology, micro-electronics, material sciences, food technology, marine sciences and non-conventional energy. These have to depend on the availability and readiness of the EC.

Science and technology co-operation with the EC has so far been a modest one due to budget constraints as well as procedural delay. The EC countries are a veritable mine of scientific and technological resources which can be tapped for the purpose. Apart from the Commission's own resources, the Community can act both as promoter and co-ordinator in soliciting assistance from individual member countries, both public and private sector, to partake in this endeavour which would be of mutual benefit.

OTHER AREAS OF CO-OPERATION

There are other areas of co-operation with the EC which ASEAN considers very significant, notably in tourism and drug problems. Tourism has already been included as a new activity in the framework of the Co-operation Agreement. ASEAN has increasingly gained substantial benefits from tourism, as a trade in service, contributing to the growth of its economies. Naturally, the co-operation of the EC with a view to promoting tourism is very desirable for ASEAN.

The ASEAN governments have experienced the menace of drug problems which have seriously endangered their social and economic development as well as their stability. Since the drug menace transcends national boundaries, they called for urgent international co-operative action to combat the threat that drug abuse and illicit trafficking posed to the international community.[24] ASEAN has raised this matter with the EC at the Fifth ASEAN-EC Ministerial Meeting in Dublin in 1984 at which there was general agreement on the need for international action to combat the drug menace. Since Europe is now facing the serious problems that the dangers of drug abuse pose to its own society, there are good prospects for effective and meaningful co-operation and concerted action between ASEAN and the EC in this area.

PROBLEMS AND PROSPECTS

To sum up, the following underline the importance of the EC for the ASEAN region.

1. Much emphasis has been placed upon EC-ASEAN political co-operation. Kampuchea and Afghanistan have been in the forefront of this co-operation for the past decade. There are now signs that such co-operation is being broadened to cover other areas such

as East-West relations, the Middle East, South Africa and international terrorism. This extension is to be welcomed as it widens the scope of ASEAN-EC relations. However, the political domain should not prevail over other issues which are of equal importance such as those in relation to economics, trade and development.

2. With reference to the EC and ASEAN as trading partners, it seems that currently, while the EC is regarded as extremely important for ASEAN from the ASEAN standpoint, the converse is not necessarily so, *i.e.* the EC does not regard ASEAN in a similar light. The political and economic will of both partners need to be reinforced to establish an equitable relationship between the two entities. In particular, the ASEAN-EC Co-operation Agreement of 1980, which provides for co-operation in economic and commercial matters, needs to be maximised to stimulate further access of ASEAN products to the European market and to alleviate tariff and non-tariff constraints.

On the question of the GSP, improvements are required and some of these have been pinpointed recently by the EC mid-term review of the GSP. These include more effective utilisation of the GSP in relation to industrial products. On another front, more flexibility is suggested for agricultural products, including further concessions in relation to quotas and rules of origin.

3. More concerted action is desirable for the EC and ASEAN in relation to the gamut of economic issues at the international level. These include the need to fight against the tide of protectionism and the interplay between tariff and non-tariff measures. High on the agenda is the instability of commodity prices and the call for the commitment to standstill and roll-back measures, as well as the implementation of the Common Fund to lessen the impact of declining commodity prices. However, since the commodity issues are global in nature, corrective strategies should thus be adopted to enhance collaboration between all those entities with a view to reducing protectionism, lessening the impact of declined commodity prices and diversifying products and markets.

4. In relation to the EC as an investor in the ASEAN region, the amount of EC investment has been disappointing so far. Reluctance on the part of investors from the EC is no doubt influenced by issues such as political instability and lengthy bureaucracy in ASEAN. Business confidence is inevitably contingent upon how ASEAN can present itself convincingly as a viable asset to potential investors from Europe. This dilemma is compounded to some extent, by the EC's

own interests in other regions for investment purposes and the contingency of world economic recovery which would enhance investors' confidence. From another standpoint, investment incentives remain a consistent challenge for ASEAN-EC relations. These include the need for more flexible laws and regulations for foreign investors. Collateral to this, greater public-private sector co-operation should be encouraged. This is reflected by the current proposal for joint investment committees in all the ASEAN countries linking European investors and their ASEAN counterparts in the public and private sectors. In this respect, existing networks, such as the ASEAN-EC Business Council should be capitalised upon. On another front, ASEAN may have to examine the question of creating a more unified internal market, but the economic and political realities indicate that the search for such unification is elusive.

5. Human Resource Development has been gaining ground as an area for ASEAN-EC co-operation. Skills development, including managerial capacity, is currently being promoted. Further needs for HRD include more concentration on raising the quality of life of the mass of the people, these being very much linked to rural development as the majority of the population live in rural areas. Future orientation should then be more favourable to the quality of life factor which is heavily influenced by basic needs, such as education, health and nutrition. This orientation is linked to the EC's own perception of its role in developing countries. While political, economic and commercial co-operation have been in the forefront of EC relations with the ASEAN group for the past decade, social development which is an adjunct of the expanded notion of HRD is now gathering momentum.

6. In the field of science and technology, there is much more room for EC assistance in the development of training and research capacities in the ASEAN region. This is inevitably linked with two questions of concern to the ASEAN countries which are now advancing towards more export-oriented strategies – 'transfer of technology' and 'development of technology'. The former is contingent upon an element of 'appropriateness' in the technology transfer and the need for a mechanism to determine the propriety of technology transfer from Europe to Asia. The latter calls for more co-ordination between public and private institutions in Europe to assist in the research and development of technology with ASEAN. In this respect, the proposed ASEAN-EC Centre for Energy Management, Training and Research is but a starting point for mutual co-operation

between the EC and ASEAN which may encompass other fields of science and technology in future.

7. Beyond the above is an array of other areas for co-operation between ASEAN and the EC which have not been dealt with extensively in this study. These include the need for more concerted efforts to promote tourism and to combat drug trafficking. Other areas in which ASEAN-EC co-operation may be enhanced comprise co-operation in insurance, environmental conservation and consumer protection. These may be explored within the formal ASEAN-EC context or beyond.

CONCLUSION

Ultimately, the issues discussed above lead to the conclusion that various 'strata' of co-operative efforts need to be advanced. The two most evident are the bilateral level and the 'regional' level. ASEAN-EC relations should capitalise upon existing bilateral agreements and relationships between the EC and ASEAN countries, while promoting a more inter-regional approach. This implies the need for maximum use of the resources available between individual countries under the umbrella of the regional group; ASEAN-EC co-operation should not neglect to explore bilateral channels which may complement and advance the regional approach. This strategy may indeed provide alternatives which a purely regional orientation would not be able to offer. The importance of the EC to ASEAN thus calls for multi-pronged alternatives to broaden the basis for *rapprochement* between the two regions.

Notes

1. Statement by Hans-Dietrich Genscher, President of the EC Council at the first ASEAN-EC Ministerial Meeting (AEMM), Brussels, 21 November 1978.
2. Joint Declaration of the First AEMM, Brussels.
3. ASEAN-EC Joint Statement on Political Issues, Kuala Lumpur, 8 March 1980.
4. See Joint Declaration of the Sixth AEMM, Jakarta, 21 October 1986.
5. Statement by Sir Geoffrey Howe, President of the EC Council, at the Sixth AEMM, Jakarta.

6. EC Statistics as quoted in ASEAN Secretariat Paper, *Overview of ASEAN-EC Economic Relations*, Jakarta, 1985.
7. Quoted from EEC, *The European Community and ASEAN*, Brussels, 1985.
8. ASEAN Secretariat Paper, *Overview of ASEAN-EC Economic Relations*, Jakarta, 1985.
9. *Ibid*.
10. Statement by Mr. Claude Cheysson at the Sixth AEMM, Jakarta.
11. ASEAN-EC Co-operation Agreement, Kuala Lumpur, 7 March 1980.
12. EEC, *The European Community and ASEAN*, Brussels, 1985.
13. See item on GSP in the Joint Press Release of the Sixth Meeting of the Joint Co-operation Committee (JCC), Brussels, 20–21 March 1986.
14. *ASEAN Memorandum on Commodities* presented to the Sixth JCC, March 1985.
15. See various statements in the Joint Declaration of AEMMs under the item International Economic Issues.
16. *ASEAN Memorandum on Commodities* presented at the Sixth JCC.
17. The figures quoted from *Europe and South East Asia*, no. 2, June 1985, Press and Information Service of the EC in Southeast Asia, Bangkok.
18. *Report of the ASEAN-EEC High Level Working Party on Investment*, Jakarta, July 1986.
19. Statement of Mr. Claude Cheysson at the Sixth AEMM, Jakarta.
20. Joint Declaration of the Sixth AEMM, Jakarta.
21. ASEAN Secretariat Paper, *Human Resource Development*, Jakarta, 1985.
22. *Report of the ASEAN-EC Expert Group on Human Resource Development*, ASEAN Secretariat, June 1986.
23. On Science and Technology see ASEAN Secretariat, *ASEAN Cooperation in Science and Technology*, Jakarta, 1985; Joint Communiqués of the First and Second Meetings of the ASEAN Ministers on Science and Technology, Pattaya, October 1980 and Jakarta, November 1983, respectively.
24. ASEAN Foreign Ministers' Joint Statement on the International Problem of Drug Abuse and Trafficking, Kuala Lumpur, 9 July 1985.

3 The Importance of ASEAN to Western Europe

Vincenzo Tornetta

I THE HISTORICAL BACKGROUND

The ties which link Western Europe and the countries of South-East Asia are very old and have had a multi-century continuity which cannot be overlooked when evaluating their present status as expressed through the institutional relationship between the EC and ASEAN, as well as through the bilateral links between the individual countries.

As for the origins of these relations, it is enough to remember the flourishing trade in spices which existed between the East and Europe and which reached its highest level during the Middle Ages. The idea of making this trade easier and faster was the original purpose of the enterprise carried out by Christopher Columbus – who discovered America by chance whilst aiming at reaching the East through a shorter route by travelling towards the West.

But it was not only trade that gave substance to the relationship between Europe and those far away regions of South-East Asia: the human component was also very important, especially at the beginning of the modern era. It suffices to think of the presence and work of the missionaries; of the intense cultural as well as religious activity which was developed thanks to their intervention, and which contributed to a better mutual understanding of the respective cultures.

In effect, for centuries the Far East was economically and culturally much more important for Europe than, for instance, the nearer African continent. The colonial era could not but leave its mark on these relations. The main European maritime powers were in fact present in South-East Asia. However, the colonial relationship was generally not traumatic, with the possible exception of Indochina. And so, too, the decolonisation process developed in a manner which allowed the continuation of deep and peaceful relations.

South-East Asia represents a crossroad between the two great basins of the Indian Ocean and the Pacific Ocean. Geographically speaking, however, its states gravitate towards this latter area. In this geographical context South-East Asia has a notable strategical and political relevance: it controls vital supply routes as well as being the source of important raw materials. From this point of view it is a vital artery, not only economically but also as an element of security balance.

Its importance has greatly increased during this post-war period. The new independent states which now comprise this region have different political, economic and cultural characteristics, which give particular complexity to the global political picture of South-East Asia.

The substantial evolution of the political and strategic balances which has taken place in the Asia-Pacific area within the last few years has contributed to making this region even more important with respect to the world balance of power. Hence a greater international interest – and consequently also of the European Community – towards this region. At this point it would seem appropriate to consider, in its general outline, the evolution of these balances during the last decades.

II THE EVOLUTION OF BALANCES IN THE ASIA-PACIFIC AREA

At the end of the Second World War the vast region usually called Asia-Pacific presented a clear-cut bipolar situation. On the one hand there was the Chinese-Soviet bloc, with a clear directive of political and ideological predominance on the continent, and on the other hand the unchallenged maritime pre-eminence of the United States in the whole Pacific area.

This situation did not last for long. On the continental level it was split by the break between China and the Soviet Union which destroyed the monolithic continental predominance of the Communist bloc. After the turmoil of the cultural revolution. China has gradually re-directed and consolidated her internal affairs and has at the same time re-emerged as an active element in Asian politics. Moreover the normalisation of her relations with the United States and Japan, brought into effect in 1978, has given a greater flexibility to Chinese foreign policy.

China has therefore re-emerged as a factor of increasing importance but not only in the continental setting. China has had a centuries' old interest in South-East Asia. This presence, though not of a military nature, has had a cultural, economic and human significance, thanks also to the existence of well-rooted and significant Chinese communities throughout the countries of this area. Undoubtedly China will try to re-affirm and develop this traditional influence, even though it is difficult as yet to guess the forms that this influence might take in the future, in relation to the general evolution of Chinese policy. However, the possible future directives of Chinese politics cannot but raise fears and preoccupations amongst some countries of the area.

The Soviet Union, whose position on the continent has been contained by the break with China, has shown a tendency to project her air and naval presence towards the South, with the aim of taking upon herself the role of both an Asian and a Pacific power. This ambition, notwithstanding the considerable military presence deployed and in spite of remarkable efforts, has not yet been followed by an equally weighty influence on an economic and political level on the part of the USSR.

However, in South-East Asia the Soviet Union has found in a unified Vietnam an important ally especially with regard to the containing of China. Lastly, the deployment in Siberia of long-range nuclear missile systems has given a new dimension to the Soviet military presence in the area.

The mainly military aspect of the Soviet presence is counteracted, to a degree, by the essentially economic and commercial nature of the Japanese one, which has gradually grown in importance, although Japan tries to prevent her increasing economic influence from taking on political and, above all, military connotations. Indeed in this context the whole Pacific area has found itself more and more at the centre of growing economic activity and trade, to the point of taking away the primacy from the Atlantic area. Moreover some of the major world traffic routes pass through South-East Asia.

At the heart of this latter area a new protagonist of political-military balances has emerged during the last decade: the unified Vietnam with her 50 million inhabitants and more than one million men in the armed forces, which represents a particularly efficient military machine. In the Indo-Chinese region Vietnam pursues her own national aims, and although still greatly dependent on Soviet assistance, cannot be regarded as a 'satellite' of the USSR.

Vietnam's objective, that is, to exercise a predominant influence in the Indo-Chinese region, is opposed to China's. If the former aims at creating a certain 'Indo-Chinese Confederation' under her control, China's interest is rather in a Balkanisation of Indo-China whose states would remain open to her traditional influence. The counter-position between Vietnam and China has deep historical roots and should be regarded as immutable, even though its aspects may vary according to circumstances.

Finally, the United States, with her air and sea power, and the weight of her economic and political relations, still remains the predominant factor in the Pacific even though her pre-eminence is no longer absolute. The increased Soviet air and naval presence cannot, however, represent a threat for the American global position. The United States has moreover acquired, through her new relations with China, new possibilities of action and influence in the Asian area.

The original bipolar counterposition which existed during the immediate post-war period, has therefore gradually given way to a new situation in which the number of political and military balance components has increased, and amongst these are five major actors: the United States, China, the Soviet Union, Japan and Vietnam. Moreover, during this period several new independent states have formed in the area.

The main sector, however, where the influence of new factors of balance has most obviously emerged is South-East Asia, more especially since the American disengagement from Vietnam in 1975. This disengagement has created a new political and strategic situation in the area, a situation determined by the emergence of a unified and ideologically motivated Vietnam with an active interest in Cambodia and Laos; and at the same time by the parallel assertion and consolidation of an important Soviet air and naval presence with equipped bases along the Vietnamese coastline.

This situation has had a considerable influence on the countries of South-East Asia and on their political directives and has reinforced, through ASEAN, the collaboration – especially political – amongst the participating countries.

III THE CONSOLIDATION OF ASEAN AS A 'DIPLOMATIC COMMUNITY'

The origins of ASEAN go back to 1967 with the declaration signed at Bangkok on 8 August of that year by the five founder countries: the Philippines, Indonesia, Malaysia, Singapore and Thailand (these countries were joined in January 1984 by Brunei.) The memorandum of agreement of ASEAN contained aims of a general character: promotion of peace and regional stability; advancement of economic development, encouragement of an active co-operation and mutual assistance on questions of common interest in the economic, social, scientific and administrative fields.

The original structure of ASEAN was composed of the Foreign Ministers' Council, of which a permanent Committee – presided over in turn by the Foreign Minister of each of the member countries and by the ambassadors accredited to the host country of the moment – represented the executive organ. Since its foundation, however, and up to the summit of the Association held at Bali in February 1976, ASEAN activity had had limited developments. The Bali meeting, held a few months after the end of the Indo-Chinese conflict, represented a turning point and the beginning of a phase of active revival of ASEAN. A 'Treaty of Amity and Co-operation' aiming at the settlement of the existing controversies amongst the associated countries, as well as a 'Declaration of Concord' proclaiming the political and economic programme of the Association, were signed at Bali. Finally a permanent Secretariat was established which was based in Jakarta.

The timing of this turning point clearly indicates how the new situation, which came about in South-East Asia following the American disengagement from Vietnam, represented the driving force for a reinvigorated political and diplomatic co-operation amongst the associated countries. Running parallel to this there was a greater external projection of ASEAN which started developing new contacts, on a political as well as economic level, in particular with Japan and the European Economic Community.

The ASEAN activity – apart from the aspects of co-operation in the fields of economics and administration – appeared mainly, to the outside world, as that of a 'diplomatic community' aiming at the adoption of common directives with regard to events likely to influence the area balances and affect some common interests. This of course does not rule out the fact that certain differences of opinion have continued to exist in the political perceptions of the associated countries. This is particularly true with regard to the respective roles of China and Vietnam in the power balance of the area. Whilst some associate countries, such as Thailand and Singapore, are more sensitive to the pressure by Vietnam and to the dangers that this might entail, other countries, such as Indonesia and Malaysia, tend to put greater emphasis on the possible consequences of a growing expansionist pressure by China towards the South, to which Vietnam in the long run might represent a cushion and a counterbalancing element.

However, in spite of these differences in appreciation, especially in the long-term perspective, the ASEAN countries have reached and shown a remarkable unity of objectives, in particular in the face of the worsening Indo-Chinese crisis after the invasion of Cambodia by Vietnam.

Political co-operation has thus assumed a major role probably becoming the area of main importance in the relations amongst the associated countries. The developments of the Indo-Chinese conflict, in particular, have fostered an increased group solidarity. The repeated successes in the votes at the United Nations and other international conferences as well as in the Non-Aligned Movement (NAM), have enhanced the international prestige of ASEAN. The institutional relations established with the United States, Japan and the European Community, have also contributed notably to this prestige.

IV THE DEVELOPMENT OF RELATIONS BETWEEN THE EC AND ASEAN

The fundamental element that characterises the European Community's attitude towards ASEAN is the assumption that – in a regional context such as that of South-East Asia, of primary importance for the stability of Asia and the Pacific – ASEAN represents an important element of stability which also corresponds to the general interests of Europe. From this angle, and in the belief that international balances should be seen interdependently and globally, the respective interests of the EC and ASEAN present a remarkable similarity from which stems the mutual interest for institutional forms of consultation and collaboration.

The first institutional meeting of the two organisations, at Foreign

Ministers' level, took place in Brussels in November 1978. Subsequently – at fairly regular intervals – similar meetings took place in Kuala Lumpur in March 1980, in London in October 1981, in Bangkok in March 1983, in Dublin in November 1984, in Jakarta in October 1986, *etc*. It is to be noted that, as from the ministerial meeting of 1983 in Bangkok, the agenda of the EC-ASEAN conferences has grown larger: besides some regional problems of common interest (mainly Cambodia and Afghanistan) a growing number of other problems of both regional and global importance were discussed, such as the Middle East, East-West relations and armaments control.

The final communiqué of the meeting in Jakarta refers, in fact, to the following problems discussed there and points out some common assessments: Cambodia, Afghanistan, East-West relations, South Africa, the Middle East, the financial crisis of the United Nations, cultural co-operation, and the international economic situation. The last part of the communiqué dwells on the problem of investments as well as on the general one concerning economic relations between the EC and ASEAN.

As can be seen, a wide variety of problems was dealt with in respect of which a considerable similarity of position was shown. The EC's interest in developing a systematic dialogue with ASEAN happens to be enhanced by the fact that the ASEAN countries are in their turn linked to other international groupings: thus Malaysia and Indonesia are members of the Islamic Conference, Malaysia and Singapore belong to the Commonwealth, and finally Malaysia, Singapore and Indonesia are part of the Non-Aligned Movement. Moreover, relations between the EC and ASEAN are not limited to the periodical institutional meeting amongst the Foreign Ministers. The EC countries, together with Japan, Australia, Canada, the United States and New Zealand, form the so-called 'dialogue partners' of ASEAN. Meetings between ASEAN and the 'dialogue partners' take place collaterally to the Ministerial Conference which is held annually, in rotation, in one of the capitals of the six states. To these meetings the EC countries have latterly been represented by a 'troika' headed by a delegate of the President in office.

Finally it must be noted that the EC's interest towards ASEAN is not limited to the problems and to the international situation of the moment. The EC countries have also shown an active interest in what represents the main long-term political objective of ASEAN: that is the project of a zone of peace, freedom and neutrality (ZOPFAN) in

South-East Asia, originally expressed in the Kuala Lumpur Declaration of 1975, which aims at the creation of a zone which would be set aside from external interference from any quarter. The ASEAN countries also hope that other governments of the area – and in the first place Vietnam herself – might decide, in their own interest, to collaborate with them in the achievement of this great, peaceful design.

Such a long-term directive of ASEAN was confirmed during the inter-ministerial meeting with the EC held in Dublin in 1984. On that occasion the ASEAN countries also requested the Community's full support for a political solution of the Cambodian crisis, the continuance of which could aggravate the Chinese-Soviet rivalry in the area with destabilising consequences for the whole of South-East Asia. The setting in motion of a conciliatory process in the region must in any case be regarded as a premise for the creation of ZOPFAN.

V THE MAIN PROBLEMS OF SOUTH-EAST ASIA

At the present time, the political interest of Western Europe towards South-East Asia is centred mainly on two problems which are of mutual interest for a more stable international balance. These problems are: the continuing Indo-Chinese conflict and the expansion of the Soviet military presence in the area.

The Indo-Chinese conflict – which today consists of the Vietnamese political and military presence in Cambodia – has its historical origins in the centuries-old tendency of the Vietnamese peoples to expand towards the fertile plains of the South, and the equally historical counter position between Vietnam and China. This counter position – dormant during the colonial epoch and the subsequent conflicts in Vietnam – has now dramatically re-emerged and its main setting has been Cambodia.

With the *coup d'état* of December 1978, actively supported by the Vietnamese forces, Hanoi installed in Cambodia a régime bound to Vietnam and fundamentally dependent on her support. Hanoi's action – although it contributed to overthrow a particularly hated and bloodthirsty régime – has generally been condemned by the international community, and the repeated United Nations decisions in this respect are evidence of this censure. China, for her part, has regarded Hanoi's political and military action as a serious threat to her own security, looking upon it as an expression of Hanoi's 'hegemonic directive' over the whole of Indo-China, a directive not only tending to exclude all Chinese influence but moreover openly hostile to that country.

Such a prospect is certainly unacceptable to China. A solid and hostile political-military unit on her southern border would prove to be for China not only a barrier to her historical influence, but also a permanent military threat. To this must be added the strengthening of the relationship between Vietnam and the Soviet Union which was developed during the recent conflict. The Soviet Union certainly has an interest in supporting a strong entity tendentially hostile to China at the latter's southern frontier, both as a check to Chinese power and as a means of dispersing her military potential. There is also a no less considerable Soviet interest in procuring air and naval support bases along the Vietnamese coastline which faces a vast region of South-East Asia along which run important commercial routes.

The above explains the motives of the sharp Chinese reaction to Vietnam's invasion of Cambodia, a reaction which in February 1979 also took on a military aspect with that 'punitive lesson' against Vietnam, which, however, did not obtain the hoped for results but, on the contrary, turned out to be a substantial failure for the Chinese military forces. The prospect of Chinese military pressure bending Vietnam – which has a well-trained army and can count on Soviet assistance – therefore, seems unlikely.

On her part Vietnam has not so far succeeded in crushing the guerilla forces that continue operating in Cambodia: these forces receive outside assistance and are headed by a government in exile presided over by Prince Sihanouk. A stalemate has ensued which presents two fundamental dangers and negative aspects: first of all this situation is an obstacle to the stabilisation of political and military balances in that important region and at the same time it encourages Soviet presence in the zone thus making Vietnam – although it cannot be considered a satellite state – more and more dependent on Soviet assistance.

In the face of these two prospects the interests of Western Europe and ASEAN undoubtedly coincide. Both have an interest in eliminating dangerous centres of tension and instability in the area, such as that represented by the situation in Cambodia. Faced with a situation of this kind it is certainly necessary to maintain positions of principle such as the non-acceptance of the Vietnamese military invasion and occupation of that country. However, while insisting on a withdrawal of those forces, possible compromise solutions are being considered; thus both ASEAN and the European Community have shown a positive interest in a possible coalition, presided over by Prince Sihanouk, between the government in exile and the present Cambodian régime, coupled with a gradual withdrawal of the Vietnamese forces from Cambodia. In this regard a specific eight-point proposal was put forward by Prince Sihanouk in March 1986. The proposal was substantially approved by the ASEAN countries and in May the EC countries adhered to it 'as a positive contribution for a political solution'. Vietnam's attitude has so far been negative, although she has expressed her intention of withdrawing her troops from Cambodia by 1990.

This is not the place for an investigation on the prospects for a solution to the Cambodian crisis; but the continuance of what is now called the third war of Indo-China threatens to worsen a military confrontation as well as the involvement of the main powers of the region with their opposed interests. All this jeopardises regional stability with negative consequences for the general international balances of power.

Finally, and independently from the direct involvement in the Cambodian crisis, careful consideration must be given to the implications of the increased Soviet presence which is now of a mainly military nature. About a third of Soviet naval forces are at present stationed in the Far East with considerable air forces and with modern nuclear units. Increasingly the Soviet Union has a tendency to behave as an Asian power and recent authoritative confirmations of this have been given. The above must not in itself give cause for alarm, but it requires a careful evaluation of possible developments and of its repercussions on the present power balances. Therefore, the situation is one that requires constant consultation.

In conclusion, we can observe that the institutional relations between the European Community and ASEAN are based on a stable parallelism of interests and seem destined to develop further in the future. These relations are given special significance thanks to historical factors as well as to the political structures of the countries concerned, who are all averse to totalitarian systems and ideologies. This parallelism of interests also represents an incentive towards stable forms of consultation and collaboration. The institutional forms which at present govern the relationship on the political level between the two groupings, based on the light of experience, can be considered an adequate setting even for the future.

Finally, the relationship which has been established between the countries of the European Community and those of ASEAN represents an important and positive example of the North-South political dialogue.

4 Western European Security and the Role of NATO

Franco A. Casadio

1. We Europeans often find ourselves questioning the foundation and credibility of the security of Western Europe. In fact, for thirty years now we have been asking the same three questions. What is Europe frightened of (from now on we shall say 'Europe' even if we mean 'Western Europe')? What is the threat which the individual countries feel to their own security? Each of them perceives it in a more or less different way, but in all cases they feel it comes from the east. This is the first question.

The second question is: up to what point will the United States be willing to go to defend its Eastern Front and in particular that sector of this front which is in Europe? In particular, are we sure that the United States is actually prepared to use the nuclear weapon in defence of Europe and thus let itself be taken up in the spiral of Soviet nuclear reprisal on North American territory?

The third question: how is it that the Soviet Union has a conventional and nuclear deployment on its Western Front so clearly 'projected' towards the West? To be more explicit, on the basis of what plans has the Soviet Union deployed such an offensive front against Western Europe?

2. I propose to break up the 'system' of international relations within which Europe is seeking its security into its component parts. These components are:

1 the type of threat which Europe feels is coming from the East;
2 the type of threat hanging over the United States, which Americans feel is coming from different parts of the world and not only the east, as is the case with Europe;
3 what the Soviet Union, for its part, feels it is threatened by. This point has to be determined in order to understand what

plans the Soviet Union has prepared against Western Europe and therefore what concrete form the Soviet threat could take;
4 what are, from a strategic viewpoint, the specific and typical features of the European theatre, that is of the area of tension existing at the point where NATO and the Warsaw Pact meet up;
5 what are and what were NATO's strategic doctrines. These doctrines have had the main aim of lessening tension and the threat from the east. We must learn if the European states belonging to NATO have considered these doctrines capable or not of guaranteeing security to Europe.

3. Among all the possible threats which Europe can see, the really important one comes from the east, that is from the Soviet Union. Since the end of World War II, and not just since the creation of the Warsaw Pact in 1955, this threat has been seen in two forms which, rightly or wrongly, are charged to the Soviet Union: military pressure and subversion.

To my knowledge, no-one has described this 'perception of threat' better than Paul Henri Spaak, in the speech he gave on 28 September 1948 in the third ordinary session of the General Assembly of the United Nations, at the Palais de Chaillot in Paris. It was the famous speech, both strong and balanced, known as the speech of 'fear', the 'fear of the USSR', the fear of its government, the 'fear of its politics', as Spaak would write in his Memoirs, eighteen years later.

Spaak speaks precisely of the two reasons for fear which I have just mentioned: military pressure and subversion. Three days before, on 25 September, the Soviet representative, Vishinsky had violently attacked Western Europe and the United States, giving one of the first examples of that Soviet 'propaganda' which is based on accusation, the more vehement the less it is justified, and the twisting of truth.

4. 'Do you know why we're frightened?' Spaak began.

'We're frightened because you're always speaking of imperialism. . . What is the current notion of imperialism? It's that of a country, generally a big country, which makes conquests and increases its influence in the world. And what is the historic reality of these past years? There's only one large country which has come out of the war acquiring other territories and this large country is

> the USSR. During the war and because of the war you annexed the Baltic countries. During the war and because of the war you took a piece of Finland . . . a piece of Poland. Thanks to your audacious and able policy, you have asserted your power in Warsaw, Prague, Belgrade, Bucharest and Sofia. Thanks to your policy, you occupy Vienna . . . and Berlin and you don't seem at all willing to leave them. Thanks to your policy, you are now claiming your rights in the control of the Ruhr. Your empire extends from the Black Sea to the Baltic and the Mediterranean. . . And you ask us why we are worried? The truth is that your foreign policy is now more audacious and ambitious than that of the Czars themselves.'

The threat which Western Europe has always perceived as coming from the east is made up of different elements: geographical Europe split in two, as had never happened before, Eastern Europe sucked up into a military and economic political system the opposite of that, ancient and deep-rooted, of the western part of Europe; the 'projection' of the Soviet Union towards the West, that is towards us. The instrument with which the Soviet Union had conquered and obtained all this was, in our eyes, force. ' . . . and you ask us why we are worried?' Spaak continued to repeat.

5. But there is a second component of the threat, which the Western Europeans are convinced they can perceive, and which comes from the Soviet Union.

'Finally you frighten us,'[continues Spaak] –

> 'because in each of the countries represented here you maintain a fifth column in comparison to which Hitler's fifth column was nothing but a boy-scout organisation. There's no place in the world in which a government, in Europe, Africa or Asia, which is facing difficulties or obstacles, doesn't have to cope with you, already there to render them more serious. . . At this moment, in each of our countries, there is a group of men who not only act as representatives and defenders of your foreign policy (which, after all, wouldn't in fact be all that bad), but who never miss an occasion to weaken politically, morally and socially the State in which they are living.'

Certainly, the atmosphere of the epoch had a great influence in explaining the echo which Spaak's words aroused in all of Western Europe.

6. Western Europe – or rather the individual countries of Western Europe – has always seen the threat from the east as a form of military pressure, supported by arms which the Soviet Union was stockpiling in ever increasing quantities. As regards the other threat, that of subversion, it has undoubtedly diminished, at least to a certain extent, with the passage from the period dominated by the Cold War to that influenced by peaceful co-existence. With the period of détente (1969–1975), the threat perceived as subversion increased instead of decreasing as would have been reasonable. What caused the lack of a 'real' détente were the social violence and terrorism factors which began in 1968 and which were concentrated in the 'five golden years' of domestic and international terrorism (1968–1972.) The continuing perception of this twofold threat inevitably forced the Western European countries into seeking the protection of the United States. If one thinks carefully, it is not in fact all that difficult to explain the fact that a sentiment was born in a more or less conscious and open manner, alongside that of fear, which consisted of anxiety about the danger of being abandoned by the United States one day or another.

7. I want to repeat that the type of analysis which we are carrying out at this moment is not 'objective', that is we are not so much worried about knowing, for example, the position which Europe occupies in the strategic lines of North American and Soviet support. We are mainly conducting a 'subjective' analysis. What we want to do, at least for now, is to demonstrate the sentiments which have influenced public opinion in West European countries and, to a large extent, the governments themselves, in their troubled search for a reasonable satisfaction of their sense of security.

From this viewpoint it is not surprising that Europeans feel gripped by two contradictory sentiments. On one side they are frightened of being abandoned by the Americans. At the same time they are frightened of being involved by the United States in tensions, crises and conflicts which do not concern them and to which they wish to remain extraneous. This can happen in many ways, but there are two which most disturb Europeans: the danger of finding themselves involved in a nuclear war, not depending on Europe, and the danger of war begun by mistake. Obviously it would either be a nuclear war or one which could easily become so.

8. The United States' perception of the threat is completely different. First of all, while Europe only sees the one coming from the

east as a military threat, the United States sees the threats to it as coming from a radius of 360°. The first reason is a geostrategic one. The Soviet bloc, although very distant (it is only in the Bering Straits that the USA and USSR are separated by a distance of a few miles), is situated the other side of the Atlantic to the east, the other side of the Pacific to the west and the other side of the Arctic to the north. There are those who say that the United States can see the threatening Soviet presence in Cuba, and especially in Nicaragua, just beyond the Caribbean. Therefore also to the south.

The United States perceives two major threats. The first – which it is sure it can control better than the other – is the possible alteration of the delicate nuclear balance in favour of the Soviet Union. The Americans take care of this threat by 'arms control', which they themselves invented. Trusting in its confirmed technological superiority, the United States is therefore sure it can easily control the 'quantitative increments' which the Soviet Union has in the past attempted to achieve to its own advantage.

But it is the other threat which the Americans fear they will not always manage to control, or control enough. They see any event which could alter the balance of power in the world as a threat. They are not so good at 'crisis management' as they are at 'arms control.'

9. Whatever the type of threat which the United States sees, the friendship and alliance of Western Europe are indispensable. The Americans cannot lose Western Europe, its vast resources of people, culture and economic wealth. For the security of the United States it would be a disaster if the security line situated in the east were to move back, that is, rest on Turkey or Israel.
From this point of view the Europeans need have no worries.

10. Let us now put ourselves in the place of the Warsaw Pact and the Soviet Union. The aggressive 'projection' of the Warsaw Pact in the direction of the West is seen in the deployment of the Soviet forces on the Western Front and the concentration of bases and depots behind this Front. We can, however, give two different explanations of this projection. We can put it down to the Soviet Union's expansionist trend, implicit in the ideology it professes and in its strategic doctrines, dependent on this ideology. Or we can explain it by the counter-move with which the Soviet Union proposes to break the containment with which the West (not only NATO, which operates in a well-defined region) has managed to halt the

Soviet bloc and in fact the Russian-Chinese bloc for many years.

11. The Soviet Union has broken the West's containment in two different ways, with its strategic lines 1 and 2. Its strategic line 1 starts from the Arctic Sea bases and goes through the northern and central Atlantic to break the line which connects North America with Europe in the Atlantic. With its strategic support line 2, also called the 'line of the fleets', the Soviet Union links up the naval theatres and relative fleets of the Black Sea, Eastern Mediterranean, Red Sea, Indian Ocean and the fleet which operates in South-East Asia to control maritime passages from Indonesia, to join up finally with the fleet of the eastern Siberian ports. With this line – which also acts as a containment of China – the Soviet Union overlaps the North American strategic line at two points, that is in the Middle East and in South-East Asia.

The threat of containment and the Soviet counter-move leave aside another 'level' of the threat, to which the Soviet Union also feels exposed: the nuclear one. I will just point out that the Soviet Union is convinced that if it should find itself in a situation of nuclear inferiority, this will mainly be due to its qualitative and technological shortcomings, especially in the field of rockets. If the Soviet Union wants to make up for its loss of security deriving from the qualitative progress made by the United States, it can only increase the quantity of its nuclear arms and point them at 'paying' objectives, such as the Western European countries.

12. The Soviet Union reacts to a perception of the threat such as this with 'doctrines' which it considers can guarantee its security. For Western Europe this 'reaction' is taken for granted, even if very often the fear of a western aggression is not really thought to be credible. However, it is natural that some action 'scenarios' are formulated in Western Europe which the Soviets could see as applied to them. For our part we will formulate some of them.

First of all, it is necessary to think of two or three cases in which Europe would be involved in an indirect, but always significant manner. I refer to side effects:

– caused by distant events such as the occupation of Afghanistan by Soviet troops

– or caused by closer events, such as a repression in Poland, and that is in the Soviet camp itself.

The new trend of Soviet foreign policy has lessened the danger of these events. But there has been no lack of episodes in NATO's history in which typical events of the Soviet camp – such as the 1968 Czechoslovak question – have aroused fear and therefore a very serious stiffening on the part of NATO.

13. We cannot exclude from the list of our 'scenarios' the fact that the Soviet Union could

– carry out a rapid and circumscribed attack on the West, taking advantage of the surprise and understandable few days' delay on the part of the European countries of NATO and the American forces in Europe. According to those who uphold this thesis, the attack would have as its sole aim the pursuit of stronger negotiating platforms, in order to obtain intermediate political results;

– manage to achieve a limited war, after it has succeeded in procuring an actual disengagement of the United States, even if only with a short-lived effect.

14. In the list of hypotheses made by experts on a possible Soviet attack, there are three other 'scenarios' which we want to mention:

– the hypothesis of an attack on Europe, within a generalised conflict. In this case the attack to the north, centre or south of the NATO line-up would be supplemented by a widespread war at sea, in the Mediterranean and in the oceans;

– the hypothesis of a classic attack, by subsequent echelons (which is the type of hypothesis adopted by the *Rogers Doctrine*) concentrated in the central theatre;

– the hypothesis of a *blitzkrieg*, which would lead to a concentration of Soviet forces in restricted sectors, thus leaving important stretches of the Front undefended;

– the hypothesis of an attack directed at individual targets, such as weapon depots, rocket-launching systems or command and control centres.

15. In the hypotheses we are formulating now the conflict would no longer be just classic or conventional, but would inevitably be nuclear. There are only two hypotheses:

– the Soviet Union forces NATO to make use of nuclear arms, whatever the rhythm and cadence of the use of nuclear arms with increasing range and power;

– the Soviet Union, contrary to its stated doctrines, takes the initiative of a surprise, preventive nuclear attack.

This hypothesis would only become real in the case in which the Soviet Union could be certain of not being submitted to a North American nuclear reprisal. And this could occur in two cases: if the USSR should guarantee the United States' abstension and if the USSR should have an unexpected superiority in the typical means of the Strategic Defence Initiative.

In more general terms there is a widespread conviction – which is also well-founded – that there will not be a conflict in Europe but if there were to be one it would inevitably be a nuclear conflict.

16. The European theatre is drawn by the line of contact between NATO's Eastern Front and the Warsaw Pact's Western one. It would be very helpful, especially for us, to try to determine the 'depth' of this theatre, on each side. The Vienna negotiations, known as MBFR, demonstrate how difficult this is. It is thus appropriate and legitimate to ask ourselves if this theatre is symmetrical or asymmetrical and, taking that it is asymmetrical, if this situation acts in itself in the favour of Western Europe and NATO, or Eastern Europe and the Warsaw Pact.

The matter is clear enough. The theatre is asymmetrical and in fact acts in favour of the Warsaw Pact. The first and most serious asymmetry (serious for NATO) is of a geostrategic nature. On the Soviet side, behind the border with the West, there is a great expanse of territory up to the Urals, very suitable for far-ranging defensive manoeuvres in that it has a relatively low density of population and industries. On the NATO side, however, the density of population and industries around the border is very high and the geographic depth considerably less. Thirty per cent of West Germany's industry is to be found within a 60-mile strip west of the border between the two military pacts. Thus one understands why, in order of time, the first strategy adopted by NATO was that of advance defence.

17. The other dominant asymmetry in the European theatre is between the strategic doctrines of the Warsaw Pact, conceived and actuated in a unitary manner, and that of NATO. Also with NATO, the different strategic doctrines which have succeeded each other over time have shown a certain unitary conception. Many of us think that this unitary conception has been enough to harmonise the use of forces and co-ordinate the contribution and support of the various contingents. Behind NATO's 'doctrines' (and unlike the Warsaw Pact's doctrines) the major strategic choices made by the European

countries and the United States, which are necessarily 'upstream' of NATO's doctrine, are affected by the moods of their respective public opinions to a much greater extent than in Eastern Europe.

In the world, only the European theatre is dominated by interdependence and also by the immediate infectiousness between the use of classic and conventional arms and the use of nuclear arms, on a regional and global level. This means that, in the European theatre, the dominant strategic problem is that of avoiding any kind of conflict, given that no power in the world can guarantee that a 'conventional' Soviet attack, that is with classic weapons, against Western Europe will not automatically start off a general nuclear conflict.

Up to now the deterrent to discourage the Soviet use of conventional weapons has been based on this automatic follow-up and the implicit threat implied in it. To raise the threshold of nuclear war – and that is to keep off the moment in which it would become inevitable to use nuclear weapons – the only thing to do seems to be that of stepping up our defence capacities in terms of classic arms, until they are the same as those of the Warsaw Pact, if they really are superior.

18. Faced with this threat, and bearing in mind the typical geostrategic and geopolitical context of the European theatre, the European countries belonging to NATO and the United States have drawn up a successive series of defence plans in the Alliance organisations. Were they well conceived and implemented? What effect did these doctrines and plans have on the sense of security which the Europeans have been pursuing for forty years now?

At the beginning of the 1950s, European security was primarily based on the hope of an advance defence, secondly on the proposal of absorbing the Soviet attack, if necessary by retreating up to the Rhine and no further, and thirdly on the certainty of an American strategic nuclear attack. In the mid 1960s, the sentiments included in NATO's strategic doctrines were still three in number but different from those of the previous years. First, the last hope was placed in a massive reaction, secondly, at the same time greater faith was placed in the intermediate range of nuclear weapons and thirdly, we entrusted our security to the uncertainty which we provoked in the adversary. Our response will not be univocal, but flexible. As long as our enemies are on their guard and do not have too much faith in themselves, we will strike them where they least expect it and, furthermore, if it comes to a nuclear conflict, it will be their fault. We will never provoke such a conflict at the highest level.

19. At the end of the 1960s the mechanism is perfected, so much so that it contains an open and clear 'game of the parties'. For many years we were even certain that we had achieved security, even if the Warsaw Pact's conventional forces were superior to ours. We had drawn up our doctrine: first, we envisaged different levels of military clashes, but all linked to the higher levels by precise escalation mechanisms; secondly, we also envisaged that there would be 'thresholds' or 'steps' between one level and the next, separated by a barrier (decoupling); thirdly, we invented the 'triads' that is, three military tools, independent of each other, and those were conventional forces, tactical or theatre nuclear weapons and strategic nuclear weapons.

20. NATO's strategic doctrines have to satisfy three requirements: first, come within the global strategy of the United States, a country which does not want to and cannot afford to lose the European 'pillar'; secondly, they have to safeguard Europe with North American nuclear power; and thirdly, they have to look after the interests of border countries, such as West Germany.

At the beginning of the 1980s, the progressive upgrading of NATO's strategic doctrines led to the *Rogers Doctrine* which introduced five novelties. First, the doctrine of active defence was accepted. However, it would be limited to striking the first Soviet echelon, which would be separated from the others with deep strike actions. This element of NATO's strategy is aimed at hitting East Germany more than the others. Secondly, greater use is made of forward manoeuvres of the defence forces. The goal is to take away the adversary's attack initiative – such as any harassing fire by the artillery – to then pass to the offensive, and anyway to exploit the depth of the space behind the enemy, an important power factor for him.

21. The element of strength was the third: the use of the air forces and new conventional technologies, in which NATO is stronger than the Warsaw Pact. It involves undermining the second, third and last echelons of the Soviet forces, before they come into contact with NATO's defences. Technically all this means putting two strategic principles into action: the acquisition of targets, and the control of

and the use of air forces not only to support the land forces but as a harassment on the battle field. Among the indirect effects of this use of strength doctrine, no less important, according to some, is the support given in this way to domestic revolt and its significance.

Finally, the last two important elements of this doctrine: fourth, making the most use of the light infantry, 'anchored' to the ground; and fifth, the 'tacticalisation' of nuclear weapons. As regards this principle, the theatre forces would be used as an actual war instrument and no longer as a cog in the escalation.

22. We have now completed the survey of the threats to which Europe feels vulnerable, the forms of attack to which it feels exposed, the different way in which the mutual solidarity of Europe and the United States is felt and the doctrines with which the European states have attempted, from time to time, to gain a sense of security.

As we said at the beginning, our task was not to speak of NATO's 'strategies' or those of the Warsaw Pact. Our task was that of indicating what anxieties have beset the Europcans over these years and why they still do. We have discovered one thing: NATO is certainly a good defence, but even if it were not its role would still be that of 'reassuring' Europeans. And this seems to me very important.

5 Regional Security: Problems and Prospects in South-East Asia

Lau Teik Soon

INTRODUCTION

The most problematic regional security issue today is Vietnam's policy towards the Indo-China states, which is aimed at establishing what Hanoi calls 'a special relationship' among Vietnam, Laos and Cambodia (or Kampuchea). Since 1975, this issue has pre-occupied all the South-East Asian governments as well as certain external powers especially China, the Soviet Union and the United States. The focus of attention has been on the specific aspect of Vietnam's Indo-China policy, that is, Vietnam's occupation of Cambodia which has deprived the Cambodian people of their independence, sovereignty and territorial integrity. By this act, Hanoi has forced through the structure of the special relationship on Cambodia, but in the process, it has violated certain principles of international relations, namely non-interference in another state's affairs, and peaceful settlement of inter-state disputes.

Vietnam's occupation of Cambodia is viewed by the ASEAN governments as a direct threat to the security of Thailand as well as an indirect threat to the other ASEAN states. There was the fear that the prolonged conflict in Cambodia might spill over into Thailand and thereby, create a wider regional confrontation. More relevant, from the ASEAN viewpoint, Vietnam's occupation of Cambodia constitutes a major constraint to the normalisation of relations between ASEAN and the Indo-China states. The ASEAN states are concerned that Vietnam should not violate the territorial integrity of another state and that the security of Thailand should not be threatened by the presence of Vietnamese troops in Cambodia.

Vietnam's policy towards Indo-China has opened the way for certain external powers to expand their influence over the internal as well as the regional affairs of South-East Asian states. Specifically, it has provided China and the Soviet Union with the opportunities to exert and promote their power and influence over the rival Indo-Chinese forces. China's influence can be felt through its military support of the anti-Vietnamese resistance movements in Cambodia. On the other hand, the Soviet Union's strong support for Hanoi has resulted in the extensive influence of Moscow in the political and military affairs of the Indo-China states. More importantly, it has led to the build up of the large military presence of Soviet forces in Vietnam.

The occupation of Cambodia by Vietnam and the subsequent political and strategic re-alignments of the protagonists have affected the strategic balance in the region. At the superpower level, the Soviet Union has strengthened its position *vis-à-vis* the United States in the Asia-Pacific region. This impact together with others mentioned above have made this issue, namely, Vietnam's policy towards Indo-China including the Cambodian problem, a matter of central concern in the South-East Asian region.

VIETNAM'S SPECIAL RELATIONSHIP WITH LAOS AND CAMBODIA

Vietnam's policy towards Indo-China states is aimed at developing a special relationship with its immediate neighbours, Laos and Cambodia. This special relationship is derived from the colonial experience, the nationalist struggles and the strategic unity of the Indo-China states. Under French colonialism, Indo-China constituted one main administrative unit and the French administrators and their Vietnamese subordinates ruled the whole region. In this way, the Vietnamese infiltrated the structures and institutions of government in the other Indo-China states.

During the nationalist struggle for independence, first against French colonialism and later American imperialism, the Vietnamese communist leaders and troops assisted and influenced the communist nationalist movements in Laos and Cambodia. But the main struggle was between Vietnam and the external forces, and in this struggle, Hanoi maintained the need for the strategic unity of the whole of Indo-China. That is to say, Hanoi considered it vital that political developments in the neighbouring states should facilitate the victory of the Vietnamese communists over their enemies. Specifically, Hanoi would feel secure if there were friendly governments in

Vientiane and Phnom Penh, and if they had easy access into Laotian and Cambodian border areas in order to pursue successfully their military objectives.

After the independence of the three Indo-China states was achieved in 1975, Hanoi maintained that the three states should be bound close together in a 'special relationship', so that their political, social, economic and security developments could harmonise with each other's national interests. The principle adopted was that no neighbouring Indo-China state should be a threat or used to threaten another state in the region. Towards this goal, various mechanisms were utilised including the following: treaty agreements providing for economic and military commitments, regular consultative meetings to co-ordinate internal and foreign policies, and a joint stand on various international issues. Over and above all, Laos and Cambodia would have to accept the dominant role of Hanoi in Indo-China affairs.

The earliest manifestation of Hanoi's policy of establishing a special relationship with its neighbours was seen in the formation of the Indo-Chinese Communist Party (ICP) in 1930 led by the Vietnamese leader, Ho Chih Minh. The premise was that the communist revolt against the colonial French rule was on an Indo-China scale and not just confined to one area. This was comparable to the Indonesian nationalists' rebellion against Dutch rule in the whole of Indonesia in the 1940s.

Subsequently, however, in 1950 the ICP was disbanded and separate communist parties were established to continue the revolt against the French and later the Americans. But these communist parties in Indo-China were to be linked together and their activities co-ordinated by the Vietnamese Workers' Party – the Viet Minh. The Viet Minh became a dominant influence over the other two Indo-China communist parties *viz*. the Pathet Lao and the Khmer Issarak in Laos and Cambodia respectively.

The culmination of this phase of co-operation among the Indo-Chinese communists was the Geneva Conference of 1954. The Vietnamese communists obtained control of half of Vietnam and the prospect of complete control of the whole country in two years' time. The Pathet Lao was recognised as a nationalists' group and given control of the southern and eastern provinces bordering Vietnam. But the Cambodian communists left the Geneva meeting empty-handed. Hanoi did not champion their cause because Ho Chih Minh needed the co-operation of Prince Sihanouk in order to strengthen the Viet Minh's struggle for the reunification of Vietnam. This was the first serious breach between the Vietnamese and Cambodian communists which was to have serious implications for Cambodian-Vietnamese relations between 1975 and 1978.

During the 1960s and 1970s, the Vietnamese communists concentrated on the reunification of Vietnam. But at the same time, Hanoi assisted the Pathet Lao and the Cambodian Communist Party – the Khmer Rouge under Pol Pot, in their struggles against their governments. But Hanoi was closer and more co-operative towards the Pathet Lao: Hanoi supported the Pathet Lao against the Royal Vientiane government. On the other hand, Hanoi's support for the Khmer Rouge was suspect: in fact, Hanoi favoured Prince Sihanouk, even when the latter suppressed the communist-led rebellion in Samlaut in 1967. The Cambodian communists had to rely on their own resources to conduct their guerilla war against Prince Sihanouk.

In 1970, Cambodian communists benefited most from the overthrow of Sihanouk by the Lon Nol forces and the subsequent American bombing of Cambodia. China assisted in the formation of an alliance between Sihanouk and the Khmer Rouge. But what swelled membership of the Communist Party and strengthened the resistance against Lon Nol was the American bombing of the country. By the early months of 1975, the communist forces in Cambodia and Vietnam pushed towards final victory as the Americans and their allies were driven back. In mid-April 1975, the Khmer Rouge achieved their victory and a fortnight later, the Viet Minh took Saigon. In Laos, the Pathet Lao declared the establishment of the People's Republic of Laos after ousting the neutralist government of Souvanna Phouma. Thus, by the end of 1975, all of Indo-China came under communist rule, and each of the states had its own separate independent and sovereign government.

Between 1975 and 1976, Vietnam mobilised all its resources to reunify the country – this was achieved in June 1976. Then, Hanoi turned its attention to the question of the establishment of a special relationship with its Indo-Chinese neighbours. Vietnam did not have much problem in forging an early agreement with Laos. In July 1977, Hanoi and Vientiane signed a 25-year Treaty of Friendship and Co-operation which bound Vientiane to Hanoi in a very close relationship economically, politically and strategically. As a land-locked country, Laos was dependent on Vietnam for access to the outside world. More importantly, in view of its backwardness, Laos needed the support of Vietnam for its economic development and defence build up. Thus, the treaty was a necessity for Vientiane, but in turn, it had to take into account Vietnamese interests in the formulation of policies concerning Laotian development. Under the treaty, Vietnam has undertaken certain obligations, including economic and technical assistance and stationing of troops in Laos. Hanoi maintains a military presence of about 50 000 troops in Laos.

In its effort to establish the same kind of relationship with Cambodia, Hanoi was to come across considerable opposition from the Khmer Rouge. The Cambodian Communist Party or the Khmer Rouge under Pol Pot was an ultra-nationalist movement which was aimed first at creating a totally self-reliant state based on agricultural production, and a closed society free from any outside influence, especially Western and Vietnamese influence. Towards this end, Pol Pot embarked on a brutal policy of eliminating all bourgeois lifestyle, emptying the cities and forcing the movement of people from the urban areas to the countryside. The dictatorship of Pol Pot was also aimed at eliminating pro-Vietnamese elements within the Party. Hence, during the period 1975 to 1978, it was estimated that more than a million people died as a result of forced labour, malnutrition, famine, hunger and execution.

In its relations with Vietnam, Cambodia under Pol Pot asserted its claims over territories both near the Cambodian-Vietnamese border and offshore islands in the South China Sea, which were occupied by the Vietnamese. In fact, soon after its victory, Pol Pot drove the Vietnamese settlers out of the disputed border areas and the island of Pulo Wai. But behind the territorial dispute, was the long standing animosity between the Cambodian and the Vietnamese communists.

Since 1960 when the Cambodian Communist Party was formed under Pol Pot, the Khmer Rouge had been at odds with the Vietnamese communists. Even earlier, the Cambodian communists had suffered humiliation at the Geneva Conference when the Vietnamese communists acknowledged Sihanouk as the legitimate ruler and refused to support the Cambodian communists' claim to be a nationalist force. Between 1954 and 1970, Hanoi continued to support Sihanouk even as the latter suppressed the Khmer Rouge. Following the overthrow of Sihanouk, there had been an uneasy relationship between the Khmer Rouge and the Viet Minh. This tension broke into open conflict immediately after the Khmer Rouge victory in April 1970.

There were other deep seated roots of the strained relations between Cambodia and Vietnam. Cambodians and Vietnamese have been traditional enemies. There are considerable differences in race, religion, language and traditions. Cambodians have always feared the Vietnamese even in pre-colonial times when Vietnam together with Thailand were the major expansionist powers who had infringed on Cambodian territorial integrity. In fact, the former Khmer empire lost considerable territories to both Vietnam and Thailand and shrank to its present size. Hence, Cambodian hostility *vis-à-vis* Vietnam has its roots in ethnic, historical and strategic factors.

Subsequent to the Vietnamese reunification, Hanoi took up the issue of the border claims with Cambodia. During the years from 1976 to 1978 there were many negotiations between Cambodian and Vietnamese officials on this issue. The Khmer Rouge who had introduced an extreme form of communism, different from the Vietnamese, resisted the latter's attempts to subordinate Cambodian interests to those of Hanoi. It was clear to the Vietnamese Communist Party that the Khmer Rouge under Pol Pot would not succumb to the policy of special relationship formulated by Hanoi.

Initially, Vietnam tried to influence the Cambodian situation by supporting the pro-Vietnamese faction within the Khmer Rouge leadership but this did not achieve the desired result. There were even threats of invasion by Vietnam. Fearing a complete split between Vietnam and Cambodia, Beijing offered to mediate and to bring the two parties to the conflict to negotiate on the issue. However, the Chinese failed to convince the Indo-Chinese rivals of the necessity to overcome their border problem and maintain socialist solidarity in the region.

Vietnam resorted to aggressive means in order to ensure its national security; specifically, to settle the border conflict and political differences with the Khmer Rouge. This was to lead Hanoi to its present economic plight and isolation from the international community. In December 1978, Vietnamese troops invaded Cambodia and in January installed a pro-Hanoi government under Heng Samrin.

The Khmer Rouge under Pol Pot fled to the north and northwestern parts of Cambodia bordering Thailand from where they have continued their struggle to liberate their country. The Vietnamese, despite their overwhelming military strength have not been able to eliminate the anti-Vietnamese resistance groups. At the same time the Cambodian nationalists are gaining strength politically and militarily. Hence, the Cambodian problem seems headed towards a long protracted struggle.

VIETNAM AND ASEAN

Following the Vietnamese defeat of the United States in May 1975 and the reunification of the northern and southern parts of Vietnam the following year, Hanoi for a very brief period concentrated on domestic issues as well as establishing friendly relations with its neighbours both in Indo-China and ASEAN. It was clear that Hanoi had the formidable task of restructuring the social and economic system prevailing in the southern part of the country. The integration of the manpower resources of the south into the administrative, economic and political institutions introduced by the Vietnamese Communist Party was a vital objective confronting the Hanoi leadership in the task of reconstruction. It was necessary for Vietnam to receive financial, technical, economic and other assistance from outside countries in the Soviet bloc as well as the West. Unfortunately, between 1975 and 1978 Vietnam embarked upon policies which were to lead Hanoi into the present quagmire in Cambodia. Firstly, there was the anti-ethnic Chinese policy in the south of the country. The introduction of extreme communist policies caused the dispossession of the bourgeois capitalist class. This meant that the Vietnamese of ethnic-Chinese background were the main victims. Consequently, this Vietnamese minority sought to flee the country either overland into Cambodia and Thailand or across the seas to the ASEAN states. Such a policy aggravated the conflict between Hanoi and Beijing as well as between Vietnam and ASEAN states. Secondly, soon after its victory against the United States, Hanoi turned its attention to the border problem between Vietnam and Cambodia. Clearly there were conflicting claims over certain tracts of land along the border which had been part of the so-called Ho Chi Minh trail of the Vietnam war period. Thirdly, Hanoi began to adopt a hostile policy towards the ASEAN states. This was first manifested in 1976 at the meeting of Non-Aligned states in Colombo, Sri Lanka.

The Vietnamese occupation of Cambodia and its military forces numbering between 140 000 to 160 000 is perceived as a threat to Thailand's security. The relations between Vietnam and Thailand have not been cordial over the years. There were a number of factors which contributed to the strained relations between Bangkok and Hanoi. They had been traditional rivals for the control of Indo-China. In North-East Thailand there are about 60 000 Vietnamese settlers who have been the subject of dispute between the two countries. Vietnam is not prepared to accept the repatriation of the Vietnamese minority back to Vietnam. In the 1960s and 1970s, the relationship became worse because of Thailand's participation on the side of the United States in the Vietnam war.

For Bangkok, a neutral Cambodia is a useful buffer against the advance of the Vietnamese. Thailand together with its ASEAN allies has been in the forefront in the resistance against Vietnam's occupation of Cambodia. Thailand has succeeded in undermining the Vietnamese dominance of Cambodia and in denying to Hanoi the fruits of its military aggression. Thailand and its ASEAN allies are firm in their resolution that the Cambodian problem can only be settled through negotiation and using the UNGA resolution together with the March 1986 initiative of Prince Sihanouk as the basis for discussion among the interested parties.

In the meantime, Thailand has improved its defence forces to face any attack from Vietnam across the border. In fact since June 1980, there have been a number of Vietnamese incursions into Thai territory. The Vietnamese, with their policy of hot pursuit of the CGDK forces into Thai territory as well as their aim of deterring the Thais from intervening on the side of the CGDK forces, have intruded into Thai territory occasionally. There have been direct contacts between Thai and Vietnamese forces but on a very limited scale. Nevertheless, there is the danger of these border skirmishes becoming a permanent feature of the situation along the Cambodian-Thai border. This could escalate into a serious confrontation and even war between Thailand and Vietnam.

The Vietnamese threat to Thailand is regarded as an indirect threat by all the other ASEAN states. Hence, ASEAN has solidly stood behind Thailand in the latter's opposition to Vietnam's occupation of Cambodia.

Between 1975 and 1978, there was the prospect of the normalisation of relations between the ASEAN states and Vietnam. The Prime Minister of Vietnam, Pham Van Dong visited the ASEAN states and professed the desire to normalise relations and adhere to the principles of non-interference in internal affairs and peaceful settlement of disputes. Unfortunately, Vietnamese aggression against Cambodia has created a heightened sense of distrust and fear of the Vietnamese by most of the ASEAN states. The strained relations between ASEAN and Vietnam were also aggravated by the view expressed by Vietnam at the Non-Aligned meetings that most of the ASEAN states were not genuinely independent. It was taken to mean that because the ASEAN governments would not adopt its socialist programme, they were therefore neo-colonialists and a threat to Vietnam's interest. Vietnam's call for genuine independence for the ASEAN states was regarded as interference in the internal affairs of the ASEAN states.

Vietnam's occupation of Cambodia constitutes the major obstacle to normalisation of relations between ASEAN and Vietnam. ASEAN has called for the peaceful settlement of the issue based on the UNGA resolution but so far Hanoi has not responded positively. Nevertheless, Indonesia and Malaysia have tried to persuade Vietnam to come to the negotiating table, but up to now they have not been successful. Both Jakarta and Kuala Lumpur have advocated the position that Vietnam's security interests must be taken into account. Further, the normalisation of relations on a bilateral basis should not be constrained by the Cambodian problem. However, Vietnam wants some guarantees including the elimination of the Khmer Rouge from any future coalition government before it would consider negotiation. Of course, this is unacceptable to the Coalition Government of Democratic Kampuchea (CGDK).

ROLE OF GREAT POWERS

The continuing conflict in Cambodia has opened the way for the intervention of the two major communist powers in the regional security affairs of South-East Asia. Both China and the Soviet Union are entrenching themselves more and more and becoming active participants in the political affairs of the region particularly in Indo-China. Vietnam perceives China as its major security threat for traditional, historical and strategic reasons. It also sees China as an expansionist power. Yet China was the major power which provided assistance to Vietnam during the war against the United States. But after the war Beijing attempted to put pressure on Hanoi to side with the Chinese against the Soviets in the Sino-Soviet conflict. However, Hanoi maintained a neutral position. Further, in the dispute between Vietnam and Cambodia, although China attempted to mediate, eventually Beijing came out in support of Phnom Penh against Hanoi. This was viewed as an attempt by China to assert its dominance over Indo-China through the Khmer Rouge.

When the Vietnamese committed the aggression against Cambodia, China sent its military troops into Vietnam in February 1979 to pressure the latter to withdraw. Although the Chinese intervention was a limited engagement, it served notice to Vietnam that China could always apply military pressure on the northern flank of Vietnam's security system. In fact, the presence of Chinese military troops along the Sino-Vietnamese border constitutes a major security threat to Vietnam.

China has become the major supplier of economic and military assistance to the anti-Vietnamese resistance forces, *viz*. the Khmer Rouge as well as the non-communists under Prince Sihanouk and Son San. Such aid ensures the capability of the Cambodian nationalists to fight a protracted war. China's policy towards Vietnam is to undermine Vietnam's objective of becoming the predominant power in Indo-China and Hanoi's role as a strong ally of the Soviet Union. Since the alignment of Vietnam with the Soviet Union, beginning with the economic agreement between them signed in September 1975, Moscow has been able to build up a strong political and military presence in Indo-China. In China's view, Hanoi has assisted the Soviet encirclement of China. Hence, China would want to continue with the Cambodian conflict in order to weaken the economic and military power of the Vietnamese. Thus, it is in China's interest to prolong the conflict in Indo-China – this is a position different from that of ASEAN which would prefer to see the Cambodian issue resolved as soon as possible.

The Soviet Union has been the main beneficiary of the Vietnamese occupation of Cambodia. After the failure of the talks with Cambodia on the border question, Hanoi apparently decided on the military solution to the dispute. Towards that end Hanoi prepared itself by first joining Comecon in June and subsequently signing a 25-year Treaty of Friendship and Co-operation with the Soviet Union in November 1978. With the economic and military support of the Soviet Union, Vietnam embarked on its aggression against and occupation of Cambodia. Soviet support for the Vietnamese policy serves its interest particularly in its objective of obtaining strategic facilities to improve its position in the Asia-Pacific area. For a long time the Soviet Union has been searching for a warm water port which could serve its Pacific fleet the whole year round and link up with the bases in Soviet Asia namely Vladivostok and Petropavlovsk. Such an achievement would strengthen the Soviet position *vis-à-vis* the United States. The acquisition of bases in Vietnam would enable Moscow to reach out to the vital Straits of Malacca as well as the

Indian Ocean, and counterbalance similar facilities of the United States in the Philippines. Soviet support of Vietnam has been estimated to cost about $1 billion in economic, technical and military assistance. But it is a small price to pay for the very significant strategic bases which Moscow has gained in Vietnam.

THE UN AND THE CAMBODIAN PROBLEM

The international community has debated the Cambodian problem in the United Nations as well as in other international fora. Since 1979, the ASEAN states have initiated the resolution in the United Nations General Assembly (UNGA) which proposes to solve the Cambodian problem through a comprehensive political settlement. In 1986, 115 member states supported the UNGA resolution and 21, mainly from the Soviet bloc, opposed it. The terms of the UNGA resolution include the withdrawal of Vietnamese troops from Cambodia, the right of self-determination for the Cambodian people, and the establishment of an independent, sovereign and neutral state in Cambodia. Towards the implementation of the UNGA resolution, an international conference on Cambodia was convened by the United Nations Secretary General in July 1981 and a committee under the chairmanship of the Austrian Foreign Minister was set up to bring the conflicting parties to the negotiating table. But up to now, the United Nations has not been a successful mediator in the efforts to resolve the Cambodian problem.

In the political and military fields, the anti-Vietnamese resistance movements of Cambodia have improved their position *vis-à-vis* the Vietnamese and Heng Samrin régime. In 1982, a coalition of Cambodian nationalists comprising the factions under Prince Norodom Sihanouk, Son San and Khieu Samphan came together to form the Coalition Government of Democratic Kampuchea (CGDK). This Government has the support and recognition of the majority of the states in the United Nations. As President, Prince Sihanouk is regarded as a symbol of the unity of the Cambodians and representative of the nationalist struggle to regain their independence, sovereignty and territorial integrity. On the battle field, the CGDK forces have obtained considerable military support from China: although the Khmer Rouge receives the most amount of military supplies, the other factions under Prince Sihanouk and Son San are also recipients of Chinese military aid. Other countries including the United States provide the CGDK especially the non-communists with economic and humanitarian assistance.

In the on-going military conflict in Cambodia, neither the Vietnamese nor the CGDK forces have been able to achieve a military victory over the other. The Vietnamese conduct occasional offensives against the Cambodian guerilla areas as well as refugee camps. But they have not been able to dislodge completely the CGDK forces from west and north-west Cambodia. On the other hand, the CGDK forces have been able to penetrate deep into Cambodian territory but are in no position to defeat the Vietnamese militarily. The solution to the Cambodian problem must lie in a negotiated settlement of the issue. In March 1986, the CGDK came forward with a proposal to resolve the Cambodian issue. An interesting feature of the Sihanouk initiative is that they are prepared to form a new coalition government with the participation of the Heng Samrin régime. To date however, the Vietnamese have rejected the peace proposal put forward by Prince Sihanouk.

ASEAN AND REGIONAL SECURITY

The security issues which I have outlined above have led to a number of responses on the part of the ASEAN states. First, they have begun to expand their national defence resources in order to improve their capability to meet any kind of regional threat. At the same time, they have relied on various security arrangements to strengthen their defences. For example, the Philippines and Thailand are still members of the Manila Pact. Both Manila and Bangkok receive considerable economic and military assistance from the United States. Most recently Washington and Bangkok have agreed to set up military stockpiles in Thailand. Although the United States does not maintain any military bases in Thailand the establishment of these stockpiles would be advantageous in the event of any hostility involving Thailand. In the case of the Philippines, the United States' assistance has been crucial in dealing with the problems of the communist and Muslim insurgencies.

Malaysia and Singapore are members of the Five Power Defence Arrangement. Under this Commonwealth defence pact, the ANZUK powers, namely Australia, New Zealand and the United Kingdom maintain a small number of forces in Malaysia and Singapore and conduct various military exercises with these two coutries. The most important part of the Five Power Defence Arrangement is the integrated air defence system under the charge of the Australians. This system provides for the air defence of the Malaysia-Singapore area.

Among themselves the ASEAN states have defence co-operation on a bilateral basis. They have been able to exchange information and intelligence on security matters particularly the problem of communist insurgency and the threat from external powers. The bilateral military exercises have been quite extensive in recent years and such co-operation covers all the branches of the armed forces. In general, ASEAN desires to see a balance of power in South-East Asia. Hence they support the continuation of the US military presence including the maintenance of the American bases in the Philippines, namely Clark airbase and Subic naval base. These are particularly crucial at a time when the Soviet build up has been progressing rapidly in South-East Asia.

The ASEAN states have differences concerning the role played by China and the Soviet Union in Indo-China. Two of the ASEAN countries, namely Indonesia and Malaysia, perceive China as a long term security threat. Their perception has to do with their own internal political situation especially the Sino-Muslim tensions and the communist insurgencies. Hence, Jakarta and Kuala Lumpur are inclined to the view that Vietnam and the Soviet Union could be useful obstacles against the influence of China in regional affairs. On the other hand, Thailand perceives China as the major regional power which can be a deterrent against further Vietnamese advance in Indo-China as well as Soviet support for the Vietnamese.

The ASEAN governments have maintained that the ultimate strategy to deal with issues of regional security lies in political stability and economic growth in their countries. Towards those goals, they have formulated development plans which are aimed at building united and cohesive nations, achieving economic growth and equitable distribution of wealth and stabilising the political system. While the ASEAN states can rely on themselves, they still require the assistance of their major economic partners, namely, the United States, Japan and the European Community (EC). The EC has provided the political and diplomatic support for the ASEAN position on the Cambodia issue, but ASEAN states do not see the Europeans as participants in the strategic equation in South-East Asia.

There is no doubt that the EC can play a vital role in promoting political stability and economic growth in the ASEAN states. The EC is a dialogue partner of ASEAN. But there has been limited progress in the dialogue talks and there is little expectation that these can produce useful and substantial economic co-operation between the two regional groupings. However, much can be done on a bilateral basis between individual EC and ASEAN states. Between them they can deal with issues of protectionism, external debt, low commodity prices and the promotion of extensive trading relationships. Economic relations constitute a means for the EC to contribute towards peace and security in South-East Asia.

6 The Relations with ASEAN as a 'Model' of a European Foreign Policy?

Elfriede Regelsberger

I THE SUBJECT IN DIFFERENT PERSPECTIVES

Depending on the level of analysis, the relationship between ASEAN and the European Community (EC) and its present twelve member states (also referred to as the EC Twelve) may be assessed differently. Those who concentrate on the bilateral links emphasise the 'natural' interest of the two groupings, which decide to tackle a number of problems on the basis of intra-regional co-operation, to apply that principle also to their external relations. To build up such an inter-regional coalition seems to be particularly appropriate at a time when international politics is marked by global inter-dependence both in the political and economic fields. Group-to-group relations can be built up more easily – and the dialogue between ASEAN and the EC Twelve confirms this development – in those cases where both partners share a common political and economic philosophy. But also if conditions are less favourable there is an increased need for co-operation among states across regional boundaries to tackle major problems and to serve their own 'national interests'.

In addition to this general argument, both ASEAN and the EC have several other good reasons to establish close links. They are primarily political. ASEAN wants to gain European recognition as a viable and important force in South-East Asia. The 'umbrella' of the 'neutral' EC thereby offers a new start – free of strains that may be inherent in some of the traditional bilateral relations between ASEAN countries and the member states of the EC due to the colonial past. The 'civilian power' Europe, eager to promote peace and stability in the world without military means and to foster co-operation among states on the basis of equal partners, had to answer ASEAN's request for co-operation positively.

Observers note overall satisfaction with the quality of the relationship. Some even go further, attributing a kind of model character to the ASEAN-EC relationship for the future development of inter-regional co-operation in general.[1] The dialogue on 'political' questions is said to be successful, covering an ever growing number of issues and leading to common viewpoints and intensified consultations. In the field of economic co-operation, results have not been dramatic despite certain dynamics, the increase of contacts at various levels and the number of activities undertaken to promote trade and investment links.[2] This may not be surprising given the relatively low rank of ASEAN in the EC's external relations in comparison to the group of ACP countries (the 66 developing countries in Africa, the Caribbean and the Pacific, linked to the Community through the Lomé Convention) or the countries of the Mediterranean region. It remains to be seen whether the 'genuine' partnership with ASEAN will progress and make full use of the economic potential of both sides during the second phase of the implementation of the co-operation agreement.[3]

Other observers, dealing primarily with the EC Twelve's overall external relations and their efforts towards a common foreign policy in the framework of European Political Cooperation (EPC), do not place relations with ASEAN among the priorities.[4] Some experts and particularly those on EPC matters go further still and tend to neglect and even overlook the political consultations established with ASEAN in an assessment of EPC activities in the 1970s and 1980s.[5]

This paper proceeds much along the lines of those latter analysts. It tries to set the political dialogue with ASEAN into the broader framework of a European foreign policy. Pointing to the premises of the Twelve's capacity as an international actor and the gradual evolution of a European profile in world affairs may help to clarify the present status and potential for future developments in the political relationship with the ASEAN countries.

II THE EC TWELVE'S CAPACITY AS AN INTERNATIONAL ACTOR

1 No transfer of competence on foreign policy matters to the supranational level . . .

About 30 years ago, when the Treaties of Rome were signed to create the European Communities, foreign policy matters remained outside the provisions. The failure of the European Defence Community and of the related creation of a political authority with responsibilities for a common European foreign policy in 1954 led the Europeans to pursue a more modest approach.[6] European integration was to start in the economic field and, to the extent that any progress would be made, 'spill over' to other 'political' areas of common interest.

According to this logic only limited competences, *i.e.* those touching upon foreign trade, were transferred from the national to the supranational level. The application of the treaty provisions in political practice, however, did not always work satisfactorily.[7] Member states frequently contested Community responsibilities on matters of external trade and called for decisions of the European Court of Justice and the Commission in its turn did the opposite. To attribute further competences to the EC in the field of international politics was entirely unrealistic. Member states were eager to preserve national sovereignty in particular on foreign policy matters which constitute one if not the major element of such sovereignty. Progress towards 'speaking with one voice' in world affairs could only be achieved through inter-governmental co-operation. But even there the obstacles proved to be insurmountable at least during the early 1960s when de Gaulle's concept of a '*Europe des patries*' ran contrary to the ideas of the other EC countries wanting to develop a common foreign policy in the framework of and in connection with those organisations such as the EC and the Atlantic Alliance which were already in existence.

The growing internal cohesion of the EC and its greater weight as an economic 'giant' led to a reconsideration of Europe's international profile in the early 1970s. The political 'dwarf' was to play a more active role and make specific contributions thus 'ensuring that international relations have a more just basis; that the independence and equality of states are better preserved; that prosperity is more equally shared; and that the security of each country is more effectively guaranteed'.[8]

Structural changes within the international system at that time (*e.g.* growing economic and political interdependence; the development of a multipolar world with an ever growing number of new states) made the Europeans aware of their vulnerability to political and economic events outside their own borders. The first use of the Arab oil weapon in 1973–74 demanded concerted European action as did the policies of the new majorities in the United Nations whereas developments in Asia were of minor importance to the Europeans in the early 1970s.

2 . . . but creating a system of inter-governmental co-operation

In 1969, the Heads of State and Government of the then six EC member states instructed their foreign ministers 'to study the best way of achieving progress in the matter of political unification' taking particularly into consideration how a united Europe would be 'capable of assuming its responsibilities in the world of tomorrow and of making a contribution commensurate with its traditions and its mission'.[9]

The result of discussions that followed during 1970 was an agreement by the Six[10] on a regular exchange of information and consultations which should lead to harmonised views and sometimes also to common actions by the EC member states. European Political Co-operation (EPC) as this new kind of co-operation was called, was purely inter-governmental based on the political will of the participating countries. Results of this new type of multilateral diplomacy could only be those to which all were able to consent. The instruments at hand were largely those of traditional diplomacy. EC member states formulated common positions on a wide range of international questions (Cyprus, East-West relations, South Africa, terrorism, the Middle East *etc.*) and made them known to the international public. Co-operation among the EC countries was also initiated at international organisations like the United Nations and international conferences, the most outstanding example of a successful cohesion of the Europeans being the Conference on Security and Co-operation in Europe (CSCE).

The weaknesses of the EPC became obvious to the extent that the '*acquis politique*', *i.e.* the substance of common positions agreed upon by all participants, had to be transformed into common action.

In order not only to react to international developments but also 'to shape' events,[11] the instruments of the EPC had to be refined and linked to those of the EC and of the national level. The so called 'fact-finding missions' of the spokesman of the EC countries, the Presidency, became a popular means of EPC diplomacy.

The visits of successive Presidents to the Middle East in the early 1980s and the ones of the foreign ministers of Luxembourg and the United Kingdom to South Africa in 1985–86 in the name of the Twelve may be well known. In the 1980s the Europeans intensified contacts with third countries in general – partly as a reaction to external requests, partly because the EC countries themselves wished to make their voice better heard internationally. Regular consultations were established with a selected group of countries (e.g. Japan and China) and a kind of normal 'diplomatic trade' developed enabling the Ten, and after the entry of Portugal and Spain in 1986, the Twelve to bring their common positions and concerns more directly to the attention of the countries and governments outside the EC.[12] Co-operation between the embassies of the EC member states grew and was extended to more than 80 countries around the world. In several of those capitals outside the EC also, contacts between the group of European ambassadors and representatives of the host government became usual. At the same time the number of *démarches*, through which the EC countries issued their common concern about concrete events in a third country became a fixed practice of the EPC. To give an example: between January 1981 and June 1986 around a hundred *démarches* were made to intervene especially in cases of violation of human rights.[13]

Connecting the EPC with EC policies and instruments (in a 'positive' way by offering trade preferences or economic aid to a third country or in a 'negative' way by restricting or blocking commercial relations for a certain time) remained rather unusual throughout the 1970s. Efforts to strengthen the young Portuguese democracy with Community aid in the mid-1970s or to grant economic assistance to the Lebanon in order to stabilise the political system of that country have to be described as an exception to the general practice of the EC. Imposing sanctions became a rather 'popular' method of attempting to achieve more consistency between the EPC and the external relations of the EC in the 1980s. This new approach of linking various instruments worked considerably well in some cases such as the Falklands crisis. In other ones, and they were in the majority, divergent national interests among the EC member states prevailed over a common stance, delaying and watering down or even preventing collective declarations and measures.

For the most outstanding examples of recent EPC history, the Twelve's poor 'performance' in giving a clear signal to South Africa (which in the end resulted in a package of 'positive' and some 'restrictive' measures) or the Twelve's dissension over a concrete answer to Syria's involvement in international terrorism may be recalled.[14] This rather negative image of the EPC's potential to act, together with some other shortcomings in the consultations (*e.g.* failure to reach consensus on topics like security policy) contrasts with developments that indicate progress in the EPC in the mid-1980s. Since its start in 1970 the EPC has gradually evolved into a 'central element' of the foreign policies of the EC member states.[15]

All participating governments stress the value of consultations which take place in a highly confidential atmosphere and almost permanently through frequent meetings at official and ministerial levels (in total more than 150 a year, plus frequent contacts between the Twelve at international conferences and organisations) and a direct telex network between the foreign ministries. In the course of a general debate in 1985–86 on how to reform the Community institutions and the decision-making process and how to enlarge the scope of common activities to reach the final goal of European Union [16], EPC received a legal basis for the first time. This step of institutionalising European co-operation on matters of foreign policy is a clear manifestation of the Twelve's constant interest towards a collective management of major international problems. The Single European Act,[17] signed by the EC member states in February 1986, in its Article 30 fixes the aims and procedural arrangements of co-operation on foreign policy matters in a legally binding way.[18] Among the provisions worth mentioning here, in the context of the EPC's external activities, are the following:

Art. 30,8 stresses the interest of the Twelve in establishing a political dialogue with non-EC member states thereby mentioning explicitly co-operation with other regional groupings, 'whenever they (*i.e.* the High Contracting Parties) deem it necessary';

Art. 30,10*g* foresees the creation of a small Secretariat located in Brussels, which would have among other functions, the charge of assisting the Presidency in contacts with the outside world;

Art. 30,5 claims that the EPC and the EC's external relations have to be 'consistent', *i.e.* the various policies and instruments at hand have to be combined and used in a co-ordinated way.

Whether or not this new legal commitment will lead to a '*saut qualitatif*' and in fact inspire member states to renounce their 'vital' national interests for the benefit of a common 'European foreign policy' (as aimed for in the Treaty provisions) remains to be seen.

Among EPC representatives the view is that consultations are marked by a new 'spirit.' In view of recent events — for example British behaviour in the US-Libyan affair or in the case of Syria (the Hindawi affair) — some doubts are justified. It may well be that an observer from inside the European borders tends to be too critical and too pessimistic about the Twelve's capacity to act and about the results achieved by the EPC so far. Conversely most outside observers usually draw a rather – and sometimes too – positive picture. The potential of Europe's international weight is easily overestimated if too much concentration is placed on nice sounding common statements of the Twelve. Behind this *acquis politique*, diverging national positions persist and interpretations of a text differ if declarations have to be translated into concrete policies. One should not forget that so far the EPC has in no way replaced other ways and means of national foreign policy. Collective diplomacy has to be seen first of all as an opportunity for the governments to preserve and enlarge their room for manoeuvre internationally. One should not forget either that even as far as the EC's external relations are concerned it is primarily the member states who have a say with other EC bodies playing a minor role. Finally one should keep in mind also that developments inside the Community such as the awkward debate about reforming the Common Agricultural Policy, solving the budgetary problems or managing the entry of Portugal and Spain into the EC as demonstrated in 1983–84, may hamper Europe's international profile and undermine its credibility as a major force and reliable partner.

III POLITICAL RELATIONS WITH ASEAN IN THE TEST

1 Asia – no priority on the EPC agenda . . .

When the foreign ministers met for their first EPC meeting in late 1970 two topics were discussed: first, East-West relations in a period of détente in general and the European role in the forthcoming negotiations on the Conference on Security and Co-operation in Europe (CSCE) in particular; secondly, and with particular emphasis by the French, the situation in the Middle East. The latter subject, and the extent to which the EC member states started to establish closer links with the countries of the Arab League (the so-called Euro-Arab Dialogue was one of the first examples of the EC's inter-regional co-operation), relations with the United States needed careful consideration. Worried about the future international engagement of the Europeans, the American Administration wished to be closely associated with the EPC.

Compared to those subjects still remaining on the EPC agenda, discussions on the situation in Asia during the period 1970–74/75 may be described as a '*quantité négligeable*'. Developments in Asia were, like those in Latin America, of much less importance to the Europeans throughout the 1970s. Discussions at official (and occasionally at ministerial) level – a working group composed of the desk officers dealing with Asia in the national foreign ministries was installed – focussed on several specific issues like the civil war in Pakistan, the recognition of Bangladesh, the admission of China to the United Nations and the role of Vietnam in South-East Asia.[19]

Compared to other topics of international politics (*e.g.* the Arab-Israeli conflict, East-West relations, Southern Africa) EPC policy towards Asia remained somewhat sporadic and declaratory until the 1980s. The Nine and, with the entry of Greece in 1981, the Ten issued their 'concern' over developments in the region – as they did on many other international problems – through unilateral statements,[20] in the speeches of the Presidency during the Sessions of the UN General Assembly[21] and also on the occasion of meetings with ASEAN.[22] Concrete actions like the European support for alleviating the problem of Indo-Chinese refugees were the exception to the rule. Instead the Europeans were eager to develop concepts and policies towards the countries in their immediate neighbourhood. Asia was located somewhat on the periphery of the EPC and this should remain so for a while in the view of certain EC member states, notably France and the United Kingdom, whose governments wanted to keep their traditional links with Asia outside the EPC framework (as so-called '*domaines réservés*').[23]

The Soviet intervention in Afghanistan in 1979 marks a certain turning-point in the Europeans' perceptions of the impact of international events even if they are geographically far away. For Europeans the Afghanistan crisis highlighted the dangers of the communist threat to Asia which had already existed there in the form of Vietnam and its expansionist policy but which had concerned the Europeans far less than Afghanistan. The fact that the Soviet Union destabilised the balance of power in the region had direct implications for the overall climate between East and West. More than anybody else the Europeans would be struck by a new period of 'Cold War'. The then Nine, confused and unable to speak with one voice shortly after the Soviet *coup*, felt the urgent need to adopt a common approach which would on the one hand satisfy the Americans who were in favour of breaking ties with Moscow and on the other hand enable the Europeans to keep the door open to the East. In their endeavours to influence the Soviet Union to withdraw its troops and to allow to the people of Afghanistan the right to self-determination, coalition partners in the western camp and in Asia were welcome.

Contacts between the EC and ASEAN had been established since the first meeting of foreign ministers in 1978 and the second meeting in March 1980 (Kuala Lumpur) offered the opportunity to raise the problem of Afghanistan at an early stage. The European side intended to seek support for its plan for a neutral and non-aligned Afghanistan to be secured through international negotiations. ASEAN could easily agree to the positions of the European partners because both sides shared identical views on the subject. The Joint Statement of the Kuala Lumpur meeting was a clear commitment to assist the Europeans and to work together to promote peace and stability in the whole region. The Europeans for their part showed solidarity with the ASEAN countries in their struggle against Vietnam and called for the recognition of international principles (territorial integrity, non-interference, national independence) which were similar to those claimed in the case of Afghanistan.

The ministerial conferences that followed the Kuala Lumpur event – London 1981, Bangkok 1983, Dublin 1984 and Jakarta 1986 – and the significant length of the joint political conclusions issued there may suggest that Asia and herewith ASEAN have become a major topic on the EPC agenda. This, however, is only partly true. Both sides – particularly at the political top, less at the officials' level – remained interested in keeping in touch on a regular and institutionalised basis. ASEAN and also the EC countries, the latter presumably to a lesser extent, profited from the relationship which enabled each party to exercise a wider range of influence on the international scene. In a longer-term perspective the advantages for the Europeans may lie more in ASEAN's role as a mediator and moderate partner in the whole area of North-South relations and questions of international trade. Seen from the point of view of ASEAN, the dialogue with the Twelve is primarily orientated towards strengthening ASEAN's role as a political force in the region and promoting intra-regional cohesion between the members of ASEAN.

Despite the mutual interest, publicly repeated by the participants several times, in continuing the dialogue, the substantive content of the political consultations have stagnated somewhat during the past few years. The topics on the agenda occurred again and again and already well-known formulae were taken up in the joint declarations. The reasons for this kind of stereotyped and repetitive communiqué were twofold. The 'classical' subjects referring to the situation in Asia like the Afghan crisis and the policy of Vietnam did not change in a positive way. Earlier principles and statements agreed upon by the two sides therefore remained valid. Another explanation for the *status quo* character of the consultations presumably was that difficulties arose when attempts were made to go beyond the initial and more general common declarations. At least several EC governments for example were more doubtful about the viability of the Kampuchea Coalition Government supported by ASEAN and were more concerned with the participation of the Khmer Rouge in it than were the South-East Asian countries. Also, with regard to Vietnam, not all EC member states shared their partners' view of isolating that country and not granting it Community or other European aid.

The discussion of new subjects at the Bangkok meeting (the Middle East problem; East-West relations), the Dublin conference (in addition to the topics mentioned already the problem of drugs and the Iran-Iraq conflict were raised) and the Jakarta meeting (also South Africa was on the agenda) may be interpreted as a 'significant' step[24] in the political consultations, considering *e.g.* the links of some ASEAN countries with the Islamic world or the political support the EC countries would get from their partners for their assessment of East-West relations. One could also say that the fact that foreign ministers meet regularly to discuss a variety of international problems is politically valuable.

It may, however, also be argued that raising *e.g.* the tricky question of the Arab-Israeli conflict, at the moment when the Ten (for good reasons) kept a very low profile in the whole affair, was a sign of embarrassment on behalf of the Ten. Given the problems mentioned above, to have gone ahead on matters directly related to South-East Asia, and introduce new subjects could have had a kind of 'refreshening' effect on the consultations. This seemed to be the hope of the protagonists of the political dialogue with the 'initiator', German

Foreign Minister, H.-D. Genscher in the forefront. But the Middle East as well as South Africa obviously were bad choices if the two sides wished to develop a substantive common strategy given the divergence of views among the Europeans and the very limited room for manoeuvre for both ASEAN and the EC countries to contribute to a resolution of those conflicts. No wonder, the outcome of discussions on these topics was poor[25] reflecting itself in the said communiqué rhetoric ('concern', 'condemnation' of a given situation). This kind of a concerted diplomacy tends to be more detrimental both to the EC's and to ASEAN's international profile than beneficial.

In 1983–84 the EPC witnessed several setbacks, one being the inability of the Ten to talk seriously enough about matters of European security, others being Greece's falling out of a common line and the impact of intra-EC disputes on the EPC. Besides, new subjects for the political consultations of the EC member states arose on the horizon – the deterioration of the situation in Southern Africa, the redefinition of relations with Latin America after the Falklands crisis and the southern enlargement of the EC, the combating of terrorism, to mention the major ones. Consensus-building in the EPC became an increasingly cumbersome undertaking.

Compared to those sometimes tricky EPC topics, Asia did not constitute a source of major controversy among the Twelve. In line with a general proliferation of EPC issues during the immediate past, developments in Asia, particularly to the extent they became more and more critical there (*e.g.* the situation in Sri Lanka), were discussed more often than in previous years.

It was mainly the experts in the EPC working group on Asia and the Political Directors, and only occasionally the foreign ministers, who exchanged views on Asian problems. Now and then the *acquis politique* was made known in public declarations, *e.g.* on Afghanistan (at least once a year since 1979), the terrorist attack on a South Korean delegation in October 1983 or on the turmoils in Sri Lanka.[26] In 1985–86 the EC countries repeated their disapproval of the Vietnamese attacks at the border with Thailand and reaffirmed their general support for ASEAN's proposals on the Kampuchean problem.[27]

New and perhaps the most striking activities towards Asia were undertaken in the course of the political changes in the Philippines. At several ministerial meetings since 1986 the situation there has been on the EPC agenda. The Twelve vigorously welcomed the new president and affirmed their support for Ms Aquino's policy not only by symbolic gestures like the EC ambassadors' attending a Mass in Manila but also by concrete offers for the economic recovery of the country.[28]

EPC policy towards the Philippines is worth noting also insofar as it constitutes one of the few or even the only reference the Twelve have made in public to internal developments in the countries of the dialogue partners in South-East Asia. On matters of the violation of human rights, where the EC countries usually conduct a kind of 'silent diplomacy', again either Asia in general or the ASEAN countries in particular have not been a major target: less than 10 per cent (seven out of around 90 to 100) of EPC *démarches*, made between January 1981 and June 1986, referred to Asia.[29] Among those known are several interventions in the case of South Korean Opposition leader Kim Dae Jung and towards Indonesian authorities to protest against the execution of several political prisoners.[30]

This neglect of Asia corresponds to a widespread thinking in the European public which concentrates on certain countries in the world, notably the Soviet Union, South Africa or on Latin American régimes, to call for the respect of human rights. Obviously in order not to disturb the excellent climate of the political consultations with ASEAN, the Europeans have been hesitant so far to criticise or even mention doubtful developments and practices in the ASEAN countries. The sixth ministerial meeting held in October 1986 in Indonesia seemed to indicate a certain turnabout in that some European participants issued concerns about the recent executions in the host country and their compatibility with the general principles of human rights.[31]

2 . . . but establishing formalised links with ASEAN

Compared to the network of contacts that exist today at the level of ministers, officials, and businessmen to discuss the questions of trade, economic and development co-operation, those of the political dialogue look rather poor. As the European move towards ASEAN was first and foremost a 'by-product' of the British accession to the EC, the links with Community institutions grew first. Afraid of losing their Commonwealth preferences on the British market after the enlargement of the EC, Malaysia and Singapore sought contacts with Brussels as early as 1972. The Community reacted promptly, and suggested discussions on economic questions and also showed interest in intensifying trade relations. Contacts were established between Commission representatives and the Special Co-ordinating Committee of ASEAN Nations (formed by the ministers of trade) and the ASEAN Brussels Committee (composed of the ambassadors of the ASEAN countries to the EC).

In 1975 a common Study Group was set up to explore the possibility of economic co-operation and two years later was accompanied by regular meetings between the ASEAN ambassadors in Brussels and the Permanent Representatives of the EC member states there. In 1978 contacts extended to the political level. From then on meetings of the foreign ministers were convened regularly and in 1985 supplemented by a gathering of the ministers of economic affairs. Since 1980 economic ties have been based on a Co-operation Agreement which designated the Joint Co-operation Committee as the central organ for implementing the provisions of the Treaty. Contacts intensified considerably in the private economic sector, one outstanding example being the creation of the Business Council in 1983. Also on the parliamentary level a dialogue was opened between the European Parliament, in particular its delegation for South-East Asia, and the ASEAN Inter-Parliamentary Organisation in 1979. And in 1981 EC representatives were invited to participate in the annual meetings of ASEAN with their partners in the Pacific. Initially the European presence there was limited to the Council President and a member of the Commission. In 1983, again pushed by the Federal Republic of Germany, the formula was changed to a European troika representation, *i.e.* the foreign minister acting on behalf of the Council was assisted by his colleagues of the preceding and incoming Presidencies and the Commission representative.

Coming to the institutional framework of the political dialogue, it can be said that ASEAN became associated with the EPC at a remarkably early stage. At the time of the first ministerial meeting in 1978 only a selected group of so-called 'allied and friendly' states had regular contacts with the then Nine. Together with the countries of the Arab League, which enjoyed a special status in the external relations of the EC Nine since the oil crisis, ASEAN represented the somewhat 'exotic' part of that group of privileged partners.

When comparing the format of contacts with ASEAN to that of other third countries (*e.g.* the United States, Turkey, and Greece) a shift in quality became obvious in the late 1970s. Consultations with ASEAN, as a sign of special appreciation of the partner, took place at ministerial level right from the beginning whereas in the other cases contacts were started at official level and upgraded later on if both sides wished to do so and if an agreement on the new format could be reached. Another particularity of the ASEAN-EPC relationship consists in the full representation of the European side which was partly also the case in the early days of the Euro-Arab Dialogue. But contrary to the latter, where the number of participants was reduced because of the divergency of views, contacts with ASEAN continued on the same basis. In the 1980s when the Ten/Twelve established political links with other regional groupings such as the Central American states in 1984 or the African front-line states in 1986, the dialogue with ASEAN in some way served as a model.

On the other hand, some of these new political relationships and in particular that with Central America grew rapidly. Consultations there were organised both at ministerial and senior official level and in 1985 the EC countries' interest towards that continent manifested itself when a communiqué was signed which was seen as a commitment to an annual dialogue at ministerial level. The document issued at the so-called 'San José II' meeting in Luxembourg[32] is unique in that EPC contacts with third countries or regional groupings have so far never been based on a formal agreement. Another aspect worth noting here is the frequency of meetings of group-to-group relations. The foreign ministers' gatherings which are at the heart of the political dialogue with ASEAN are organised every 18 months only whereas ministerial conferences with the Central American states are held annually.

In view of the Twelve's obligations to contact third countries which have an 'inflationary' tendency and given the fact that foreign ministers today already have a considerable work-load to carry, one may well ask whether the existing formula of the dialogue with ASEAN still fits into their calendars. The answer seems to be 'no', if one compares the present composition of the European delegation with that of the past and if one takes the EPC officials' numerous complaints about when and where to organise the ministerial dialogue into consideration. In the not-too-distant future the Twelve will have to decide on the priorities of their consultations with third countries if they want to conduct their external relations in a serious way. It does not satisfy either side if a ministerial meeting is convened but attended by a majority of junior ministers in the end. This happened in the case of the contacts with the front-line states and there is a similar trend in the meetings with ASEAN. To avoid disappointment on behalf of the partners and to reduce the danger of static contacts in which nobody would be interested in any longer, the Twelve should think about suitable reform proposals. If it becomes increasingly difficult to fix the date of a ministerial conference, in particular if it is to be held in South-East Asia, it might be possible to meet at the end of the UN General Assembly or other international conferences. Another suggestion might be to reduce the European participation and charge the Presidency, possibly enlarged to the troika, to act in the name of the Twelve. Another possibility could be to hold the meetings with the ambassadors of the EC countries accredited to South-East Asia instead of the foreign ministers who seem to feel more and more uncomfortable with their status as 'appendages' to the Presidency during the meetings.

If the dialogue with ASEAN is to develop in quality it should be broadened at the working level. In addition to the collaboration of the two sides in the UN framework[33] the contacts between the diplomats of the ASEAN countries in European capitals and those experts in the foreign ministries of the Twelve who co-operate in the EPC working group on Asia might be intensified. The new EPC secretariat in Brussels may also help to establish more permanent links. Another suggestion could be to organise regular briefings between the ambassadors of ASEAN and the Political Director of the country holding the EPC Presidency; whereas meetings, on a similar basis to those of the ministers, at directorial level seem to be hardly practicable due to the workload of those senior officials, at least of several governments in Europe. If one places the political dialogue with ASEAN into the general framework of EPC contacts with other countries in Asia, the relationship that initially seemed privileged takes on a somewhat different character. Since the late 1970s, Japan has shown a clear interest in a political coalition with the Europeans. It was born out of the desire to counterbalance US claims of Western solidarity in the Afghan crisis and in the matter of US hostages in Iran in 1979–80. The Europeans as well were very much in favour of this new partnership and, after several *ad hoc* contacts in 1979, consultations were formalised and broadened in 1983. Today they range from six-monthly meetings at ministerial level (the Twelve being represented according to the troika formula) and similar ones at senior official level. Consultation is said to be intensive also between the ambassadors of the Twelve in Tokyo and the Japanese foreign ministry and contacts between the respective embassies also exist in some other capitals around the world. At present, the Twelve are considering how the existing links can be strengthened in the future.

In the past few years the EC countries continued to diversify their contacts towards Asia by establishing a political dialogue with China and India. Today bi-annual consultations take place at ministerial level reflecting the importance the Twelve attach to these countries. In 1986, the foreign ministers also raised, though very briefly so far, the question of relations with the members of the South Asian Association for Regional Co-operation (SAARC): Bangladesh, Bhutan, India, Maldives, Nepal, Pakistan, Sri Lanka. To the extent those countries manage to co-operate they may become another partner for a (presumably economically orientated) dialogue with the Twelve.

IV PERSPECTIVES

To conclude, there is a certain discrepancy today between the solemn declarations of the Europeans on the importance of Asia in general and ASEAN in particular and the steps the Europeans take to demonstrate their belief in it. The time has come to define the priorities of a truly 'European' foreign policy (as proclaimed in the Single European Act of 1986) for the late 1980s and to decide where Asia and ASEAN fit into it. If the countries of that region are to be of vital interest the existing institutional basis of the political dialogue with ASEAN has to be broadened. If, however, the Twelve are going to turn to other parts of the world, and there are indications that this is likely to be the case, contacts with ASEAN will be weakened. The political dialogue would then lose its part as the role-model for Europe's relations with certain other groupings. This guiding character has, however, always been a limited one. It could set the framework for some 'latecomers' to the EC's external (economic) relations such as the countries of the Andean Pact and the Central American States whereas the political dialogue with the latter group has been organised differently. Also for the present debate on how to co-operate with the Gulf Co-operation Council (GCC) and the Eastern European countries of the CMEA (Comecon), individual formulae have to be developed.

Given the heterogeneity of positions among the EC countries on a number of foreign policy matters, which became obvious in the mid-1980s, one may be pessimistic about the prospects of a future 'European' foreign policy. There are signs of a reverse trend in

Western Europe, *i.e.* concerting national foreign policy with selected partners instead of or at least parallel to the EPC and EC framework. Third countries and regional groupings should carefully observe this evolution and develop a strategy to answer the new intra-European coalition-building.

Notes

1. Andreas Lukas, *Regionale Wirtschaftsgemeinschaften im internationalen System*, Frankfurt, 1985, p. 276.
2. Jürgen Schmid, 'Die Beziehungen zwischen ASEAN und der EG. Bericht über die interdisziplinäre Tagung des Arbeitskreises Europäische Integration', 20–22 February 1986 in Passau, manuscript; Kommission der EG, Generaldirektion Information, *Die Europäische Gemeinschaft und ASEAN*, No. 81/85, Brussels 1985.
3. Hans-Christian Reichel, 'Die Europäische Gemeinschaft und ASEAN', in *Außenpolitik*, 1985, No. 2, pp. 189–96; here pp. 194.
4. See, e.g., the (yearly published) contributions on the EC's external relations and on EPC, in: Werner Weidenfeld and Wolfgang Wessels (eds), *Jahrbuch der Europäischen Integration 1980–1985*, Bonn. Wichard Woyke, 'Außenbezienhungen der EG', in *Pipers Wörterbuch zur Politik*, Vol. 3 Europäische Gemeinschaft, München, Zürich 1984, pp. 19–21. Gianni Bonvicini, 'The Major Challenges of Political Cooperation', Paper presented at an international conference on 'The Priorities of Community Action and Political Cooperation'; Brussels, 20–22 Nov. 1986.
5. Philippe de Schoutheete, *La coopération politique européenne*, first and second editions, Brussels 1980 and 1986. David Allen, Reinhardt Rummel and Wolfgang Wessels (eds), *European Political Cooperation*, London 1982, briefly mentioned in Reinhardt Rummel, *EPZ – Erfolgsformel für gemeinsame westeuropäische Außenpolitik*, Entwicklungsmöglichkeiten der Europäischen Politischen Zusammenarbeit auf der Basis der Einheitlichen Europäischen Akte, Ebenhausen 1987.
6. For the history of a European foreign policy see Philippe de Schoutheete 1986, op. cit. p. 11. Texts of the documents in: European Parliament, Committee on Institutional Affairs, *Selection of Texts Concerning Institutional Matters of the Community from 1950 to 1982*, Luxembourg 1982, pp. 109.
7. Jean-Victor Louis, 'La Communauté et ses Etats membres dans les relations extérieures', in *Journal of European Integration* 1983, No. 2/3, pp. 203–35.
8. Extract from the Foreign Ministers' Declaration on the European Identity. Text published in: Press and Information Office of the Federal Government (ed.), *European Political Cooperation (EPC)*, fourth edition, Bonn 1982, p. 60.

9. Points 3, 15 of the Communiqué of The Hague Summit, 2 Dec 1969. Text published, in: Press and Information Office, op. cit., pp. 24, 28.
10. First report of the Foreign Ministers on EPC, 27 Oct 1970 (Luxembourg Report). Text published, in ibid., pp. 28.
11. As the Ten had already claimed in 1981. See the Third Report of the Foreign Ministers on EPC, 13 Oct 1981 (London Report). Text published, in ibid., p. 272.
12. For further details see Elfriede Regelsberger *et al.*, *The external relations of European Political Cooperation*, EUI Working Paper No. 85/172, Florence 1985.
13. See Memorandum submitted by the President-in-Office of the Twelve to the European Parliament. Text in *Report Guimon Ugartechea*, Doc. A2–208/86.
14. Elfriede Regelsberger, 'Die Europäische Politische Zusammenarbeit', in Weidenfeld and Wessels, op. cit., pp. 239–48.
15. Ibid., p. 272.
16. For details on the reform debate and the various proposals, see: Werner Weidenfeld, 'Die Einheitliche Europäische Akte', in *Außenpolitik*, 1986, No. 4, pp. 375–383.
17. The text of the Single European Act which contains the final results of the reform debate is published, in *Bulletin of the EC*, Supplement No. 2/1986.
18. For an assessment, see Wolfgang Wessels, 'Die europäische Zusammenarbeit in der Außenpolitik', in *Integration*, 1986, No. 3, pp. 126–32.
19. More details are to be found, in Reinhardt Rummel, *Zusammengesetzte Außenpolitik: Westeuropa als internationaler Akteur*, Kehl, 1982, pp. 124; Philippe de Schoutheete 1986, op. cit., pp. 302; William Wallace, 'Political Cooperation: Integration Through Intergovernmentalism', in William Wallace, Helen Wallace and Carol Webb (eds), *Policy-Making in the European Community*, London 1983, pp. 373–402; here p. 384.
20. See Statement by the Nine, 19 Feb 1979. Text published in: Press and Information Office, op. cit., p. 159; Declaration of the Foreign Ministers, 25 April 1983. Text published, ibid. (German version, sixth edition, Bonn 1984), p. 247.
21. Cf. Speech by G. Thorn on behalf of the Nine, 23 Sept. 1980, ibid., p. 220; Statement of the Presidency at the 36th Session, 19 Oct. 1981, ibid., p. 284
22. Joint Statement of the Ministerial Meeting, 7/8 March 1980, ibid., p. 188; Communiqué of the Ministerial Meeting, 13/14 Oct 1981, ibid., p. 279; Declaration of the Ministerial Meeting, 25 March 1983, ibid. (German version), p. 243.
23. Philippe Moreau Defarges, *Quel avenir pour quelle Communauté?*, Paris, 1986, p. 204
24. Andreas Lukas, op. cit., p. 208.
25. See Points 20, 21 of the Joint Declaration of the Bangkok Meeting. Extracts published in: Press and Information Office, op. cit. (German version), p. 245.
26. *Bulletin of the EC*, 10/1983.
27. *Bulletin of the EC*, 1/1985; 6/1985.

28. *Bulletin of the EC*, 2/1986; 5/1986.
29. *Report Guimon Ugartechea*, op. cit. (n. 13).
30. Reinhardt Rummel, op. cit., p. 136; *Agence Europe*, 11 Oct. 1986.
31. Embassy of the French Republic in Bonn, *Bulletin d'informations*, 22 Oct. 1986.
32. *Bulletin of the EC*, 11/1985.
33. As to the voting behaviour of the two sides, see the contribution of Kusuma Snitwongse in this volume.

7 EC-ASEAN in the Context of Inter-regional Co-operation

Andreas Lukas

INTRODUCTION

In the last 40 years, a lot of countries have tried to promote their national development by forming economic communities or regional groups. They built integrated communities in order to play their part in the international system as one unit. In addition to the economic aspect, political reasons are of considerable significance. For many of the new regional groups the European Community (EC) seems to have become a model for regional economic co-operation because of the high increase of the intra-regional trade in the EC after its formation.

Compared to the nation states, the role of these Regional Economic Communities (RECs) has become more important within the international system. In this context, the increasing links between regional groupings are of substantial relevance.

This paper is divided into five parts. After the introduction, a short account of the most important RECs as partners of inter-regional co-operation will be given. Secondly, the present system of inter-regional co-operation or the system of relationship between these RECs will be examined. Thirdly, a representation of ASEAN as an important partner of inter-regional co-operation for the EC will follow. In the fourth part, an attempt will be made to assess EC-ASEAN co-operation, which was institutionalised by the Co-operation Agreement in 1980. The last part will analyse the political dimension of EC-ASEAN co-operation.

Partners in inter-regional co-operation

'The concept of regional economic co-operation is commonly viewed in the Third World as a "good thing" likely to promote peace and stability of a region and so foster its economic development to the benefit of all countries concerned' (Wong 1985, p. 79). For developing countries the conditions and the implementation of integration are completely different from those of industrialised countries. There are, of course, many reasons for forming regional communities. 'Each regional group is the product of different environments, different forces and different motivational mechanisms' (Indorf 1983, p. 106). In the Third World, for example, some groupings have come into being as a result of political changes in regional geo-political constellations, *e.g.* the increasing influence of the super-powers or the declining influence of the former colonial powers. Co-operation between developing countries and integration play an important role in a wide range of fields, *e.g.* culture, politics, economics, transport and communications. This means, co-operation and integration do not have to be confined to the economic aspects.

Economic integration intertwines national, regional and worldwide integration. It also varies in appearance and intensity: preferential area, free trade zone, customs union, common market, economic union and complete integration. These main forms of economic integration can be considered as different steps in the process of integration. 'By 1950, however, "economic integration" was coming to be used more specifically as a term to denote a state of affairs or a process involving the combination of separate economies into larger economic regions' (Robson 1980, p. 1). Most regional economic groupings are established for political reasons. As a factor in understanding the progress of economic integration the political element should not be under-estimated or ignored.

A Regional Economic Community, in the sense of this paper, is a group of different sovereign states that are bound by an agreement. Within the framework of this agreement, they start to co-operate with the final aim of integration. They participate in the international system and one of their common characteristics is the aspiration for economic integration or political co-operation. The establishment of these regional integrations strengthens the international position of the member countries in both political and economic terms.

At present, the following can be cited as the most important examples of such RECs with varying degrees of integration and success (see Table 7.1):

EC, European Community (founded in 1957, 12 member countries, attempted form of integration: common market and economic union)

Table 7.1 The most important Regional Economic Communities

Community	*Foundation*	*Present Members*	*Integration*
EC (European Community)	25.03.1957	Belgium, Denmark, France, Federal Republic of Germany, Greece, Ireland, Italy, Luxemburg, Netherlands, Portugal, Spain, United Kingdom	Common Market, Customs Union
EFTA (European Free Trade Association)	04.12.1960	Austria, Iceland, Finland, Norway, Sweden, Switzerland	Free Trade Area
Comecon/CMEA (Council of Mutual Economic Assistance)	25.01.1949	Bulgaria, Cuba, German Democratic Republic, Mongolia, Poland, Romania, Czechoslovakia, Hungary, Vietnam, USSR	Zone of selected preferences, cooperation
Andean Pact	26.05.1969	Bolivia, Ecuador, Colombia, Peru, Venezuela	Common Market, Customs Union
ECOWAS (Economic Community of West African States)	28.05.1975	Benin, Ivory Coast, Guinea, Mali, Mauritania, Niger, Burkina Faso, Senegal, Togo, Gambia, Ghana, Liberia, Nigeria, Sierra Leone, Guinea-Bissau, Cape Verde	Common Market, Customs Union
ASEAN (Association of South-East Asian Nations)	08.08.1967	Brunei, Indonesia, Malaysia, Philippines, Thailand, Singapore	Free Trade Area, Customs Union
MCCA (Mercado Común Centro Americano)	13.12.1960	Costa Rica, El Salvador, Guatemala, Honduras, Nicaragua	Common Market
GCC (Gulf Co-operation Council)	25.05.1981	Saudi Arabia, Bahrain, Qatar, Oman, Kuwait, United Arab Emirates	Common Market
SAARC (South Asian Association for Regional Co-operation)	1985	Bangladesh, Bhutan, India, Maldives, Nepal, Pakistan, Sri Lanka	Economic, scientific and technical cooperation

EFTA, European Free Trade Association (1960, 6, free trade zone)
Comecon, Council for Mutual Economic Assistance (1949, 10, selected preferences)
Andean Pact (1969, 5, common market)
MCCA, Mercado Común Centro-Americano (1960, 5, common market)
ECOWAS, Economic Community of West African States (1975, 16, common market)
ASEAN, Association of South-East Asian Nations (1967, 6, customs union)
GCC, Gulf Cooperation Council (1981, 6, common market)

These RECs have been selected because of their special significance in inter-regional co-operation. This will be analysed in the next paragraph. Three of the RECs – EC, EFTA, Comecon (Comecon without the non-European member states) – are groups of industrialised countries. The other five are groups of developing countries in the Third World with some typical drawbacks of integration (Lukas 1985, p. 18):

1 the one-sided external trade with raw material and primary products (*e.g.* the ASEAN-countries compete with similar products for the same markets, the GCC-members with their oil-products or the MCCA-countries with agricultural products);

2 the domination of one country in a group (*e.g.* Nigeria in the ECOWAS with 58 per cent of the population of the group and 75 per cent of the GNP, Saudi-Arabia in the GCC, 70 per cent and 61 per cent);

3 the various levels of development, which can be demonstrated by the relation between the poorest and the richest country in the group (the relation of the GNP per head in 1984 between the ASEAN members Indonesia and Singapore is 1 : 13.4, between Bolivia and Venezuela in the Andean Pact 1 : 6.3, (see Table 7.2);

4 different basic conditions of the member states, *e.g.* population, geographical position, raw material or territorial factors; and

5 ethnic, cultural, religious and national problems, because these nations became independent fairly recently, most of them are still

Table 7.2 Regional economic communities in comparison

	EC	*EFTA*	*Comecon*	*Andean Pact*	*MCCA*	*ECOWAS*	*ASEAN*	*GCC*
Foundation	1957	1960	1949	1969	1960	1975	1967	1981
Members	12	6	10	5	5	16	6	6
Area (sq. km)	2 259 000	1 339 000	25 403 000 23 303 000 (a)	4 719 000	423 000	6 142 000	3 069 400	2 564 000
Population (Mio, 1984)	321.6	31.24	441.1 375.5 (a)	78.7	23.5	167.3	280.3	15.9
Percentage of world population	6.82	0.66	10.1	1.7	0.5	3.5	5.9	0.3
GNP (Mio, US$ 1984)	2 597 071	384 986	1 716 534	137 297	21 783	93 556	217 103	191 073
GNP per head (US$ 1984)	8 075	12 323	3 891 4 507 (a)	1 745	927	559	775	12 017
Relation poorest and richest country	1 : 6.7 (Port./ Luxemb.)	1 : 1.8 (Austria/ Switzerl.)	1 : 3(a) (Romania/ GDR)	1 : 6.3 (Bolivia/ Venezuela)	1 : 1.7 (Honduras/ Costa Rica)	1 : 4.6 (Burk. Faso/ Nigeria)	1 : 13.4 (Indonesia/ Singapore)	1 : 3.4 (Oman/ United Arab Emirates)

Source: World Bank, *World Development Report 1986*; author's calculations
a) European Members of Comecon

involved in the process of nation-building or their own political integration

In the ASEAN region, for example, there were many conflicts before the foundation of the Association, such as the conflict between the Philippines and Malaysia over Sabah, or the non-recognition of the new federal state of Malaysia by Indonesia in 1963 (Shee 1977, p. 754). Indonesia had not even finished the nation-building process until the 1980s. The all too-short period of sovereignty has given rise to many such problems. The border conflict between Ecuador and Peru in 1981 is just another example. The potential for political and territorial disputes still exists within most of the developing RECs. Generally, they have been established to reduce their political and economic dependence on other countries and the vulnerability to foreign dominance. Political or economic events from outside the region have promoted the co-operation and integration in the beginning:

> *e.g.* the war and the increasing influence of the communists in Indo-China were conducive to the development of ASEAN;
> the political change in France in 1974 and the United Kingdom's entry to the EC influenced the ECOWAS positively;
> the great economic dependence on foreign countries, particularly the USA, supported the foundation of the Andean Pact; and
> both the Soviet invasion of Afghanistan and the war between Iran and Iraq led to the formation of the GCC.

Although the external pressure on the RECs still exists, a wide range of common interests constitutes the basis of their unity, so that the above mentioned disputes do not play a dominant role.

In the MCCA and the GCC the differences between the poorest and the richest country are not so evident. Compared to this, the relationship among the member states of the EC has completely changed with the membership of Spain and Portugal. Whereas it used to be 1:3.3 between Greece and Luxembourg, it has changed to 1:6.7 between Portugal and Luxembourg. Apart from the larger number of member states, this economic slope within the EC indicates a serious problem of integration. This will be one of the main difficulties facing Turkey in its bid to gain membership of the EC. The ECOWAS, with its numerous member states and different groups of English-speaking, French-speaking and Portuguese-speaking countries and different links to each other, has probably more problems of integration than ASEAN. From the beginning, only a few states joined the ASEAN, although the association was open to all states in South-East Asia (ASEAN Documents, 1983, p. 2). In the early years, the ASEAN countries attached more importance to a common identity, which is demonstrated by terms like 'think ASEAN' or 'ASEAN-spirit', and the principle of consensus.

It has taken centuries to reach the present stage of integration in Europe. Ever since the Middle Ages the idea of a unified Europe has appealed to many Europeans. Further, the European countries were relatively homogeneous regarding their cultural background, and a historical aspiration for integration was always prevalent. In spite of their common heritage the three decades of the EC's and EFTA's existence have been marked by disputes, difficulties and threats of withdrawal. Therefore, it is not surprising that the development of a regional identity and organisation in the Third World also faces difficulties and is a slow and deliberate process. This particular aspect is discussed by Harris/Bridges for the ASEAN (Harris/Bridges 1983, p. 78). But it is also applicable to the other RECs.

The present system of inter-regional co-operation

The links between the RECs have increased since the co-operation agreement between ASEAN and the EC in 1980. The degrees of interaction can be categorised as follows:

0 there is no interaction between the RECs
1 there is only an indirect interaction between two RECs
2 the attempt of an interaction has failed
3 there are contacts and regular dialogues
4 there is a formal agreement
5 the agreement has been put into practice to a great extent.

These categories can be interpreted as steps towards increasing interaction. The present system of relationships between the RECs can be described as in Figure 7.1.

Number 1 characterises a relationship which is formalised by an agreement, but the agreement is not directly formed between the RECs concerned, *e.g.* EC–ECOWAS. The ECOWAS member states belong to the ACP-Group which is not a regional community. The EC-ECOWAS links are laid down in the Lomé Convention applicable to all 66 ACP countries.

Figure 7.1 The present system of relationships between Regional Economic Communities

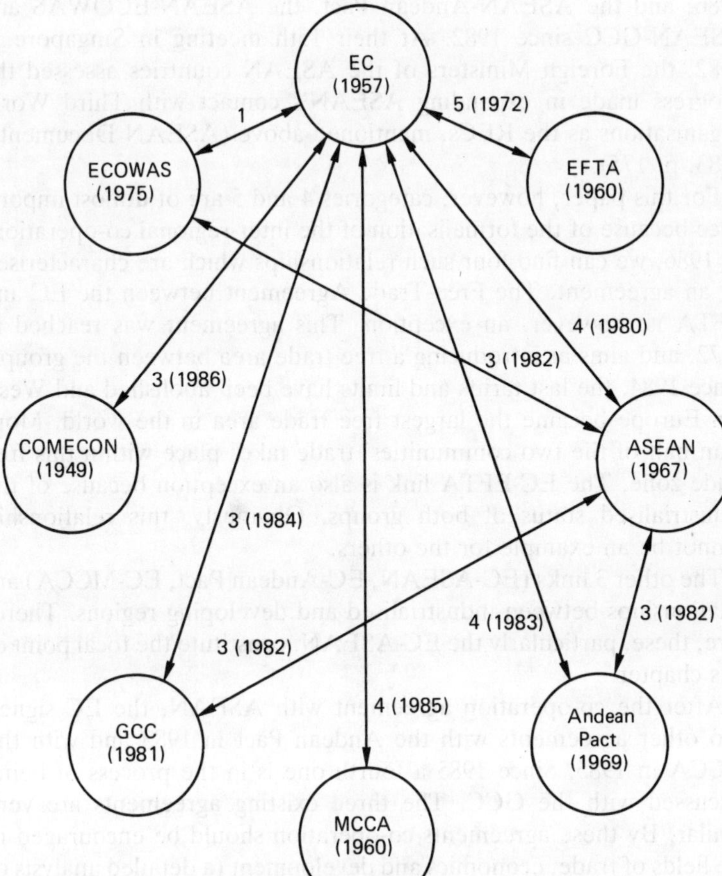

Number 2 describes an interaction between RECs which had been attempted by both sides but which failed, *e.g.* EC-Comecon before 1985. But in the last two years all the signs are that the EC-Comecon interaction will be improved.

Number 3 stands for the first real interaction in the sense of inter-regional co-operation which starts with official contacts, dialogues, conferences or meetings between the RECs. The regional groups act as communities and strive for more intensive links, *e.g.* the EC-GCC since November 1984, the EC-Comecon since September 1986, and the ASEAN-Andean Pact, the ASEAN-ECOWAS and ASEAN-GCC since 1982. At their 15th meeting in Singapore in 1982, the Foreign Ministers of the ASEAN countries assessed the progress made in expanding ASEAN's contact with Third World organisations as the RECs, mentioned above (ASEAN Documents, 1983, p. 175).

For this paper, however, categories 4 and 5 are of utmost importance because of the formalisation of the inter-regional co-operation. In 1986, we can find four such relationships which are characterised by an agreement. The Free-Trade Agreement between the EC and EFTA is, however, an exception. This agreement was reached in 1972, and aims at introducing a free trade area between the groups. Since 1984, the last tariffs and limits have been abolished and Western Europe became the largest free trade area in the world. More than half of the two communities' trade takes place within this free trade zone. The EC-EFTA link is also an exception because of the industrialised status of both groups. Obviously, this relationship cannot be an example for the others.

The other 3 links (EC-ASEAN, EC-Andean Pact, EC-MCCA) are relationships between industrialised and developing regions. Therefore, these, particularly the EC-ASEAN, constitute the focal point of this chapter.

After the co-operation agreement with ASEAN, the EC signed two other agreements with the Andean Pact in 1983 and with the MCCA in 1985. Since 1985 a fourth one is in the process of being discussed with the GCC. The three existing agreements are very similar. By these agreements co-operation should be encouraged in the fields of trade, economics and development (a detailed analysis of the EC-ASEAN and EC-Andean Agreement is given by Lukas 1985, p. 210–15 and p. 262–5). The international regulation of GATT can also be found in each agreement. The EC-ASEAN agreement is not only the first inter-regional one, it is also a model for the other RECs. In this context, ASEAN is the most important and the most attractive EC partner for inter-regional co-operation.

ASEAN as a partner of inter-regional co-operation

Apart from the EC, only ASEAN specified inter-regional co-operation as an aim of the agreement reached when this community was founded. The seventh point of the Bangkok Declaration states: 'To maintain close and beneficial co-operation with existing international and regional organisations with similar aims and purposes, and explore all avenues for even closer co-operation among themselves' (ASEAN Documents 1983, p. 2). This quotation can be interpreted as the basis of the EC-ASEAN cooperation.

As compared to most other communities of the Third World, ASEAN, after nearly two decades of its existence, is regarded as the most successful developing REC, despite numerous problems and the low rate of integration compared to the EC. Within the theory of integration, ASEAN has agreed a preferential area and a selective free trade zone. A customs union has been discussed in the last few years. With the exception of Indonesia, all other ASEAN countries plead for the implementation of a customs union by the year 2000.

The intra-regional trade, however, is today less than 20 per cent of the whole trade of ASEAN. Within the EC, 15 years after its foundation, this rate had already grown to over 50 per cent. But one has to consider that it is only since the Bali Summit in 1976, that the ASEAN countries have pursued an active integration policy. This policy can be differentiated in intra-regional co-operation (trade and economics) and in extra-regional co-operation with the six dialogue partners Japan, the USA, Canada, Australia, New Zealand and the EC. The intra-regional co-operation was extended by four common agreements: the Preferential Trading Arrangement (PTA) to liberalise trade, the Agreement on ASEAN Industrial Projects (AIP), the Agreement on ASEAN Industrial Complementation (AIC) and the ASEAN Industrial Joint Ventures Programme (AIJV) (see Lukas 1985, p. 147 and Wong 1985, p. 87).

For the time being, the progress of these programmes is quite slow. But as long as the rate of economic growth in the ASEAN countries was high, the progress of economic integration was not of considerable importance. This has changed completely with the declining prices of oil and other raw materials, with the increasing debt problem of the developing countries, with the worldwide influence of economic changes and technical development and with the increasing problem of protectionism. For the first time since the Bangkok Declaration, most of the ASEAN member states registered a negative economic development in 1985. The growth of GNP in Singapore showed –1.8 per cent and in the Philippines –4.5 per cent. At the same time, it declined in Malaysia from 6.7 per cent in 1984 to 2.7 per cent, in Indonesia from 5.8 per cent to 2.9 per cent, and in Thailand from 6.2 per cent to 4.0 per cent (see Lukas 1986b and Asian Development Bank 1986). The need to strengthen economic co-operation and integration within ASEAN was therefore discussed as a main topic at the ASEAN summit held in Manila in December 1987. All ASEAN governments agree that the organisation only has a future, if it is possible – besides the political solidarity – to intensify economic integration and to become an economic community (*Handelsblatt* 27.5.1986).

Apart from these problems, the unified approach of the ASEAN nations towards other countries has strengthened the regional identity. The risk of military conflicts between the countries has been minimised, firstly by the renunciation of military power to solve conflicts, and secondly, by the growing regional identity. The ASEAN member countries know that it is vital for their community to supplement political solidarity by economic integration. From the beginning, ASEAN has been characterised by a careful and continuous integration policy. This policy takes into account the balance between the special interests of the young nation-states and the new approach of integration. ASEAN's co-operation is a flexible and open-minded one with unique consensus-based decision-making procedures. There is not a fixed schedule of integration as in the EC and the Andean Pact. Therefore Wong calls ASEAN 'a *laissez-faire* type of regional scheme. This is both the weakness and the strength of ASEAN's approach to regional economic co-operation' (Wong 1985, p. 86).

In accordance with economic development, the ASEAN member states belong to the most important newly industrialising countries (NICs). They are among the world's most dynamic and rapidly growing economies. During the past two decades, the ASEAN region has experienced an impressive real GNP growth rate of 2.6 per cent in the Philippines to 7.8 per cent in Singapore (World Bank 1986, p. 206). With the exception of Singapore, the ASEAN countries are also richly endowed with natural resources. For the EC, they are very important as suppliers of raw material.

In addition to this, the Pacific Co-operation currently being discussed, is yet another challenge for the EC. With the exception of the EC, such co-operation affects all the other dialogue partners of ASEAN. Singapore's Ambassador to the EC referred to the EC as ASEAN's first but not its only love, because of the other five (Chiang 1986, p. 3). In the trilateral competition on the ASEAN markets between the 'Big Trilaterals' – USA, Japan and the EC – in the last 13 years, the EC lost a lot of its importance as a trading partner of ASEAN (see Table 4 and the trilateral competition issue in Lorenz 1986). Langhammer and Hiemenz conclude, 'the longer it takes manufacturing industries in the EC to regain the offensive, the more difficult it will be to recover lost ground' (Langhammer/Hiemenz, 1985, p. 118).

From the point of view of the EC, however, the ASEAN countries are something like a bridge to the Pacific Region. They have a market-orientated economic policy. In the North-South Dialogue, ASEAN is a partner of the EC too, because of its pragmatic policy. Neither the EC nor ASEAN strives for hegemony. By co-operating within the international system they want more participation and a more important part compared to the super-powers, *e.g.* in the UN (Afghanistan, Cambodia) and in the GATT negotiations. Within the UN, both communities constitute a group of 18 countries which represent more than a tenth of the UN members and a population of more than 600 million. The common line adopted by the EC and ASEAN at the UN indicates that they are a factor in world politics. The formalised relationship should contribute to diversifying the political and economic relations of ASEAN. This is one of the essential meanings of this partnership.

The relationship between the EC and ASEAN

With the co-operation agreement signed in March 1980, the EC and ASEAN pursued a new way of inter-regional co-operation. It was not only the new era of the EC-ASEAN relationship as was envisaged by the agreement, but it was the first time that inter-regional co-operation was formalised between an industrialised and a developing REC. As in the case of the development of ASEAN, the agreement was also signed without a fixed schedule or aim. Therefore, the permanent dialogue between the groups has an important function (Lukas 1985, p. 215). Using the above categories of interaction, the development of an EC-ASEAN partnership can be divided into three phases:

phase 1: 1967 – 1972
phase 2: 1972 – 1980
phase 3: 1980 –

The first period started with the foundation of ASEAN in August 1967. At that time, one could not describe the relationship between

Table 7.3 ASEAN's most important trade partners (percentage)

	Imports					*Exports*				
	1973	1980	1982	1983	1984	1973	1980	1982	1983	1984
USA	16.0	15.3	14.6	15.7	12.7	16.9	17.2	14.2	18.3	21.3
Japan	25.2	22.1	22.1	21.6	18.6	27.3	26.9	28.0	26.0	27.7
EC	16.5	12.7	12.4	12.2	11.9	15.7	12.8	10.7	10.1	9.8

Source: EC Commission 1985.

the groups as an example of inter-regional co-operation because an interaction between the RECs did not exist. The first years of ASEAN's existence were characterised, as set out above, by conflicts and disputes. This did not allow an outward-looking policy, and ASEAN had to concentrate on the internal situation. At the same time, the external activities of the EC were confined to the ACP countries because of historical colonial links.

In 1972, the second phase began with direct contacts between the groups. This change in the relationship coincided with internal changes within the groups: on the one hand, the change of politics from conflict to co-operation and the beginning of an external political orientation within ASEAN, and on the other hand, the first expansion of the EC. From ASEAN's point of view, the purpose was to reduce their trade dependence on Japan and the USA. Table 7.3 shows that in 1984, Japan held a 27.7 per cent share in ASEAN exports and 18.6 per cent in ASEAN imports; corresponding figures for the USA were 21.3 per cent and 12.7 per cent . Both countries together covered more than 40 per cent of the whole ASEAN trade. The EC trade share, however, worked out at about 11 per cent. Taken together, the 'Big Trilaterals' have more than 50 per cent. We have already discussed the Bangkok Declaration which states that co-operation with other international and regional groups is one of ASEAN's aims. Therefore, as the most integrated REC the EC could be mentioned as a natural partner of ASEAN in the inter-regional field. With the entry of the UK in 1972, the EC itself had to rearrange its relationship with the former British colonies in South-east Asia. This included a number of countries of the region and was laid down in an annex to the UK's Treaty of Accession.

In the beginning, the second phase was characterised by dialogues

Table 7.4 Trade between EC and ASEAN 1973–1985 (value in Mio. ECU)

	1973	*1980*	*1981*	*1982*	*1983*	*1984*	*1985*	*Index 85–73*	*Index 85–80*
EC-Import	1.787	6.920	6.642	7.076	7.873	9.630	9.932	556	144
EC-Export	1.687	5.321	7.081	8.358	9.050	9.634	9.648	572	181
Balance	−100	−1.599	439	1.282	1.177	4	−148		

Source: Eurostat.

within the Special Co-ordinating Committee of ASEAN-Nations (SCCAN), the ASEAN Brussels Committee (ABC) and the joint study group of representatives of the EC-Commission and the ASEAN governments. In 1975, the EC-Commission decided to extend the principle of the cumulative regulation of origin to imports from regional groups as ASEAN, Andean Pact and MCCA. This was a demonstrative step designed to encourage regional integration between developing countries and inter-regional trade co-operation. With the first meeting of foreign ministers of both groups in November 1978, the relationship received a political dimension at ministerial level. The EC recognised ASEAN as a regional organisation which constitutes an important factor of stability and balance, and which contributes to the maintenance of peace in South-East Asia. Furthermore, the EC recognised ASEAN as a developing region, and agreed that co-operation between them should be expanded in such a manner as to contribute to ASEAN's efforts in enhancing its self-reliance and economic resilience (ASEAN Documents 1983, p. 235–240). The EC also underlined the importance of ASEAN as a region with important and rich natural resources. The two sides agreed to place their relations on a more formal footing. This should initiate a new formal and institutional era in EC-ASEAN relations.

The third phase started with the signing of the Co-operation Agreement during the second ministerial meeting in March 1980. Relations reached the fifth step of interaction (number 4 in our system of inter-regional relations). Since 1980, the EC has had a trade surplus with ASEAN. EC exports to ASEAN rose by 81 per cent and EC imports from ASEAN increased by 44 per cent (see Table 7.4). Since 1973, the trade between the groups on the whole increased by about six times. Within the group of Twelve, West

Germany is the most important trade partner of ASEAN, followed by the UK, which has traditional political and economic relations with this region.

However, the EC-ASEAN economic co-operation lags behind the other Trilaterals, Japan and the USA. ASEAN's volume of trade increased by about eight times. During this time the share of the EC in ASEAN imports declined from 16.5 per cent to 11.9 per cent. A similar fall can be observed in ASEAN exports from 15.7 per cent to 9.8 per cent. Compared to Japan and the USA, the EC lost some of its importance. But on the other hand ASEAN's importance to EC trade is still low (2.5 per cent). This is less than the share of the ACP countries or Latin America (EC Commission 1985, p. 4). In spite of the high economic growth in the ASEAN-region, one has to consider that ASEAN's GNP corresponds to the GNP of the Benelux countries.

The political dimension of the EC-ASEAN co-operation

The inter-regional co-operation between the EC and ASEAN has been mostly developed with regard to political co-operation. Since the signing of the agreement, an institutional structure of the relationship came into being. One can distinguish between the political and the economic level. The political level is composed of the Ministerial Meeting, the annual EC-ASEAN dialogue, the meeting between the members of the European Parliament (EP) and the ASEAN Inter Parliamentary Organisation (AIPO), and of the Joint Co-operation Committee (JCC). At the political level the framework of the relationship is institutionalised. The economic level comprises the EC-ASEAN Trade Council and the different programmes, conferences, seminars and exhibitions held in both regions (Lukas, 1986a).

The joint Ministerial Meeting became the central and most important body of inter-regional co-operation. This meeting was the first inter-regional one and the first the EC had held with non-associated countries at ministerial level. The first meeting with ASEAN had taken place before the agreement was signed whereas the first ministerial meeting between the EC and EFTA was held twelve years after the EC-EFTA Free-Trade Agreement. This indicates the importance of the meeting for the EC-ASEAN partnership. The meetings, held about every 18 months, were primarily dedicated to political topics. The Foreign Ministers of both groups take important decisions on inter-regional co-operation and make international declarations (Indochina, Cambodia, Afghanistan) at this highest level. But during the sixth meeting, held in Jakarta in October 1986, economic problems were in the forefront, *e.g.* co-operation between the groups, the joint position at the GATT negotiation and the promotion of European investments in ASEAN. This corresponds to the recent ASEAN efforts, mentioned above, which hold internal economic co-operation and integration to be a vital factor in ASEAN's future. The main economic focus of this EC-ASEAN meeting goes together with the rapidly changing international situation because of economic and technical development.

The EC-ASEAN dialogue after the annual ASEAN meeting of Foreign Ministers can be seen as the second institution of inter-regional co-operation. Despite the importance of this dialogue, the EC is only one partner, as explained above. In the long run, this dialogue can be regarded as a connection between the European and the Asian-Pacific Region, in which ASEAN has a role as mediator and a source of information (Tengku 1986, p. 150).

The third institutional form, the EP-AIPO dialogue, is not governed by the Agreement. But these meetings, which have taken place five times, have become an important forum for the political exchange of views below government level. It is one of the tasks of the EP to show clearly that inter-regional co-operation is not possible without large and continuous transnational communications between the groups at every level. The EP can also give advice and support to the AIPO in the process of forming an ASEAN Parliament similar to the EP.

The JCC was created by the Co-operation Agreement. It is the main instrument by which the Agreement is implemented.

Finally, three factors could be said to be characteristic of the EC-ASEAN co-operation:

1 In the face of the increasing political and economic interdependence of the world, the EC and ASEAN member states are a successful example of co-operation between industrialised and developing countries at many different levels.

2 By co-operation, both communities gain a stronger position and influence in international politics and development. They are of increasing importance in world politics.

3 Both groups as regional communities could contribute to the stability and development in their regions and the EC could play a decisive role in North-South and South-South co-operation.

In the context of international politics, a new way of communication and interaction between RECs can be implemented by the EC-ASEAN co-operation. Regional unity, which is the primary aim of ASEAN, is also welcomed and supported by the EC. By means of internal and inter-regional co-operation, ASEAN strives to reduce the confrontation of foreign powers in South-East Asia and, simultaneously, its vulnerability to foreign dominance. The development of South-East Asia is subject to various confrontations such as:

the confrontation between the USSR and China,
the confrontation between the USSR and the USA and
the economic collision between the USA and Japan.

By promoting inter-regional co-operation one of the functions of the EC is to reduce ASEAN's dependence on this foreign influence, to diversify ASEAN's political and economic relations and to enhance stability and security in South-East Asia. In international politics this is the main political dimension of this inter-regional co-operation. The renewal of the EC-ASEAN Agreement during the first meeting of the Economic Ministers in Bangkok in October 1985 called for more intensive economic co-operation. The 1986 meeting of EC-ASEAN Foreign Ministers emphasised that this must be achieved within the framework of the political co-operation which had been agreed upon. The conference also proved that the institutional organisation of this inter-regional co-operation is in a position to provide the necessary context and to intensify this co-operation.

Conclusion

States as interacting units are gradually being replaced by RECs. Among these RECs, the EC-ASEAN inter-regional co-operation is a pragmatic and successful one. It is a good example of North-South co-operation. But in the long run, this inter-regional co-operation is in its initial stages. The increasing number of Co-operation Agreements throw light on a pattern of development in international relationships. Like the EC-ASEAN agreement, two similar agreements have been signed (the EC-Andean Pact and the EC-MCCA), further agreements are being discussed (EC-GCC and EC-

Comecon). Because of the specific situation of ASEAN, the very recent nature of formalised EC-ASEAN co-operation and the internal situation and problems of the other RECs, identical forms of inter-regional co-operation cannot be forecasted exactly. But there are many similar problems and starting positions, *e.g.* the impetus to strengthen their own position and to reduce political or economic dependence through integration within the groups and through inter-regional co-operation. There is no doubt that the EC-ASEAN co-operation, which is certainly in the process of formation, depicts a new system of international relationships that could contribute to stability in general. The aim of the EC is to reduce polarisation in the regions. Inter-regional co-operation between RECs can therefore be regarded as a new approach in international politics.

References

ASEAN Documents, (1983) Ministry of Foreign Affairs, Bangkok 1983.

Asian Development Bank, (1986): *Annual Report 1985*, Manila 1986.

Chiang Hai Ding, (1986) *Development of the ASEAN-EC Co-operation Programme, as seen from ASEAN*. Working paper on the interdisciplinary conference 'The relations between ASEAN and the EC', organised by the Arbeitsgemeinschaft Europäische Integration e. V., Bonn and Gesellschaft für Asienkunde e. V. Hamburg, 20–22 February 1986, Universität Passau.

EC Commission, (1985) *The European Community and ASEAN*, (Brussels: Europe Information, External Relations, No. 81/1985).

Harris, Stuart and Bridges, Brian, (1983) *European Interests in ASEAN*, (London-Boston-Henley: Routledge & Kegan Paul).

Indorf, Hans H., (1983) 'Political Dimensions of Inter-Regional Co-operation: ASEAN and the EEC,' *Asia Pacific Community*, Tokyo: No. 19, Winter 1983), pp. 89–107.

Kraus, Willy und Lütkenhorst, Wilfried, (1984) *Wirtschaftsdynamik im Pazifischen Becken. Entwicklungstendenzen, Handelsverflechtungen und Kooperationsansätze*, Stuttgart: Thienemanns 1984.

Langhammer, Rolf J. and Hiemenz, Ulrich, (1985) 'Declining Competitiveness of EC suppliers in ASEAN Markets: Singular Case or Symptom?', in: *Journal of Common Market Studies*, vol. XXIV, No. 2, (December), pp. 105-119.

Lorenz, Detlef, (1986) 'International Division of Labour or Closer Co-operation? A look at ASEAN-EC economic relations', *ASEAN Economic Bulletin*, vol. 2, no. 3 (March), pp. 168–185.

Lukas, Andreas, (1985) *Regionale Wirtschaftsgemeinschaften im internationalen System. Eine Analyse ausgewählter Wirtschaftsgemeinschaften und ihrer Interaktionen, insbesondere zwischen der EG und der ASEAN*

(Saarbrücker Politikwissenschaft Bd. 6), Frankfurt a. M. – Bern – New York: Lang 1985.

Lukas, Andreas, (1986a) 'Entwicklung, Stand und institutionelle Organisation der EG-ASEAN-Beziehungen' in: *Asien* (German Association for Asian Studies), Hamburg, Nr. 20, Juli 1986, pp. 51–58.

Lukas, Andreas, (1986b) 'Wirtschaftliche Situation in den ASEAN-Ländern' in: *Blätter für deutsche und internationale Politik*.

Robson, Peter, (1980) *The Economics of International Integration*, (London: Allen & Unwin 1980).

Shee, Poon-Kim, (1977) 'A Decade of ASEAN, 1967–77', *Asian Survey*, (August) pp. 753–770.

Tengku, Ahmad Rithauddeen, (1986) 'Probleme und Aufgaben der Länder Südostasiens', *Europa Archiv*, Folge 5/1986, pp. 145–150.

Wong, John, (1985) 'ASEAN's Experience in Regional Economic Co-operation'. *Asian Development Review*, vol. 3, no. 1, pp. 79–88.

World Bank, (1986) *World Development Report 1986*, (Washington D. C.).

8 EC-ASEAN Trade and Industrial Co-operation: The Pros and Cons

Rolando Valiani

1 My aim is to draw attention to the difficulties in increasing trade relations between the European Community countries and those of the South-East Asian area. It is easy in circumstances like this to get carried away with declarations of principle, invoking the great advantages which free trade brings to everyone. But we know that the reality is often more complex than the theories and that the options of principle have to contend with the interests of enterprises and states. This is why I am convinced that instead of imagining bold designs, destined to remain on paper, it is perhaps preferable to rely on the policy of small steps, and circumscribe the debate to what actually can be done at this stage. In the light of these considerations, which take into account the interests of Italian industry and its economy, I will analyse the obstacles to the expansion of trade between the two areas and I will make some brief reflections on the policies to adopt in order to start overcoming them.

2 The first and greatest obstacle to the development of trade between the EC and ASEAN is represented by the progressive slowing down of the world economy. The commercial relations between the two areas are languishing also because international demand is slackening, monetary disorder is increasing and protectionism is more widespread. In this framework, the most realistic road to take is that of avoiding the worst, and preventing the consequences of the economic crisis jeopardizing what has been achieved up to now. But even if it were possible to avert the risks of a recession and relaunch world demand, as I hope, it will not, in the short term, be equally easy to impose a decisive turning point on the commercial relations between the two areas. Many products of ASEAN countries are by now in open competition with major sectors of European industry. Suffice it to mention textiles, clothing, the timber and food industries,

and a series of intermediate goods including electronic components. These are products requiring relatively simple technology, whose competitiveness is almost exclusively linked to the price. Here the ASEAN countries start with a clear advantage. Their industries pay salaries much lower than European ones and they can count on standards of working flexibility (and therefore also of productivity) unimaginable in Europe.

The relative advantages of the South-East Asian industries are also stressed by the most recent evolution of exchange rates. The ASEAN currencies have always fluctuated with the US dollar and in the years 1985–6 they have been devalued with respect to the ECU to the same extent as the American dollar. In fact, by a good 30 per cent. Low labour costs, favourable exchange ratios: that is all it needs for the European enterprises most exposed to competition to find themselves suddenly out of the market with all the easily imaginable economic, social and political consequences. The third cause which hinders a more decisive growth of trade is represented by the dominant position which the United States and especially Japan have gradually assumed in South-East Asia. Many large multinationals of the two countries, attracted by the low costs and high productivity of labour, have made massive investments in that area, transferring their simpler productions there. A choice which has swept European competition off world markets and which is sometimes also used to attempt rather unfair dumping practices. It is only natural that, when faced with such situations, European enterprises multiply the pressures on individual states and on the European Community to be defended and only recently the EC had to intervene to check these practices.

3 As can be seen, there are objective difficulties in achieving spectacular openings within the short term. It is true that in principle we would all benefit from a liberalisation of trade, but it is also true that the interests at stake are considerable and that it just needs a rash move to provoke serious repercussions which could hinder the cause of free trade instead of advancing it.

Therefore, it seems preferable to tackle the question in a very gradual manner, beginning by removing the obstacles one by one. In this view, the first step to take is that of defining a common reference framework in which the needs of the two areas are respected.

There is no lack of mutual meeting points. Allow me to point out a few of them. There is a European interest in readjusting the dominant positions which the Japanese and Americans have in the South-East Asian countries and in competing on equal terms on a commercial and productive level. A supremacy which is not always due to the attention which Japan and the United States have devoted to that area, but which is sometimes also the result of preferential agreements and special treatments. Removing the political and legal obstacles which have caused this state of affairs is a first step. The fact that major European enterprises have invested very cautiously in South-East Asia, although the potential exists, and have never decisively aimed at that area is singular and merits reflection. There is evidently something which still does not work and which makes ventures in those countries not very appealing or profitable.

Another meeting point could be represented by the EC and ASEAN's common battle in international centres to avert the world recession. If no country has anything to gain from a crisis, the most damaged will certainly be the weaker countries; from those of the Third World to the newly industrialised ones. Everything which can be done to liberalise trade is paltry in comparison with a strong recovery of world demand. Without counting on the fact that the temptation to limit international trade increases when each area has to reckon with the social and political problems which the recession imposes. If these considerations are correct, the thesis that the regulation of the world economic crisis depends only on the big Seven and their ability to reduce the US public deficit and relaunch domestic demand in Japan and Europe should be contended. Problems such as clearing up international debt or creating a new currency order are no less decisive than the recovery of demand, because they allow the Third World and newly industrialised countries to reduce the burden of servicing their foreign debt and ease off the internal constraints to which many economies have been subjected for currency reasons.

4 Whilst admitting that it is difficult to imagine substantial progress as regards trade relations between the two areas if a more favourable general context is not constructed first, it is however possible to define a route which, step by step, leads to concrete results. Europe has a moral and political duty to help South-East Asian countries to strengthen their industrial system and reinforce their still rather precarious institutions. In this framework, the potential meeting points could concern a greater European opening to the import of raw materials and especially agricultural ones, the development of

forms of countertrade, and greater co-operation in the field of technical assistance and development of human resources.

A considerable proportion of the South-East Asian countries' exports is made up of agricultural foodstuffs and food products which often run up against the Community protection system. A greater opening as regards these products, as well as greater co-operation with the ASEAN countries to develop agro-industry is possible and does not injure vital Community interests.

Another possible line of action is that of countertrade. A specific tool for stepping up opportunities for the trade of countries which, like the ASEAN ones, have serious problems of hard currency. By now almost a third of world trade is carried out by barter. The EC, which has more evolved marketing techniques and financial structures, can and must develop trading in kind which will help these countries to increase their exports and pay for their imports. The advantage is mutual because the development of countertrade could ensure a greater penetration of Community products and provide opportunities which would otherwise be lost, for the major European plant and civil engineering enterprises to work in that area.

But it is above all in the field of industrial co-operation and technical assistance that the relations between the two areas can be improved in this phase. The ASEAN countries, like almost all the newly-industrialised ones, have great problems of technology, know-how, and training and development of their human capital. This is the field which the Europeans cannot leave to an American or Japanese monopoly. And not only for the necessary reasons of solidarity but also for economic benefit. Co-operation and technical assistance are today the main vehicles for setting up good trade relations. Those who take advantage of this course, end up also becoming privileged partners in the economic field.

5 The model of industrial co-operation which has had the most fortune in the South-East Asian area is the one experimented with by Japan. Japanese producers, commercial and financial undertakings have descended in force on the ASEAN countries, bringing projects, capital, technological knowledge, management skills, specialised trades and assistance not in one single commodity sector but in all those where there are opportunities for economic enterprise.

The massive, well-prepared and planned Japanese strategy has by now supplanted the traditional American influence, because the undertakings of the 'Rising Sun' have done better than the US in helping the South-East Asian countries to construct a primary nucleus of industrial activities in the sectors with the highest labour intensity and in the first ones to industrialise, also demonstrating a great willingness to adapt themselves to the plans of local government and the indigenous production and organising skills.

In fact, this is in many ways an exemplary model of global co-operation on an equal standing between an advanced industrialised country and a group of countries which are aspiring to their own industrialisation, in which the former assists, finances and gives commodity and technical support to the aspirations of the latter, achieving a higher standard of production and commercial abilities to the benefit of both partners.

If this is the framework, it will be difficult for the EC to set itself ambitious goals of industrial co-operation with the ASEAN countries which can affect the Japanese influence in the short term. However, even without pursuing global co-operation aims, some attempts at partial collaboration can be made. There are sectors, such as that of preserved food, timber, clothing and electronic components in which it is possible to try out forms of productive integration among the firms in the two areas. It is an operation which must be prepared with care and taken gradually and which belongs more to the medium term than the near future, also because it is first necessary to set up the political and legal instruments suitable for giving certainty and safeguarding the interests of both partners. But on which, precisely for this, it is perhaps advisable to make a start right now.

9 The Link Between Trade With and Investment in ASEAN Countries: Lessons for EC Suppliers and Policymakers*

Rolf J. Langhammer

I INTRODUCTION

A view on EC economic relations with third countries in Europe and overseas gives a puzzling result. In terms of *institutionalised* relations, the Community is among the most active entities in the world. Major trading partners are linked institutionally to the Community through preferential or non-preferential trading arrangements. EC member countries have additionally negotiated investment guarantee agreements with the most important host countries. National and 'Euro' chambers of commerce provide substantial information on investment opportunities and trade possibilities supported by permanent representatives of the Community in major partner countries. Such intensive activities contrast strikingly with the *performance* of the Community in world trade and investment. Since 1970 the share of the Community in developed countries' exports has declined; most visibly in industries like machinery and transport equipment where one would have expected EC suppliers to have comparative advantages, and less visibly (or even with rising shares) in sectors like food where such advantages do not seem to exist.[1] Deteriorating competitiveness *vis-à-vis* Japanese suppliers in sophisticated products on one hand, and rising competitiveness in food products because of subsidising exports and protecting local production on the other hand provide keys towards explaining such shifts in trade shares.

Trends in international investment – as far as the limited data base allows – do not reveal a much more positive picture for the EC. During 1967 and 1976, the share of the EC members in the stock of direct investment abroad of developed market economies declined from 31 per cent to 28 per cent (OECD, Paris, 1981, p. 39). Estimates up to 1983 supplementing stock data by flow data suggest no major change in the EC share of total investment abroad as increases of German, Dutch and French investment were outweighed by decreases of UK shares in investment (UN, Centre on Transnational Corporations, 1985, p. 16).

Such discrepancies between intensive institutionalised relations and international economic performance do not only emerge on a worldwide scale but also on the much more disaggregated level of economic relations between ASEAN and the EC. Intensive bilateral relations in the context of the ASEAN-EC co-operation agreement contrast with declining shares of the EC in ASEAN markets and relatively insignificant EC investment in ASEAN outside the petroleum sector and banking.[2]

This paper discusses various hypotheses about poor trade and investment performance and proposes remedies to turn the tide.

II MORE INVESTMENT AS THE KEY TO MORE TRADE

The hypothesis that foreign investment generates more home country exports than it replaces has been supported by quite a number of empirical studies (Bergsten *et al.*, 1978; Donges, Juhl, 1979; Lipsey, Weiss, 1981; Lipsey, Weiss, 1984; Milton, 1984; Arnaud-Ameller, 1985). This positive impact has three major determinants and all of them are technology-linked.

First, investment is partly financed in kind through purchases of plant equipment and intermediates from home countries. Recent estimates for the implementation of foreign investment in Indonesia yield a 50 per cent share of investment financed in kind (Langhammer, 1986c).

Second, in the initial process of production deliveries of capital goods, raw materials and intermediates from parent companies to their foreign affiliates (intra-firm trade) are sizeable (Dunning, Pearce, 1985; Groß, 1986). Intra-firm trade implies first a demonstration effect and later on an imitation effect as foreign technology embodied in capital goods will be used by local investors either through joint ventures or independently provided that this technology successfully adapts to local conditions.

Third, foreign investment has a 'follow-the-leader' and a 'follow-up-effect.' In the latter case traditional suppliers of the initial investor will join the finished goods' producer in host countries if the local market meets both supply and demand prerequisites. Local content requirements may force suppliers into joint ventures if appropriate local partners are at hand. In the former case, home country competitors may follow the pioneer investor in the same market. The chemical industry provides examples of the former case, whereas the car industry is typical of the latter one. Both sequences of foreign investment have important trade effects in both directions. They help to open new markets and to defend old ones.

III REASONS NOT TO INVEST IN ASEAN

Disadvantages relative to competing suppliers from the US and Japan

Given such relationships between investment and trade the crucial question is why EC-based producers have been reluctant to invest in ASEAN (and elsewhere in developing Asia). Several explanations have been brought forward, especially by entrepreneurs who were asked for their motives to engage or not to engage.

First, administrative barriers, exchange risks, restrictions on capital repatriation *etc.* are reportedly prohibitive. This argument cannot easily be rejected as investors from other home countries, for instance from Japan, have also stressed the validity of this argument for important host countries like Indonesia recently (Kinoshita, 1986a, 1986b). However, as investment legislation applies to all home countries and – at least officially – does not discriminate against selected investors, the 'red tape' argument could only explain a decline of investment in ASEAN countries relative to other host areas where such impediments do not exist. It cannot explain shifts in investment shares between home countries in ASEAN countries. Furthermore, it is rather likely that host country policies towards newcomers like the EC-based investors are less restrictive than those towards dominating investors from Japan or the US, if governments aim to diversify private capital inflows.

Second, the importance of 'remoteness' factors has been stressed. In geographical terms, this argument can be rejected on empirical grounds. Costs of transportation from Europe to ASEAN countries have been estimated to be higher than those for *identical* goods shipped from Japan to ASEAN countries. However, such transport cost differentials which amount to about 4 to 5 per cent of cif import prices fail to explain the differences in the export performance of European, US and Japanese suppliers. They are not systematic but random (Langhammer, 1985). Technical innovations in transport media as well as the rise of import values per weight unit will make transportation costs in trade with South-East Asia increasingly unimportant. What remains as factors of remoteness is the relevance of costs of market exploration. This argument can be related to the lack of a long-established business community of EC member states through which such costs could be externalised. Unlike in Latin American countries as Argentina, Brazil and Chile, where, for instance, German or Italian emigrants maintained personal links to their home countries and transferred them into commercial relations for almost a century, such a community in ASEAN countries is still in the making.

It is not surprising that an overproportionate intensity of EC economic relations with ASEAN exists mainly for the UK in the two Commonwealth members Malaysia and Singapore and – less distinct – for the Netherlands in Indonesia. Given the increasing interdependence between firms which are vertically or horizontally integrated, the argument of a business community matters as the Japanese way of 'team achievement' demonstrates. It is obvious that EC-based investors suffer from disadvantages in this respect as the level of integration among firms from different member states is still below the level obtained by Japan or the United States as fully integrated entities.

Third, there is the argument of stronger governmental support for investment in South-east Asia from the Japanese side than from European governments. Empirically, this argument has to be discussed thoroughly. A recent comparative study on home country incentives concludes that all major home countries grant the same kind of incentives, *i.e.* double taxation agreements, subsidised loans for small and medium-sized investors, investment guarantee schemes, and export credit insurances (Agarwal, 1986). Their efficiency in stimulating investment cannot be isolated from other determinants to invest and are therefore difficult to quantify. Yet, there is evidence that this efficiency does not seem to be dependent on the amount of government funds but on their allocation and concentration. Japanese official agencies concentrate the aid allocation on ASEAN countries. They have established institutions specialised in economic relations only with ASEAN, and furthermore they seem to concentrate the assistance to private firms on loan and equity investment commitments.

During 1961 and 1984, for instance, Japanese corporations conducted projects funded by official aid loans and equity investment in a range of 7 per cent of total Japanese aid commitments (OECF, 1985) and almost 40 per cent of the commitments was concentrated on ASEAN countries. Neither the amount of assistance given to private firms nor its regional concentration seem to have been matched by other home country agencies, such as the German DEG (German Development Company) or the British CDC (Commonwealth Development Corporation).

Economically, public assistance to loan and equity financing of foreign investment means shifting investment risks from the firms to the taxpayer. Furthermore, investors receive a direct investment subsidy measured by the grant element. In the Japanese case it seems that the concentration of Japanese public aid and investment assistance on the resource-rich ASEAN region has signaled to Japanese private firms a political priority of this region in Japan's external economic policy and a willingness of Japanese public agencies to share risks. There has been an equivalent of massive qualitative and quantitative public assistance in EC policies towards a specific developing region, that is Sub-Saharan Africa. Both ASEAN and Sub-Saharan Africa are resource-rich, but it is the additional considerable human skill element in ASEAN countries still lacking in African countries which attracts private investors beyond the primary sector and makes Japanese public assistance effective. There is no way for the EC to copy the Japanese model unless the recipient countries do not enlarge and upgrade their factor endowment as ASEAN countries did in the past.

Fourth, Japanese 'package' strategies in general and the role of the trading houses (*sogo shosha*) as an amalgam for Japanese production and marketing have been reported to act as a deterrent for European investors. Stressing the importance of this argument highlights the weaknesses of European competitiveness rather than the strength of Japanese competitors. Weaknesses exist with respect to lacking the ability to adjust the product mix to local demand. In other words, EC-based firms supply high-income consumer goods instead of mass consumer goods, and capital goods both at top quality and top prices. However, quality advantages *vis-à-vis* Japanese suppliers fail to outweigh price differentials which sometimes exceed 50 per cent, not to speak of new suppliers of capital goods such as Taiwan or South Korea, where price differentials are higher. Limiting the product range to the top segment, of course, makes it difficult to open markets outside joint ventures and fully-owned affiliates.

Further weaknesses are reported to exist with respect to the marketing of European firms being less aggressive, responsive and adaptive than Asian or US competitors (Kirchbach, 1985). Whether this is due to isolated actions of individual firms contrasting to concerted actions of Japanese firm groups is difficult to assess. Cases can be raised against simple black and white explanations for two reasons. European and Japanese firms have increasingly entered joint ventures, sub-contracting arrangements or licensing agreements. Second, Japanese trading houses offer their services to European firms too and have become important clients of theirs.

Fifth, information costs are often assumed to be higher for EC-based firms than for US or Japanese suppliers. Apart from the existence of permanent European information services in ASEAN countries, both private and public ones, this argument can also be challenged by factual evidence. In recent years, ASEAN countries have proven to be an important location for outward processing of electronics commissioned by EC-based firms. In 1985, about 40 per cent of total EC exports of electronics designed for outward processing prior to re-exports to the EC was directed to ASEAN countries, especially Malaysia and Singapore. This relatively high share clearly demonstrates that EC-based firms do have information on how to use the abundance of skill and labour in ASEAN countries for processing labour-intensive parts of production abroad. It is interesting to note that this high share of ASEAN countries in outward processing of electronics originating in the EC had no equivalent in the other important industry in which outward processing is most common, that is clothing. In this industry EC-originating clothing was processed particularly in Mediterranean countries and in European socialist countries, not in ASEAN countries. It seems rather unlikely that high barriers against the flow of information among various EC-based industries exist thus excluding one industry from region-specific know-how which another industry has collected and applied. Instead, the argument of industry-specific determinants of an optimal 'location-mix' of production between ASEAN hosts and other potential hosts appears to be more convincing.

Considering this argument leads us to the common weakness of all previous approaches to explaining the low production engagement of

EC-based firms in ASEAN, that is the reference system of competing suppliers and the relative position of the EC-based firms. However, this is not – or at best is only partly – the relevant reference system in the decision making process of firms. Firms decide on terms of *their* potential alternatives, that is, for example, to produce locally and to export instead of investing abroad. Or, the decision can be made to invest in region *X* and not in region *Y* if both regions have similar resource endowments but different affiliations to the European Community. Tracing the different alternatives open to individual firms and the underlying policy incentives allows for a realistic assessment of firm behaviour.

Disincentives relative to alternative locations

One of the most effective disincentives to EC investment in developing countries (not necessarily only in ASEAN) has been the process of European integration, that is the removal of internal barriers to trade and – perhaps even more important – the shelter of domestic producers against outside competition through the common protection level. The effect of European integration on investment abroad was twofold:

First, integration opened the markets of neighbouring countries to exports and directed the attention of EC producers to high-income products. Both the importance of intra-EC trade (about 50 per cent of total EC trade) and of exports instead of investment rose.

Second, EC protectionism against third-country suppliers of labour-intensive goods helped EC producers of competing goods to postpone the necessary adjustment steps. One of these steps would have been to shift production to the newly industrialising countries or other developing countries and to use these countries either as export platforms as the Japanese did or as a place for supplying the local markets.

The undervaluation of major European currencies against the US dollar in the final stages of the Bretton Woods system (until 1971) led to a further incentive to direct exports and to a disincentive to foreign investment. Both the European integration process and the currency disequilibrium until the early 1970s seem to have had a long-run effect with respect to the formation of human (entrepreneurial) capital in the Community. Managers of EC-based firms were trained 'to look West' from the home base and to exploit the economic potential of the Common Market enlarged by new members in 1973 and in the early 1980s. It has been this attractiveness of the Common Market and – after realigned exhange rates – of the US market too which in some cases gave rise to the 'fortress Europe' perception and made EC investors latecomers in developing Asia.

As human entrepreneurial capital has a fairly long gestation period, lack of experienced managers able to run affiliates in countries of developing Asia has remained a bottleneck factor until today. Besides internal trade liberalisation and external protection, European integration has resulted in a third disincentive to produce abroad, that is the policy of regional subsidies for backward areas within the Community. Subsidies were paid to attract new local and foreign investment in backward areas in order to erode regional disparities in the growth of income and the income level. As backward areas dispose of a relatively similar resource endowment as advanced developing countries, that is, relatively cheap skilled labour and lack of investment capital, regional subsidies may have influenced the decision of potential investors to establish plants in backward areas of the EC instead of in developing countries. EC member countries which either partly or wholly (Ireland) are eligible for receiving regional subsidies are mostly those who urge for more protection of their industries against competition from developing countries.[3] This may indicate how substitutive investment in backward member states and developing countries appears to be and how effective regional subsidies can be in influencing investment decisions in favour of backward EC areas.

However, European integration has not been the only disincentive to investment in ASEAN countries. There are two groups of countries already mentioned above which are located 'next door' to the Community and dispose of a similar resource endowment relative to the Community as the ASEAN countries. One of the groups comprises the centrally planned economies of Eastern Europe, and the other one is the group of those Mediterranean countries which have become important exporters of manufactures (Turkey, Malta, Morocco, Tunisia, Israel). To begin with the latter group, the considerable amount of clothing exports from the Community to Mediterranean countries for outward processing does not only reflect the international competitiveness of these countries, but also considerable advantages in market access relative to ASEAN countries. Almost all countries of the Mediterranean basin enjoy duty-free access for their manufactured exports to the Community under preferential trading arrangements. Furthermore, special trade régimes exist for outward processing which mitigate the restrictive effects of the Multifibre Arrangement. Such advantages do not exist for exports from ASEAN countries. They give Mediterranean countries a clear competitive edge in activities like sub-contracting, licensing production and assembly. However, access privileges would have been ineffective if the Mediterranean countries – at least some of them – had not pursued outward-oriented trade régimes, so that exports were not significantly discriminated against compared to production for the local market.

The former group, the European socialist countries, have proved to be important partners in sub-contracting activities because of their pricing practices and also because they offer private foreign firms risk-sharing through state-owned companies. Though their resource endowment differs from that of developing countries their state-owned companies have specialised in labour-intensive consumer goods thus bringing their factor price ratios (in international prices) close to those of developing countries. The need to earn foreign exchange not only by exporting commodities has often resulted in pricing labour in socialist countries as if labour were as abundant as in developing countries. Though a number of obstacles exist against the way of bilateral trade, socialist countries seem to prefer (buy-back arrangements, industrial co-operation schemes); many European firms operating in light industries (textiles, footwear) as well as in chemical industries and transport equipment have integrated socialist companies into their production chain.[4] The role of public agencies – both from home and host countries – as risk-absorber in East-West co-operation agreements cannot be underrated. Such agencies provide insurance services against both commercial and political risks which in many developing countries cannot be obtained at equivalent terms as in socialist countries.

Finally, apart from manufactured goods the lack of European engagement in resource exploitation in ASEAN is noticeable. Again, this lack addresses an incentive problem. EC government incentives to exploit natural resources are clearly concentrated on Sub-Saharan Africa. The countries of this region are closely linked to the Community through the Lomé Convention which contains specific aid provisions for resource exploitation. However, regardless of such explicit incentives, important implicit advantages to exploit mineral and agricultural resources in Africa instead of in ASEAN countries are relevant too. Sub-Saharan Africa enjoys a political priority in EC development policy as ASEAN does in the Japanese policy, and especially in monetary affairs many African countries are still tied to their former metropolitan country, particularly the Francophone ones. This 'public umbrella' gives private investors a shelter for which they do not have to pay and which allows them to repatriate funds without large currency risks or other restrictions. Given the present state of a buyer's market for major primary commodities and the gloomy market prospects for many raw materials it is rather unlikely that European commodity producers who are well established in Sub-Saharan Africa will start to exploit new resources in ASEAN unless the old sources are exhausted or otherwise unprofitable.

IV MORE EC ECONOMIC ENGAGEMENT IN ASEAN: HOW TO ACHIEVE IT

More direct funding of public information services is the usual manner in which EC officials try to cope with the apparently low interest of EC businessmen in economic engagement in ASEAN. Moral persuasion in the sense that Europe should respond to ASEAN's good will *vis-à-vis* the Community (Chiang Hai Ding, 1986) is another method. Both methods demonstrate how helpless public authorities in market economies are if price signals and other incentives act against specific bilateral economic relations irrespective of how much they are welcomed by politicians.

It has often been forgotten that to a large extent, such incentives are not outside the influence of the authorities, but have been installed directly through political decision-making. To be specific, for years the objective of EC common policies has been to promote intra-EC trade and investment by means of harmonising national regulations, removing border levies on intra-EC trade, protecting the Common Market, and subsidising backward areas. All these measures were and are the core of the integration process which is still in the making and which has received further priority through political initiatives launched by the heads of governments. Parallel to the deepening of European integration has been its widening through the second enlargement. The indispensable outcome of inward-looking integration was the benign neglect of outward-looking integration, and it is by no means certain that this neglect has not been the explicit objective of some of the members.

It is important to note that stressing internal integration meant the neglect of outward integration in relative but not in absolute terms.

Where markets were opened to third countries beneficiaries were mostly neighbouring rest-of-EFTA countries which are not as aggressive sellers as the Asian NICs or very poor countries such as the Sub-Saharan countries. Aggressive exporters soon became victims of their own strategy, that is growth rates of their exports were curtailed by quantitative restrictions and other non-tariff barriers (NTBs).[5] Recent empirical evidence indicates that compared with Japan and the United States, the EC has the highest relative level of manufactured imports facing NTBs and also the greatest increase of such trade restrictions (Nogués, Olechowski and Winters, 1985, p. 62; Balassa and Balassa, 1984). Notwithstanding the qualifications which have to be made with respect to such estimates, it is beyond any doubt that protectionism not only restricts imports but taxes exports as well. It contributes to binding resources in import-competing industries and prevents them from shifting to new export-oriented production. Thus, protectionism indirectly impedes product innovation which has been analysed as an important disadvantage of European suppliers *vis-à-vis* Japanese competitors in ASEAN countries (Kirchbach, 1985). In general, protectionism is the easy but in the long run costly way to avoid the shift of production capacities to a more competitive location. In other words, protectionism serves as a break to foreign direct investment. And finally, protectionism curtails export demand, reduces economic growth in developing countries and consequently cuts the demand for imports from developed countries.

The two-way character of trade in manufactured goods between advanced developing countries and the old industrialised countries follows a simple logic: without allowing imports to penetrate more rapidly as in the past, there will be no acceleration of export growth. This logic is also valid for bilateral trade relations such as between ASEAN and the EC. Bilaterally, imports and exports are often interdependent as a result of firm-specific links (intra-firm imports of intermediates and capital goods from home countries and exports of manufactured goods from host to home countries).

The conclusion from these arguments is straightforward: if the Community wants to intensify economic relations with the ASEAN countries in both directions the most promising way to do so is by the removal of EC trade barriers to imports.[6] However, such a policy should not be pursued discriminatorily by giving preferences to ASEAN exclusively, for this runs counter to the multilateral trading order and provokes efficiency losses. If the shelter to domestic industries and agriculture in the Community were to be reduced, the

ASEAN countries would certainly gain their share of the cake because of their developmental dynamism. This strategy would not sacrifice the EC internal integration process in absolute terms, but would only shift the balance from internal to external integration. Yet, the strategy is not without some cost. It requires more flexibility to cope with adjustment pressures which will be exerted upon certain sectors in the EC economy by ASEAN suppliers.

Compared to the overwhelming importance of opening the markets, so-called 'direct measures' to promote trade and investment with ASEAN are of secondary importance. If information costs, for instance, would really constitute a barrier to EC investment in ASEAN, private sources of information such as the Japanese trading houses would supply information at market terms, and investors would demand such services if this were the key to profitable investment. Public suppliers of information sponsored by the Community would eventually distort the competition with private suppliers by offering the same information as the private suppliers on cheaper terms without running the same risk. Such subsidisation of a politically desired but economically 'normal' exchange of goods and services between two regions would indeed give rise to some critical questions. What should the Community do in the case of the Andean Pact or the Central American Common Market, two regional groupings which formally enjoy the same privilege of cumulative rules of origin in the EC Generalised System of Preferences as ASEAN? Should co-operation with these two groupings also be promoted directly? Obviously not.

Thus, integration efforts cannot be the reason why EC-ASEAN relations enjoy such a high political profile. Nor can economic dynamism be the reason, because then more attention should have been devoted to economic relations with the East Asian NICs (Taiwan, South Korea, Hong Kong) instead of with the ASEAN Four plus Singapore. The main reason for 'co-operation' seems to be politically rooted. The EC follows a 'picking the winner' strategy, that is concentrating political efforts on a few countries which promise to be politically congenial with respect to their western orientation, relatively stable and prepared – at least intentionally – to deepen economic integration. If cases for more ASEAN-EC co-operation are mainly politically rooted it would be logical to concentrate the privileges on political measures so as 'to speak with one voice' rather than on economic ones. This would indirectly promote EC trade and investment in ASEAN *via* diminishing political risks for private businessmen. It is very likely that the indirect effects of pronounced concerted political action of both communities in addition to the opening of EC markets would be more instrumental to deepening economic relations than direct financial promotion through public funds.

Notes

* This paper reports on research carried out in a project on causes of different success of European, American and Japanese suppliers on ASEAN markets. The project has been sponsored by the VW Foundation.

1. Table 9.1 allows for more details on winners and losers in developed countries' exports to the world disaggregated by developed and developing countries. Limiting the coverage to developed countries' exports has the advantage of not distorting the picture by suppliers from newly industrialising countries or other developing countries. Shifts in trade shares, as recorded in the table, thus only occur among the developed market economies.
2. Trade figures are well-known and are, therefore, not repeated here. Due to poor investment data the trend in investment cannot easily be detected but available information does not give rise to the conclusion that the EC has augmented its share in total realized foreign investment in ASEAN during the last decade. For statistical details see Langhammer, 1986a and 1986b; Langhammer/Groß, 1986.
3. The Irish clothing industry serves as a good example.
4. For more details see UN Economic Commission for Europe, *Economic Bulletin for Europe*, 1981 and 1982.
5. Defenders of the EC trade policy frequently state that growth rates of imports have been impressive compared with those of other developed countries. It should go without saying that this is not the right reference system. Instead, it should be stated how much trade has been foregone because of trade restrictions.
6. It is often claimed by EC officials that economic relations with *ASEAN* rather than with ASEAN countries should be intensified. Such a claim neglects reality. One can deepen institutional relations with ASEAN but as long as ASEAN does not really enter the integration process economic relations between traders and producers will be between the Community and individual ASEAN countries, or – even more realistic, if one bears the actual state of European integration in mind – between private enterprises from individual EC member states and ASEAN member states.

Table 9.1 Shares of the EC, US and Japan in developed countries' world trade, 1970–1984

Shares of.. in DC Exp to..	*Y1970*	*Y1975*	*Y1980*	*Y1982*	*Y1984*
EC/World 0–9	50.0	51.6	52.5	49.8	46.9
EC/World 0+1	45.8	49.2	52.7	52.5	51.7
EC/World 5	57.9	60.4	60.5	59.1	59.3
EC/World 7	51.3	50.5	50.3	46.0	40.1
EC/World 6+8	53.5	56.0	55.3	52.5	52.5
EC/DCEX-DC 0–9	52.9	55.5	57.5	55.0	51.1
EC/DCEX-DC 0+1	55.6	58.7	61.6	61.3	61.0
EC/DCEX-DC 5	61.5	71.9	67.8	67.9	64.4
EC/DCEX-DC 7	53.4	53.3	54.8	50.2	42.6
EC/DCEX-DC 6+8	57.1	61.2	61.0	58.1	57.4
EC/DCEX-LDC 0–9	36.6	39.9	39.9	38.8	36.2
EC/DCEX-LDC 0+1	25.0	35.7	38.7	37.9	35.7
EC/DCEX-LDC 5	50.0	46.2	40.6	46.2	46.4
EC/DCEX-LDC 7	41.2	42.2	41.4	38.5	34.2
EC/DCEX-LDC 6+8	36.4	38.2	39.0	38.7	39.1
US/World 0–9	18.8	18.4	16.8	17.6	17.2
US/World 0+1	20.8	24.6	23.3	21.7	23.3
US/World 5	15.8	15.1	17.1	17.4	17.9
US/World 7	21.8	21.2	19.5	20.2	19.3
US/World 6+8	9.9	9.5	9.6	9.1	9.5
US/DCEX-DC 0–9	16.9	15.9	13.9	14.4	14.4
US/DCEX-DC 0+1	16.7	17.4	12.8	16.3	15.6
US/DCEX-DC 5	15.4	12.5	12.6	14.1	14.9
US/DCEX-DC 7	20.7	19.3	17.6	17.3	17.5
US/DCEX-DC 6+8	8.9	8.3	8.3	7.5	8.3
US/DCEX-LDC 0–9	29.3	26.8	25.9	25.8	26.0
US/DCEX-LDC 0+1	25.0	42.9	35.5	34.5	35.7
US/DCEX-LDC 5	25.0	23.1	31.3	26.9	28.6
US/DCEX-LDC 7	29.4	25.0	25.0	25.9	23.9
US/DCEX-LDC 6+8	18.2	14.7	15.6	14.7	15.6
JA/World 0–9	8.5	9.5	10.2	11.8	13.8
JA/World 0+1	2.5	1.1	1.2	1.2	1.2
JA/World 5	5.3	7.5	4.7	5.2	5.7
JA/World 7	9.0	12.7	16.2	18.1	24.2
JA/World 6+8	12.7	13.1	12.3	15.3	13.5
JA/DCEX-DC 0–9	5.8	5.7	6.8	8.4	10.7
JA/DCEX-DC 0+1	1.7	0.9	0.6	0.5	0.8
JA/DCEX-DC 5	3.1	2.8	2.3	2.7	3.1
JA/DCEX-DC 7	6.9	8.9	12.8	14.8	21.8
JA/DCEX-DC 6+8	8.9	7.4	7.2	10.1	8.3
JA/DCEX-LDC 0–9	17.1	19.6	19.8	21.0	23.4
JA/DCEX-LDC 0+1	7.5	2.1	3.2	3.1	2.5
JA/DCEX-LDC 5	12.5	16.9	11.3	12.7	13.2

Table 9.1 *continued*

Shares of.. in DC Exp to..	*Y1970*	*Y1975*	*Y1980*	*Y1982*	*Y1984*
JA/DCEX-LDC 7	17.6	20.3	23.4	24.4	31.6
JA/DCEX-LDC 6+8	27.3	29.4	28.6	29.3	28.1

Abbreviations: DC = Developed Market Economies; LDC = Developing Market Economies; EC = European Community; US = United States; JA = Japan; SITC 0–9 = total trade; 0+1 = food, beverages; 5 = chemicals; 7 = machinery and transport; 6+8 = other manufactures.

Sources: Calculated from *UN Monthly Bulletin of Statistics*, February 1985 and February 1986.

References

Agarwal, J.P. (1986) 'Home Country Incentives and FDI in ASEAN Countries', Kiel Working Paper no. 258, (June).

Arnaud-Ameller, P. (1985) 'Investissements Directs et Flux Commerciaux – Compléments ou Substituts? Le Cas Français 1968–1978', *Revue d'Economie Politique*, 95, pp. 299–319.

Balassa, B. and Balassa C. (1984) 'Industrial Protection in the Developed Countries.' *The World Economy*, (June), pp. 179–196.

Bergsten, F.C., Horst, T., Moran, T.H. (1978) *American Multinationals and American Interests*, (Washington: The Brookings Institution).

Chiang Hai Ding (1986), 'ASEAN-EC Relations: An ASEAN View,' *Euro-Asia Business Review*, vol. 5, no. 3.

Donges, J.B., Juhl, P. (1979) 'Deutsche Privatinvestitionen im Ausland: Export von Arbeitsplätzen?' *Konjunkturpolitik*, 25, 1979, pp. 203–224.

Dunning, J.H. and Pearce, R. D. (1985) *The World's Largest Industrial Enterprises, 1962–1963*, (Aldershot: Gower).

Groß, M., (1986) 'Ausländische Direktinvestitionen als Exportmotor – das Beispiel der ASEAN-Länder.' *Die Weltwirtschaft*, H. 1, pp. 156–172.

Kinoshita, T. (1986a), 'Investment Environs in Indonesia as Viewed by Japanese Investors', *Management Japan*, vol. 19, 1986, no. 1, pp. 17–26.

Kinoshita, T., (1986b), 'Japan's Direct Investment for Asia with Emphasis on Investment in Manufacturing Industries.' *Monthly Bulletin of the Research Institute of Overseas Investment*, (The Export-Import Bank of Japan), June 1985.

Kirchbach, F. von, (1985) 'The Role of Marketing Strategies in Penetrating South-East and East Asian Markets.' Kiel Working Paper no. 249, (November).

Langhammer, R.J.(1985), 'On the Importance of Transport Costs in International Trade Flows – An Analysis of European, Japanese and US

Exports to the Philippines.' Kiel Working Paper no. 247, (November), (forthcoming in *ASEAN Economic Bulletin*, Singapore).

Langhammer, R.J. (1986a), 'ASEAN-EC Economic Relations on a Side-Track', *Euro-Asia Business Review*, vol. 5, no. 4.

Langhammer, R.J. (1986b), 'EEC-ASEAN Relations : Institutional Deepening but Modest Economic Impact', in: Christopher Stevens and Joan Verloren van Themaat (Eds.), *EEC and the Third World. A Survey*. vol. 6, ODI/IDS, (London : Hodder & Stoughton, forthcoming).

Langhammer, R.J. (1986c), 'Financing of Foreign Direct Investment and Trade Flows – The Case of Indonesia.' Kiel Working Paper no. 261, (July).

Langhammer, R.J. and Martin Groß, 'EC Foreign Direct Investment in ASEAN and its Impact on Trade.' Forthcoming as CEPS Working Document, Centre for European Policy Studies, Brussels.

Lipsey, R.E. and Weiss, M.Y. (1981) 'Foreign Production and Exports in Manufacturing Industries'. *The Review of Economics and Statistics*, vol. 63, pp. 488–494.

Lipsey, R.E. and Weiss, M.Y. (1984) 'Foreign Production and Exports of Individual Firms.' *The Review of Economics and Statistics*, vol. 66, pp. 304–308.

Milton, A.-R., 'Direktinvestitionen – Eine Konkurrenz deutscher Exporte?' *Mitteilungen des Rheinisch-Westfälischen Instituts für Wirtschaftsforschung*, 35, 1984, pp. 73–98.

Nogués, J.J., Olechowski, A. and L.A. Winters, (1985) 'The Extent of Non-Tariff Barriers to Industrial Countries' Imports.' World Bank. Discussion Paper, Report no. DRD 115, (Washington D.C.), (January).

OECD, (1981) *International Investment and Multinational Enterprises. Recent International Direct Investment Trends*, (Paris).

OECF, (1985) 'The Overseas Economic Co-operation Fund', *Annual Report for Fiscal Year 1984*. (Tokyo).

UN Centre on Transnational Corporations (1985), 'Trends and Issues in Foreign Direct Investment and Related Flows', (E.85.II.A. 15), (New York).

10 Science and Technology in ASEAN Countries: An Agenda for Trade and Growth*

Florian Alburo and W. Colozo

I INTRODUCTION

The decisive role of science and technology (S and T) in economic development is now universally recognized. Science and technology have come to be accepted as a strategic variable for national progress, an organic part of the engine of growth in the economy.

History has shown the importance of science and technology in the development process. The productive utilisation of technology has been associated with the tremendous rise in the standard of living in the developed countries over the last two hundred years, whereas the absence of this capability has been associated with a stunted development. The presence of a strong capacity to develop new knowledge (science) and transform it into useful applications (technology) has indeed become a common feature of all advanced economies.

This paper discusses some dimensions in science and technology within the context of promoting growth within developing countries with reference to ASEAN and trade with developed countries. While we will not be exhaustive here, we attempt to consider broad policy issues especially within the framework of understanding the relationship between science and growth.

The next section is a cursory picture of S and T in developing countries. Several indicators of the progress in the use of S and T are briefly explored. To illustrate the dimensions of the summary, S and T in the Philippines is quantified.

In the third section two recent phenomena within the realms of S and T are noted. Our purpose is to highlight what we consider to be important parameters in designing a policy agenda for growth and trade.

A final section defines a broad policy agenda bearing in mind the need for accelerating growth and expanding trade. We close by trying to tie up an agenda in view of the recent developments.

II S AND T IN DEVELOPING COUNTRIES

There is a growing awareness among the developing countries of the significance of the technology factor in economic growth and development. As many of these economies reach the limits of import substitution and begin to reach out into competitive world markets, the improvement of production efficiencies through technological upgrading of product designs and manufacturing techniques has become particularly important. Likewise, technology is viewed as the key to more extensive and effective use of mineral, energy and agricultural resources, which abound in these countries.

Many developing countries have succeeded, at varying degrees, in setting up an institutional framework for S and T development. Technology policies have been enunciated and these are closely interwoven with economic and development priorities. Policy-making bodies for science and technology have likewise been established by many developing countries, such as those in South and South-East Asia. In countries like India, Bangladesh, Indonesia, Malaysia, Pakistan, Singapore, Thailand and the Philippines, separate ministries or departments of science and technology have been set up. In China and Mongolia, State Commissions and Committees have been entrusted with the responsibility of managing technological development. Certain other countries have national bodies for science and technology.

Notwithstanding such explicit recognition of S and T's role in the economy and the attempts by developing countries to provide the institutional mechanism and proper environment for S and T development, the fact remains that the level of S and T capability in the developing world continues to be way below that of the industrialised nations. Consider, for instance, the following indicators:

1 In terms of resources devoted to research and development (R and D) (or to the discovery of new knowledge and its transformation into something useful to man), the developing countries continue to lag behind. Of the more than US $175 billion spent

Table 10.1 Estimated R and D expenditure as percentage of GNP in some developing and developed countries

Developing Economies	*1979*	*1980*	*1981*	*1982*	*1983*
Philippines[a]	0.26	0.26	0.17	0.19	0.19
Malaysia	–	–	–	0.64	0.50
Indonesia	0.50	0.48	0.52	0.41	0.45
Thailand[b]	0.24	0.22	0.33	0.40	0.18
Singapore	0.25	–	0.31	–	–
India	0.64	0.71	0.71	0.76	0.85
Nepal	–	–	0.25	0.30	0.68
Sri Lanka[c]	–	–	–	–	0.14
Developed Economies					
Japan	–	2.41	–	2.78	–
United States	–	–	–	2.86	–
USSR	–	–	4.85	–	–
West Germany	–	–	3.04	–	–
France	–	–	2.28	–	–
United Kingdom	2.47[d]	–	–	–	–

[a] The Philippines' R and D percentage for 1986 was estimated at 0.14 per cent of GNP.
[b] Thailand's R and D percentage for 1984 was estimated at 0.34 per cent of GNP.
[c] R and D expenditure as a percentage of GNP.
[d] 1978 figure
– Data not readily available.

Source: *Country Study Series*, Asian and Pacific Centre for Transfer of Technology (APCTT), ESCAP, Bangalore, India, 1986.

on R and D every year in the whole world, about 70 per cent is accounted for by only six countries, namely: France, West Germany, Japan,[1] the United Kingdom, the United States and the Soviet Union. It is not a coincidence that these same six countries today account for about close to 70 per cent of the total GNP of all countries in the world.

Furthermore, while these six countries spend about 2 per cent to 4.8 per cent of their GNP on research and development, many developing countries like those in South and South-East Asia could only manage to set aside 0.14 per cent to 0.85 per cent (or less than one per cent) of their GNP for the same purpose (Table 10.1). The latter figure is even below the standard set by UNESCO which has recommended that for a

Table 10.2 Science and technology manpower in some ASEAN and other developing countries

Country	*Year*	*Scientists and engineers with degrees*	*Number per 10 000 population*
Philippines[1]	1979	40 433	8.5
Indonesia[1]	1982	24 251	1.7
Malaysia[1]	1980	97 620	68.7
Singapore[1]	1981	724[a]	3.0[a]
Thailand[1]	1980	55 790	12.1
India[2]	1981	2 089 300	30.5
Pakistan[2]	1981	3 238	0.4
Sri Lanka[2]	1983	5 622	3.7

[a] Only those engaged in R and D on a full-time equivalent basis.

Source: [1] Official country sources as compiled by NSTA.
[2] Country Study Series, APCTT/ESCAP, 1986.

country to break away from underdevelopment, it must spend on R and D an amount approximately equal to about 1 per cent of its GNP. If we take the quality of R and D facilities in developing countries into account, the technological gap between the rich and the poor nations would definitely be much wider.

2 Technological research and development in many developing countries is also characterised by a low manpower pool compared to those in industrialised nations. For instance, the number of scientists and engineers in certain developing countries of South and South-East Asia range from less than one to 68 per 10 000 population (Table 10.2), compared with 500 to 600 in the United States and in the Soviet Union.[2] In the case of Japan, the number of researchers in 1981 was about 3.3 million or 277 per 10 000 population.[3] The numerical disparity is aggravated by the fact that the efficiency of the linkages necessary to convert scientific research into productivity is much greater in those industrialised economies than in the developing countries.

It can be seen that the technological gap between developed and developing countries lies in the state of their knowledge base, of which R and D is a decisive factor. Industrialised countries tend to be knowledge-intensive societies. In contrast, less developed nations are characterised by poverty of knowledge. The situation is identical with respect to technology which is knowledge-based.

There is also an element of a vicious cycle involved here. The prevailing social conditions exacerbate our ability to break out of this poverty. For instance, poor communications infrastructure (measured by radio or TV sets per thousand population or daily newspaper circulation per capita or even number of teachers at the tertiary level) limit technology diffusion.

In the Philippines, notwithstanding the various strides made in a number of technological areas (*e.g.* in agriculture, energy), much remains to be done to upgrade the local S and T capability, at least to the level of other developing countries. The Philippines was the first among the ASEAN countries to make science and technology a major concern of the government through the creation of a national science body (the defunct National Science and Development Board or NSDB, now the National Science and Technology Authority or NSTA) in 1958. Ironically, however, the country at present trails behind most of the ASEAN countries in the quality of research and development activities and the amount of resources spent on science and technology.

Philippine expenditures on R and D in 1979–1983 averaged 0.21 per cent of GNP. This was significantly less than that of Malaysia, Indonesia, Thailand and certain South Asian countries like India and Nepal. Furthermore, R and D expenditure followed an erratic movement, declining at a steady rate beginning in 1979 with a negative growth rate registered in 1981 (Table 10.3).

Table 10.3 R and D expenditure of the Philippines, 1972–1982 (at constant 1972 prices)

Year	*R and D Expenditure (in million ₱)*	*Percent of R and D to GNP*	*R and D Expenditure Growth Rate (%)*
1972	62.4	0.11	–
1973	79.8	0.13	27
1974	95.9	0.15	20
1975	129.6	0.17	35
1976	124.4	0.17	(4)
1977	188.1	0.24	51
1978	201.5	0.24	7
1979	228.2	0.26	13
1980	242.3	0.26	6
1981	166.6	0.17	(31)
1982	184.5	0.19	10

Source: 1984 *Philippine Statistical Yearbook*, NEDA.

In terms of S and T manpower, the Philippines also trails behind Malaysia and Thailand in ASEAN. The Philippines in 1979 had about eight scientists and engineers per 10 000 population while Malaysia had about 68 and Thailand 12. The Philippines, according to UNESCO, had one of the lowest number of scientists and engineers per million population.[4]

As in other developing countries, support for R and D in the Philippines comes mostly from the government. In 1982, 84 per cent of R and D was financed by public funds. In contrast, the share of government in R and D activities in many developed countries like Japan, the United States, West Germany and the United Kingdom has been declining as their well-developed private sector increasingly assumes the bigger role (Table 10.4).

Table 10.4 Ratio of private to public investment in R and D in some developing and developed countries

Developing Economies	*Year*	*Percentage Financed by Public Fund*[a]
Philippines[1]	1982	84.0[b]
Indonesia[1]	1981	Almost 100%
Malaysia[1]	1984	92.8
Thailand[1]	1983	98.4
India[1]	1983	43.5
Sri Lanka[1]	1983	93.0
Developed Economies		
Japan[2]	1982	23.6
United States[2]	1982	46.7
USSR[2]	1981	45.8
West Germany[2]	1981	43.1
France[2]	1981	57.6
United Kingdom[2]	1978	48.1

[a] Includes official foreign assistance.
[b] The non-government sector includes private industry and non-profit organisations.

Sources: [1]*Country Study Series*, APCTT/ESCAP, 1986
[2]*Japan: An International Comparison, 1984*, Keizai Koho Center, Japan Institute for Social and Economic Affairs, September 1984.

III S AND T AND RECENT GLOBAL TRENDS

The present global interdependence has underscored the need to take full account of major international development in the formulation of national plans and policies, whether on trade and economic development or on science and technology. In recent years, we have witnessed the emergence of two significant techno-economic trends which have far-reaching implications on the future direction of science and technology development in developing countries.

The first development refers to what Peter Drucker[5] argues are three fundamental changes that have taken place in the very structure of the world economy, namely:

> The 'uncoupling' of the primary-products economy from the industrial economy;
> the 'uncoupling' of production from employment in the industrial economy itself; and
> capital movements, rather than trade (in both goods and services) increasingly becoming the driving force of the world economy.

The uncoupling of the raw material economy from the industrial economy is evidenced by the following changes. The share of the raw materials' sector in most developed countries has been declining. Primary products are becoming of marginal importance to the economies of the developed world as the amount of raw material input for a given economic output has been dropping for the entire century. Relatedly, industrial production is steadily switching away from heavily material-intensive products and processes to new high-technology industries.

On the other hand, the uncoupling of production from employment in the manufacturing sector is evidenced by the fact that while manufacturing production has risen steadily in the United States, manufacturing employment has dropped steadily. This trend is the same in all developed countries and is even more pronounced in Japan where production automation is widely applied.

For the developing countries, whose economies continue to depend essentially on raw material export, the implications of the said changes will certainly be far-reaching. For instance, adjustments will have to be made in order to overcome the worsening threat of declining raw materials, markets and prices or to take advantage of new opportunities created by such structural changes in the industrialised economies, such as the growth of information and knowledge-based industries which some developing countries have proved capable of engaging in.

The other development pertains to the reverse flow of human-embodied technology from the developing to the developed countries, otherwise popularly known as 'brain drain.' This form of reverse transfer, however, has assumed greater significance in recent years as it involves not simply lower-level technologists but also highly-qualified scientists from developing countries who are employed in R and D institutions in developed countries.

In the United States, for instance, the National Science Board has reported that, with fewer American citizens electing to work in technical fields, the United States is becoming increasingly dependent on foreign nationals for the supply of doctorates in engineering, mathematics and physics, certainly the core disciplines of a technological society. In 1982 alone, over 53 per cent of the engineering doctorates awarded by US universities were granted to citizens of foreign countries, as were over one-third of the doctorates in mathematics. Although these graduates were expected to leave the United States after receiving their degrees, a great majority of them had found employment in the host country.[6]

It is obvious that unless the developing countries are able to develop their absorptive capacity in terms of S and T facilities and general environment for the practice of science and technology professions, the problem of 'brain drain' would persist and the developing economies would continue to lose their valuable talents to the developed nations.

IV A POLICY AGENDA

The upgrading of the S and T capability in developing countries will require a comprehensive set of policies and strategies that address each and every aspect of science and technology development, from research and development to commercialisation and dissemination of S and T outputs to the strengthening of linkages between R and D and the production sector.

Before going into specific agenda items, it is useful to review the implications of the dimensions of science and technology summarised by this paper. First of all, the dramatic changes in the world structure of production brings out a question about the path of development that most developing nations are confronted with. This is whether it is possible to 'leap-frog' what has been accepted as natural stages of growth. For countries characterised by large rural sectors, high population growth rates, concentrated tradeable products and markets, highly unbalanced income distributions, *etc*. can agricultural modernisation, labour-intensive manufactures, be short-circuited on the road to high incomes? How pervasive the changed world economic structure becomes will, in part, define the spectrum in which S and T lays out a context for a new development path. The increasing rate of obsolescence in products, the competitiveness of countries in edging market shares *via* the prompt use of new technological advances may define new modalities in comparative advantage.

Second there will be an inherent conflict between a need for a more outward-looking approach even within a narrower vision of the advances in S and T circumscribing trade and growth choices, and a more protectionist stance in view of the increasing protectionism especially in the US and Europe.

Finally while it may be true that there is a decline in the indigenous resource pool of scientists in the US and an increasing number of them are of foreign nationalities (especially developing countries) it is unlikely that an actual reverse flow will take place without a critical environment for scientific advancement and technology.

Let us now turn to several items that constitute an agenda for growth and trade. Many, if not all of these, have been forcefully articulated before and are therefore not new. But we will nevertheless itemise them by way of conclusions.

One is that if it comes to a matter of choice between incurring external debt, and technology imports through foreign direct investment, the latter is actually superior, under certain conditions both of which entail subsequent foreign exchange outflows. Given the experience of a number of highly indebted countries it is obvious that unless these exchange resources were used to build up capacities for repayments, an exchange crisis is bound to take place. One can of course argue that perhaps investments and technology imports would not be forthcoming thereby requiring another form of capital flows. But this is not an argument against such imports but an even stronger argument for correcting the source of the problem (*e.g.* political stability).

Another is that there are self-limits to public R and D if not in financial terms then certainly in terms of the substance of R and D.

Commercial technology which partly carries the frontiers of S and T is necessary for some countries even at the tail end of the product cycle, since this gets developing countries into the flow, if not the frontier of technology.

Then there are trade-offs to the encouragement of transfers of commercial technology through Transnational Corporations (TNCs) from transfer pricing to other social costs. But this must be weighed up in the narrower context of indigenous entrepreneurship and its parochial limitations.

There is also the question of trade promotion, diversification and incentives. Market familiarity if not concentration allows expanded modes of transactions that ultimately facilitate S and T development or at least technology transfer. Intra-firm transactions are major sources of payment for technical services. Would concentration be more conducive to this? Certainly expanded investment and other arrangements (equity, joint ventures, licensing, trade marks, *etc.*) with more countries (especially Europe and Japan) would yield an expanded S and T base.

In the final analysis, how is one to stimulate demand for technology? We must recognise that this demand would be a derived demand from products and processes that are in themselves profitable as reflected by the private sector markets. Therefore policy must facilitate this behaviour. One must then look at macro economic policy to see the extent to which S and T is enhanced. This includes traditional market indicators such as exchange rates, tariff structure and protection, government participation in the economy, and others – apart from the social, physical and political infrastructure. Indeed the consistency and stability of overall foreign investment rules are an equally important régime. But there are two crucial areas which we believe should be given priority attention in terms of policies and programmes.

The first is the strengthening of science and technology education. In S and T development, human resources constitute the most decisive factor. Technology, no matter how sophisticated, will be useless if it cannot be assimilated; effective assimilation and adaptation of technology can be achieved only with the presence of adequately trained and educated population. The S and T education envisioned here goes beyond specialised training. It must be incorporated in the whole education system (starting from the lower grades) for the purpose not only of developing skills but, more importantly, for the propagation of a science-oriented national culture.

The other area concerns the acquisition of imported technology. The various instruments used in this regard must be reassessed in order to improve the process of technology transfer from foreign suppliers. It is observed, for instance, that technology assessment in many developing countries has been deficient, resulting in haphazard importation of technology. Technology screening boards in many developing countries are often limited to the legal and contractual aspects of technology transfer, and the assessment of technological appropriateness is neglected.

Notes

* The views expressed here are those of the authors and do not necessarily reflect official government positions.

1. In 1981, the research and development activities of both the public and private sectors in Japan were valued at US$ 22.35 billion. This figure accounted for about 10 per cent of the total R and D expenditures in the world. This huge investment in both human and capital resources has given Japan a 10 per cent share in total world output.
2. *Economic Impact* (No. 26), 1979, p. 19.
3. *Japan: A Technology-Based State*, RCTT/ESCAP, 1984, p. 1.
4. UNESCO, *Statistical Yearbook*, 1984.
5. 'The Changed World Economy', *Foreign Affairs*, Spring 1986, pp. 768–91.
6. National Science Board, *Science Indicators, The 1985 Report* (Washington, D.C.) November 1985, p. 3.

11 ASEAN Relations with Japan

Kamal Salih

There have been indications of a dramatic shift in economic relations between Japan and ASEAN in the 1980s, particularly in trade and investments, which seems to suggest some difficulty in the future for ASEAN as it tries to cope with adjustment pressures within the present world economic environment. While Japan remains the largest single export market for ASEAN as a whole, and its single major source of imports, in comparison with the United States and the European Community, in the 1980s that share has been declining. In the area of direct foreign investment, the high rate of investment growth in the 1970s has now in the 1980s begun to slacken as Japan redirects its investments to the advanced and newly industrialised countries. While the Japanese presence in ASEAN remains strong these signs of shifts in ASEAN-Japan economic relations do not augur well for the region's future growth prospects unless it is replaced by improved links with other regions such as the US and the EC. In this regard, in the 1980s the US appears to loom as the new trade partner in the coming decade, if trading régimes remain open, while ASEAN-EC trade remains stagnant.

Before we sound alarm bells, it is necessary first to examine these recent trends in ASEAN-Japan economic relations in order to determine whether these shifts reflect long-term structural changes or merely the result of the cyclical downturn and adjustment to particular short-term problems which once resolved will restore ASEAN-Japan relations to its former footing. These shifts must also be seen in the proper perspective of the ongoing global adjustments, as well as in the light of the different tacks being taken by individual ASEAN countries in dealing with their external relations and domestic political-economic problems. In order to provide a broader context to ASEAN-Japan economic relations, it is best perhaps to examine first the economic performance of ASEAN in the 1970s and early 1980s.

A PERSPECTIVE ON ASEAN ECONOMIC PERFORMANCE

The spectacular growth rates achieved by ASEAN in the 1970s, averaging 7–8 per cent per annum in real terms, were only second to the Asian NICs (consisting of South Korea, Taiwan, Hong Kong and Singapore). This growth was largely export-led; for ASEAN countries riding mainly on the back of a commodities boom led by oil prices. On looking back, unlike the export substitution strategy of the Asian NICs which enabled them to export consumer products mainly to the United States by taking advantage of lower labour costs, the ASEAN economies on the whole, which were still basically primary producers, experienced higher export receipts not because of increased real demand for their commodities but rather because of the higher prices. This pecuniary effect results from the inflationary environment prevailing in the advanced industrialised countries during the 1970s. Some ASEAN countries, like Malaysia and Singapore, did achieve increased exports of light manufactured goods, particularly in electronics and textiles, but on the whole have relied on primary exports.

A combination of the 'Dutch Disease' and export optimism among ASEAN countries had also contributed to government-led growth which boosted economic performance to the commanding heights of the 1970s. Ambitious publicly-funded projects aimed at reducing import dependence, which had risen commensurate with the growth of export receipts, were undertaken during this same period particularly in the substitution of imports of intermediate goods. In addition these public investment outlays were aimed at modernising physical infrastructure and diversifying the industrial base into primary-processing exports in order to increase the value-addedness of exports. The financing of these projects had increased government deficits in the early 1980s still further as exports began to stagnate, compelling the respective governments to resort to foreign borrowing to reduce the gap. These public sector activities, however, provided a major impetus to private sector investment growth particularly in the construction sector. Thus along with the commodities boom, a property boom in most ASEAN countries, particularly as seen in the capital cities, contributed much to the high growth performance in the 1970s.

Trade, foreign investment, foreign borrowings and aid have been, in various proportions, important to the growth of ASEAN countries. Complementarity and comparative advantage had driven

ASEAN trade with its partners during the 1970s. Government incentives have induced direct foreign investment in various sectors, and foreign participation, either as investors, suppliers or lenders, have had a considerable impact on ASEAN economic performance. The OECD markets, in spite of recession, had remained fairly open through the 1970s; even when quotas were imposed as through the Multifibre Arrangement (MFA), they were quite reasonable toward ASEAN. Aid money continued to flow, while the Eurodollar market responded favourably to ASEAN loan syndications and yen credit sources remained positive, despite high interest rates. Foreign investment, particularly from US and Japanese sources, increased considerably through the location of offshore production facilities in light assembly products for re-export to OECD markets.

Major difficulties had emerged which ASEAN countries had to face in the 1980s. First, with the long-term stagnation of the OECD countries, and the impact of deflationary policies and adjustments to energy-related problems created by the 1970s oil shocks, the ASEAN countries in the same boat as other primary commodity producers are confronted with weak demand and lower prices for commodities, particularly oil but also the other raw materials. They also face conditions of over-supply and excess capacity in these products, while price support schemes no longer generally have the support of consumer nations. Secondly, a number of the ASEAN countries, such as the Philippines, Malaysia and Indonesia, have accumulated large foreign debts which could no longer be adequately serviced by export receipts alone with current accounts being in deficit. While long-term real interest rates are declining, enabling some ASEAN countries to refinance their loans, the huge debt overhang and declining credit worthiness suggests continued problems with debt obligations liquidity for these ASEAN countries. Third, while new export orientation especially in manufactured products may be one way out for ASEAN, the threat of protectionism remain high for as long as budget and trade deficits persist in the OECD countries, especially in the US. Finally, the inflow of long-term capital also appears to have been affected in the first half of the 1980s as during this period of slow recovery, the advanced industrialised countries rationalise their portfolios and other investment plans for the rest of the century.

During this period, Japan along with West Germany had emerged as the strongest economies upon which hopes of recovery had been pinned. Japan in particular is seen by ASEAN as the major market for its commodities as well as manufactured goods, through various 'market opening initiatives'; as their major source of foreign investment, particularly through the relocation of 'sunset industries' to South-east Asia; as their major creditor, especially given the estimated $500 billion to one trillion surplus expected by the year 2000; and the source of technology transfer and technical assistance. How Japan will respond to these expectations, which will determine the nature of ASEAN-Japan economic relations, will depend very much on how Japan sees its international role and on the importance it attaches to ASEAN economic performance in the future. This prospect may be examined according to what is happening in the area of ASEAN-Japan trade, investment and finance, to which we will now turn.

ASEAN-JAPAN TRADE

In the 1970s ASEAN exports to Japan grew at an annual rate of 27 per cent, about the same rate as the region exports to the rest of the world. The share of their exports to Japan rose marginally to 26 per cent of their total exports in 1981 from 24 per cent in 1971. The rapid growth of exports to Japan really occurred in the 1960s when it grew at twice the rate ASEAN was exporting to the rest of the world, and Japan's share of ASEAN exports rose from 16 per cent in 1961 to 24 per cent in 1971. The marked slowdown in ASEAN export growth to Japan was due to the marked decline in Japan's economic expansion in the 1970s. In the early 1980s, Japan's share of ASEAN exports had shown no increase, in fact it declined slightly (Table 11.1). At the same time between 1982–84 the US share had shown a four per cent increase from the 1982 level, while that of the EC stagnated at around 10 per cent.

The import-export value of Japan with ASEAN for the period 1970–83 is shown in Table 11.2, with Japan's imports from ASEAN rising from $1.87 billion in 1971 to $21.22 billion in 1980 and declining to $17.36 billion in 1983. ASEAN as a whole has maintained a favourable trade balance with Japan throughout this period. However, Table 11.2 indicates that only Malaysia and Indonesia had achieved a consistent trade surplus with Japan, whilst Thailand, the Philippines and Singapore had a trade deficit over the same period. This situation is largely explained by the fact that the bulk of Japanese imports over the period, in value terms, is made up of crude oil,

Table 11.1 ASEAN's major trading partners – share of its trade value by destination/origin

(Unit: %)

Year / *Country*	*1982*	*1983*	*1984*
Japan			
(X)	26.5	26.2	26.1
(M)	22.1	21.5	21.5
US			
(X)	15.2	18.3	19.1
(M)	14.6	15.6	16.4
EC			
(X)	10.7	10.2	10.3
(M)	12.4	12.5	10.5
Intra-ASEAN			
(X)	17.1	20.1	18.6
(M)	14.0	17.9	17.4
Others			
(X)	30.5	25.2	25.9
(M)	36.9	45.3	34.2

Note: (X) means exports and (M) imports.

Source: IMF *Directory of Trade*.

petroleum products and gas, as Table 11.3 shows. The next major item is foodstuff, which is Thailand's major export item. Japan's exports to ASEAN cover mainly machinery and equipment, metal products particularly iron and steel, chemicals and light industrial products, nearly half of which are textiles.

The structure of trade between Japan and ASEAN thus reflects the complementarity and vertical specialisation consistent with the industrial structure of ASEAN and Japan. This can be seen more clearly by referring to Figure 11.1 which shows the production-induced trade links between ASEAN and Japan and the US. Lower inducement coefficients are registered for consumer products while higher ones are achieved for intermediate goods. The strikingly low values for the US suggest that ASEAN-US trade tended to be in light manufactured consumer goods, and reflect the protection of the Japanese market from final goods. In fact if trade in crude oil, petroleum products and Liquified Natural Gas (LNG) is removed,

Table 11.2 Import-export of Japan with ASEAN

($ billion)

Year / Country	1970		1972		1974		1976		1978		1980		1982		1983	
	Exp.	*Imp.*	*Exp.*	*Imp.*	*Exp.*	*Imp.*	*Exp.*	*Imp.*	*Exp.*	*Imp.*	*Exp.*	*Imp.*	*Exp.*	*Imp.*	*Exp.*	*Imp.*
ASEAN	1.81	1.87	2.56	2.44	5.41	7.96	6.06	7.74	8.65	9.92	13.03	21.22	14.85	19.46	15.02	17.36
Thailand	0.45	0.19	0.52	0.25	0.95	0.69	1.07	0.85	1.53	0.84	1.92	1.12	1.91	1.04	2.51	1.02
Malaysia	0.17	0.42	0.26	0.40	0.71	0.98	0.70	1.36	1.16	1.90	2.06	3.47	2.50	3.01	2.77	3.13
Singapore	0.42	0.09	0.70	0.12	1.39	0.62	1.53	0.65	2.32	0.87	3.91	1.51	4.37	1.83	4.45	1.47
Philippines	0.45	0.53	0.46	0.47	0.91	1.10	1.11	0.79	1.55	1.06	1.68	1.95	1.80	1.58	1.74	1.31
Indonesia	0.32	0.64	0.62	1.20	1.45	4.57	1.64	4.09	2.09	5.25	3.46	13.17	4.26	12.00	3.55	10.43

Source: White Paper On International Trade: Japan, 1972, 73, 74, 75, 76, 77, 79, 80, 81, 82, 83, 84, JETRO

Figure 11.1 Production of Japan and the United States Induced by Industries of East and South-East Asian countries

Induced Countries	Japan						USA					
Inducing Countries / Industrial Sector	IDN	MYS	PHL	SGP	THA	KOR	IDN	MYS	PHL	SGP	THA	KOR
Food, beverage, and tobacco	o											
Textile and leather products	O	O	O	o	o	O	o	o	o			o
Lumber and wood products				O						o		o
Pulp, paper products, and printing	O	O		O	o	o				o		o
Chemical products	O	o		O	O	**O**				o		o
Petroleum refining												
Rubber products			O		o	**O**			o			o
Non-metallic mineral products				o								
Metal products	**O**	o	**O**	O	O	**O**						O
Machinery	**O**	O	o	O	O	**O**	o	o		O		O
Transport equipment	**O**	O	O	**O**	**O**	**O**			o	o		o
Other manufacturing industries	O	o	O	O	o	O			o			o
Construction	O	O	o	O	o	o				o		

Notes:
O Inducement coefficient of more than 0.4.
O Inducement coefficient of between 0.2 and 0.4.
o Inducement coefficient of between 0.1 and 0.2.

Source: Shunichi Furukawa, *International Input-Output Analysis*, Institute of Developing Economies, Tokyo, 1986.

ASEAN trade with Japan will be small indeed, and trade will be in Japan's favour for all ASEAN countries.

This state of ASEAN-Japan trade relations is being affected by a number of recent developments which will have considerable implications for the future. First, since the oil shocks of 1973 and 1979 Japan has been taking steps to reduce the resource and raw material content of its industrial products, reflecting the change in its industrial structure to knowledge-based and service-oriented technologies. Therefore, raw material imports from ASEAN are expected to be reduced, and have contributed, apart from the slowdown in the Japanese economy, to the stagnation of ASEAN export growth in the 1980s. Thus, while the development of high value added and low-unit cost products have led to a rise in production of these new products, imports of raw material have not even increased. On the other hand, Japan only imports 5 per cent of its intermediate goods requirements,

Table 11.3 Annual change in Japan's imports from ASEAN by main product item

(in million US dollars)

Product Item \ Country / Year	ASEAN 1980	1981	1982	1983	1984
Total imports from ASEAN	21 216	20 968	19 458	17 356	22 024
Foodstuff	1 282	1 228	1 328	1 291	1 314
Natural ore & scrap	1 397	1 089	925	903	777
Natural rubber	635	523	342	485	521
Wood	2 927	1 887	2 047	1 623	1 701
Mineral fuels	16 449	17 378	15 845	13 684	15 520
(Crude oil)	10 719	10 825	9 460	7 531	7 302
(Petroleum products)	1 924	2 340	2 132	1 807	2 336
(LNG)	3 713	4 123	4 196	4 269	5 767
Machinery & transport equipment	268	350	253	261	423
Textiles	63	58	94	94	96
Chemicals	184	196	221	221	260

compared with 20 per cent for Germany. This is one area where pressure to open up Japan's domestic market is relevant, particularly for light manufactured goods and for intermediate goods for which ASEAN nations have an increasing comparative advantage. It is also suggestive of the need to relocate these intermediate goods industries to South-East Asia if ASEAN-Japan trade is to be maintained at its present level, if not to expand further.

A second factor is the appreciation of the yen against ASEAN currencies. While this makes ASEAN manufactured exports more competitive and Japanese products more expensive in ASEAN markets, the impact on the reduction of the trade gap between Japan and the ASEAN countries which are running a deficit with it is marginal unless it opens up its domestic market further. This is the argument of ASEAN countries in their dialogue with Japan. The fact is that the depreciation of ASEAN currencies has improved their manufactured exports recently but with other OECD markets rather than Japan.

A final point is that the internationalisation of Japan is apparently geared towards improving its economic relations with other OECD countries, particularly with the US in view of its huge trade surplus with the latter country and the threat of protectionism and countervailing strategies. The liberalisation of financial markets to foreign participation, for instance, does not have any bearing on ASEAN-Japan trade. Thus the reflation of Japan has to take into account needed industrial adjustments and more market opening measures to cover manufactured goods as well.

JAPANESE INVESTMENTS AND FINANCIAL FLOWS TO ASEAN

Japan's direct investment in ASEAN countries increased from $490 million to $12 534 million in 1985, an increase of more than two and half times (Table 11.4). As a percentage of total Japanese direct foreign investment (DFI), this represented a change from 13.2 per cent of Japanese foreign investment in 1971 to 17.1 per cent in 1985. Indonesia took the bulk of Japanese DFI, followed by Malaysia and Singapore.

Japanese foreign investment has followed two growth phases, according to the Bank of Tokyo, following the initial phase period of

Table 11.4 Japan's direct investment in ASEAN

(Unit: million dollars, %)

	3/31, '71		*3/31, '74*		*3/31, '80*		*3/31, '85*	
	Value	*Share*	*Value*	*Share*	*Value*	*Share*	*Value*	*Share*
Total Investment Value	3 577	100.0	12 662	100.0	36 496	100.0	71 431	100.0
ASEAN	490	13.7	2 040	16.2	7 020	19.3	12 534	17.6
Indonesia	242	6.8	1 189	9.4	4 423	12.1	8 015	11.2
Malaysia	50	1.4	249	2.0	649	1.8	1 045	1.5
Philippines	74	2.1	191	1.5	615	1.7	832	1.2
Thailand	91	2.5	195	1.5	397	1.1	711	1.0
Singapore	33	0.9	222	1.8	936	2.6	1 930	2.7

Note: Value shows cumulative balance based on authorizations issued since fiscal 1951.

Source: Ministry of Finance.

1951–1971. The first growth phase took place between 1971 and 1981 mainly in steel, non ferrous metals and chemical industries, especially in Latin American and Asian sites to reduce energy costs. In South-East Asia, including ASEAN the focus is on textiles and electrical appliances. The expansion of Japanese DFI during this period was induced by the oil crisis and motivated in terms of securing stable supplies of raw materials, as well as by deregulation in Japan regarding controls of DFI. The second half of this phase also saw investments in the advanced countries, particularly in the production of electrical machinery for the United States. Labour cost factors, which are lower in Asia and Latin America, contributed to the lower proportion of manufacturing investments by the Japanese in the advanced countries.

The second growth phase, beginning in 1981, marks an ominous shift, as far as ASEAN is concerned, in the pattern of Japanese foreign investments. The overall annual growth rate was two and a half times higher than in the previous growth phase, adding some \$8 billion a year. There are several characteristics of this second phase which differentiate it from the first growth phase. First, in terms of the regional distribution of investment, there is a shift in emphasis of investment to the advanced industrialised countries especially the US and Europe, a decline in share of investment to the developing countries, and as we have mentioned ASEAN in particular. Between the first and second growth phase, the share for the US and Europe had increased from 45.3 per cent to 50 per cent, while correspondingly for the developing countries it declined from 54.7 per cent to 50 per cent. The factors behind this shift include the need to ameliorate the growing seriousness of trade frictions, and therefore the establishment of overseas production facilities, in electrical machinery, general machinery and automobiles, in order to fend off protectionist threats; and an increase in Japanese investment in the service sector such as banking and insurance, and other financial services including securities trading and leasing, and other services, hotel management and real estate.

The second feature of Japanese foreign investment after the 1981 fiscal year that affects ASEAN more directly is the shift of investment out of the resource sector and into the 'other' industries category, namely in leasing activities and hotel operations. There are also new pressures to allow Japanese investment in the distributive trade, and some have taken root although there is considerable local investor resistance.

A third feature of Japanese overseas investment in the 1970s, as referred to earlier, was in offshore manufacturing units of the assembly type including electronic products and components and textiles and other light manufactured goods. While these offshore activities are expected to continue so long as the incentives offered by ASEAN continue to be attractive and the political climate remains stable, the initial labour cost advantage in the 1970s which made these investments rational decisions seems to have been lost as rising labour costs in some ASEAN countries, such as Malaysia, have reduced the gap between these and the advanced countries which are also offering incentives to promote their depressed areas. The wage cost advantage also appears irrelevant as production methods are increasingly automated through new microelectronic control. Also in recent years the investment climate in ASEAN deteriorated somewhat with political instability, such as in the case of the Philippines, and leadership succession uncertainties in Malaysia and Indonesia, with rising resource nationalism and the mounting debt problems.

Finally, in the area of Japanese investments in ASEAN, there is a possible shift in the scale of industries involved. While ASEAN expectations for the relocation of large scale capital intensive Japanese industries producing intermediate goods may not be realised easily because of the powerful Japanese domestic lobby, it is the smaller and intermediate scale industries. that are likely to respond and locate new investments in ASEAN because of cost disadvantages due to the rising yen. The alternative to Japanese intermediate goods sourcing through ASEAN production facilities is the involvement of Japanese investors in ASEAN-wide joint venture projects. As ASEAN proceeds with second phase import substitution projects taking advantage of regional scale economies, the scope of Japanese, and other OECD countries', involvement would be increased. At the same time greater competition among ASEAN countries to attract foreign, not only Japanese, investments is also expected in the intermediate future, should the overall world economic growth outlook continue to be grim.

The overall structure of Japanese financial flows to the developing countries, covering official development assistance as well as other official flows and private capital flows, is shown in Table 11.5. South-East Asia, mainly ASEAN, receives the largest share of Japanese bilateral assistance representing 38.4 per cent of the total bilateral aid funds of $2.4 billion in 1984. China had the single largest amount of aid ($389.35 million), followed by Malaysia ($245.14 million),

Table 11.5 Flow of financial resources to developing countries (in $ million; net disbursement base)

	1972	*1973*	*1974*	*1975*	*1976*	*1977*	*1978*	*1979*	*1980*	*1981*	*1982*	*1983*	*1984*
1. Official development assistance (ODA)													
Bilateral grants	170.6	220.1	198.6	201.7	184.9	236.7	383.4	560.2	652.6	810.4	805.2	993.4	1063.9
Capital grant aid	135.0	162.9	135.1	114.5	76.8	88.8	162.2	318.2	374.8	432.0	412.3	535.1	543.4
Technical assistance	35.6	57.2	63.5	87.2	108.1	147.8	221.2	241.9	277.4	378.4	392.9	458.3	520.5
Direct loans	307.2	545.1	681.8	648.7	568.1	662.6	1147.6	1361.0	1308.2	1450.0	1562.1	1431.8	1363.5
(Refinancing & debt loans)	(23.7)	(68.6)	(54.6)	(186.1)	(96.6)	(13.2)	(13.2)	(4.8)	(5.6)	(24.7)	(6.8)	(0.7)	(–2.0)
Bilateral ODA subtotal	477.8	765.2	880.4	850.4	753.0	899.3	1531.0	1921.2	1960.8	2260.4	2367.3	2425.2	2427.4
Multilateral ODA	133.3	245.8	245.8	297.3	352.0	525.2	684.4	716.3	1342.9	910.5	656.0	1335.8	1891.4
Sub total	611.1	1011.0	1126.2	1147.7	1104.9	1424.4	2215.4	2637.5	3303.7	3170.9	3023.2	3761.0	4318.7
2. Other official flows													
Export credit (over one year)	266.3	245.0	8.3	339.0	471.0	1061.6	1286.5	–235.1	822.9	1410.4	849.5	472.1	493.0
Direct investment	264.7	569.8	798.5	1015.5	776.8	417.4	703.8	675.4	767.0	1489.5	2094.9	1441.5	380.2
Multilateral loans	325.4	355.1	–17.9	14.9	85.6	123.6	162.4	–230.2	–111.9	122.7	–30.7	40.7	–130.4
Sub total	856.4	1178.9	788.9	1369.5	1333.4	1622.6	2152.6	210.1	1478.0	3022.6	2913.7	1954.3	742.8
Official flow total	1467.5	2189.9	1915.1	2517.2	2438.3	3047.0	4368.2	2847.6	4781.7	6193.5	5937.0	5715.3	5061.5

3. Private flows													
Export credit (over one year)	190.6	440.1	148.7	82.7	319.0	913.8	412.1	642.5	73.7	721.3	–1762.4	–2068.6	–655.2
Direct investment (including portfolio)	844.3	3072.1	874.8	273.3	1184.1	1233.6	5014.5	3405.8	1566.3	3698.8	3162.3	5272.9	9241.9
Multilateral loans	217.4	135.3	15.1	6.9	45.0	332.2	890.1	640.7	317.8	1599.5	1528.5	1574.2	2359.7
Grants by private voluntary agencies	5.6	6.8	8.7	10.1	16.2	18.3	18.9	19.0	26.4	27.3	23.3	29.7	40.7
Sub total	1257.9	3654.3	1047.2	372.9	1564.3	2487.9	6335.6	4708.0	1984.2	6037.9	2951.8	4808.2	10987.1
Grand total	2725.4	5844.2	2962.3	2890.1	4002.6	5534.9	10703.8	7555.6	6765.9	12231.1	8888.8	10523.4	16048.6
GNP ratio of total flow (%)	0.93	1.44	0.65	0.59	0.72	0.80	1.11	0.75	0.65	1.08	0.84	0.91	1.30
GNP ratio of ODA (%)	0.21	0.25	0.25	0.23	0.20	0.21	0.23	0.26	0.32	0.28	0.28	0.32	0.35
(Reference)													
GNP ($ billion)	299.7	412.1	459.4	497.8	558.7	686.6	963.1	998.7	1040.1	1139.3	1063.1	1158.8	1232.7
Exchange rate (Yen per US$)	308.00	272.84	291.49	297.04	296.55	268.51	210.47	219.17	226.74	220.53	249.05	237.52	237.52

Note: 1) Exchange rate based on DAC figures.
2) Including part of administrative costs.

Source: Ministry of Foreign Affairs, cited in *Japan Economic Almanac*, 1986.

Thailand ($232.02 million), Indonesia ($167.69 million) and the Philippines ($160.07 million). The early 1980s also saw a big increase in the availability of yen credit facilities giving rise to Japan as a major creditor nation and the emergence of Tokyo as an international financial centre. With greater internationalisation of the yen, and the relaxation of eligibility requirements and filing procedures, yen-denominated loan syndications (samurai loans), as well as public offering and private placement of yen-denominated bonds are expected to increase in the future. ASEAN countries are expected to avail themselves of these credit sources as they seek to finance future growth.

CONCLUSION: THE FUTURE OF ASEAN-JAPAN ECONOMIC RELATIONS

Given these economic trends in ASEAN-Japan relations, what can we say about the future. Any prognosis of bright prospects would have to be tentative. At this stage, one could say that the role of Japan in ASEAN future economic growth will depend on several factors:

1 the success of the internationalisation and reflation of Japan, particularly as they affect ASEAN directly in terms of the 'market opening' initiatives, and indirectly as they contribute to the lessening of Japanese trade frictions with the US and the EC and to the expansion of trade in the world economy,
2 the diversion of foreign investments to ASEAN, in spite of the attractions of the advanced countries, in particular the relocation of resource processing and the intermediate goods industry,
3 the success of economic co-ordination and greater economic co-operation among ASEAN members in terms of tariff rationalisation, foreign investment codes and industrial policy,
4 the success of domestic structural adjustments in the context of regional and global adjustments, and
5 the maintenance of political stability and security in the region.

These are crucial elements in shaping the future of ASEAN-Japan economic relations, as well as the possibility of greater multilateralisation of ASEAN external relations.

12 The Japanese Economy in the 1980s and its Relations with ASEAN

Noboru Hamaguchi

The purpose of this paper is to review critical issues concerning Japanese relations with ASEAN countries. EC – Japan relations will be examined only briefly. As is obvious from Table 12.1 Japan – ASEAN relations are distinctively significant among the triangular relationships between Japan, the EC and ASEAN.

Trade with ASEAN countries has important implications for Japan not just because of its volume, but also because of its impact on changing Japanese industrial structure. ASEAN countries have been rapidly increasing their exports to Japan of light manufactured products such as textiles, simple electric and electronic appliances. Japan

Table 12.1 Export and import shares

Importer	*Export shares*			*Import shares*		
Exporter	*EC*	*ASEAN*	*Japan*	*EC*	*ASEAN*	*Japan*
EC 1970	48.67	0.85	1.11	50.86	10.52	6.35
1975	54.83	1.07	0.93	57.42	13.57	5.50
1980	52.69	1.12	0.96	50.17	11.26	5.14
1985	51.95	1.20	1.24	53.30	12.69	6.60
ASEAN	10.90	19.11	24.23	0.78	16.10	9.52
	13.90	16.60	26.59	0.96	13.83	10.39
	12.75	16.71	26.80	1.22	16.94	14.42
	11.19	17.67	26.09	1.31	21.31	15.90
Japan	6.75	9.36		1.53	24.99	
	10.18	10.62		1.99	25.10	
	12.83	10.04		2.41	19.95	
	11.40	6.41		3.34	19.31	

Source: IMF *Directory of Trade*

is losing comparative advantage in these relatively labour-intensive products. The 'catching-up' by ASEAN countries (more importantly, by Asian NICs, Korea, Taiwan, Hong Kong, and Singapore) will accelerate shifts of labour and capital out of Japanese import competing industries.

On the other hand, Japan has contributed to the economic development of ASEAN countries as a significant supplier of capital goods through both exports and direct investment. One of the keys for the fast growth of ASEAN countries is a favourable interaction between domestic investment and exports. Thus, availability of efficient and inexpensive capital goods is vital for ASEAN countries.

This review comprises the following features. First, it focusses on developments in the 1980s. As described below in detail, the world economy, particularly the Japanese economy, has experienced in this period extraordinary changes which were seldom if ever experienced before. These developments include the sharp appreciation of the yen, the rapid decline in prices of crude oil and other raw materials, the fast expansion of Japanese direct foreign investment (DFI), and the large and rapidly increasing Japanese current account surplus (of the balance of payments), which is causing trade friction between Japan and its partners, particularly the United States.

Second, this review focusses on the Japanese viewpoint on Japan – ASEAN economic relations. It does not examine in detail the development of ASEAN economies themselves nor their relationship with the EC and other countries.

Third, among the many kinds of economic relations this review focusses on trade, trade policies, and direct investment. Therefore, some important aspects of Japan–ASEAN relations are not examined in this paper. These aspects include Japanese economic cooperation with ASEAN countries and short-term financial capital flow between Japan and ASEAN countries.

APPRECIATION OF YEN AND JAPANESE CURRENT BALANCE

As depicted in Table 12.2, the Japanese current balance has almost always been in surplus since the mid-1960s except for the two oil crisis periods. However, the rapid increase in current and trade surpluses in the 1980s is extraordinary. The Japanese current balance in 1985 was $49.2 billion, more than ten times greater than in 1980. This

Table 12.2 Japanese current and trade balance

	Current Balance				Trade Balance				
	World		*US*	*EC*	*World*		*US*	*EC*	*ASEAN*
	$million	/GNP(%)	$million	$million	$million	/GNP(%)	$million	$million	$million
1961	−982	1.79			−557	1.01			80
62	−49	0.08			402	0.67			59
63	−779	1.10			−166	0.23			34
64	−480	0.59			375	0.46			17
65	931	1.00	366	50	1 901	2.05	559	166	130
66	1 254	1.15	710	94	2 275	2.09	832	238	37
67	−190	0.14	221	−94	1 160	0.91	399	100	176
68	1 048	0.69	829	−62	2 529	1.67	1 204	20	230
69	2 119	1.17	1 270	8	3 699	2.04	1 641	225	230
70	1 970	0.94	857	69	3 963	1.89	1 465	303	478
71	5 797	2.44	2 756	348	7 787	3.27	3 374	599	508
72	6 624	2.08	3 351	562	8 971	2.82	3 950	934	648
73	−136	0.03	104	−189	3 688	0.86	1 312	382	1
74	−4 693	0.99	−693	983	1 436	0.30	1 893	1 468	1 499
75	−682	0.13	−935	500	5 028	0.98	1 045	2 500	309
76	3 680	0.63	3 437	1 838	9 887	1.71	5 531	3 907	688
77	10 918	1.54	6 770	2 686	17 311	2.45	8 661	4 703	921
78	16 534	1.67	8 668	3 014	24 596	2.48	10 611	5 451	68
79	−8 754	0.85	4 861	1 355	1 845	0.18	7 637	4 751	3 823
80	−10 746	0.99	6 251	4 959	2 125	0.20	9 846	9 313	4 741
81	4 770	0.41	13 871	3 965	19 967	0.17	16 297	10 816	3 127
82	6 850	0.63	14 334	4 848	18 079	1.65	15 131	9 929	3 198
83	20 799	1.75	19 151	6 620	31 454	2.65	21 211	11 048	3 667
84	35 003	2.74	35 018	6 878	44 257	3.47	36 704	10 648	6 454
85	49 169	3.69	41 727	7 993	55 986	4.20	42 988	11 089	7 146

Source: The Bank of Japan *Balance of Payments Monthly*

amount is the largest in world history, preceded by the former record of $41.4 billion made by Saudi Arabia in 1980.

The proportion of current surplus to nominal GNP has also increased sharply to 3.69 per cent in 1984. The periods of rapid increases in this proportion tend to coincide with the periods of 'trade friction' between Japan and its trading partners. The proportion exceeding 2 per cent is sometimes considered to be a 'crisis level'. The present Japanese situation may be considered far more serious. It is also noteworthy that Japan recorded current and trade surpluses against almost every country except for a few oil-exporting countries. Another important aspect of the recent Japanese current imbalance is that the invisible trade deficit, which has traditionally been so large that it sometimes exceeded trade surplus, has rapidly decreased due to an increase in investment income receipts.

Figure 12.1 Japanese current account balance

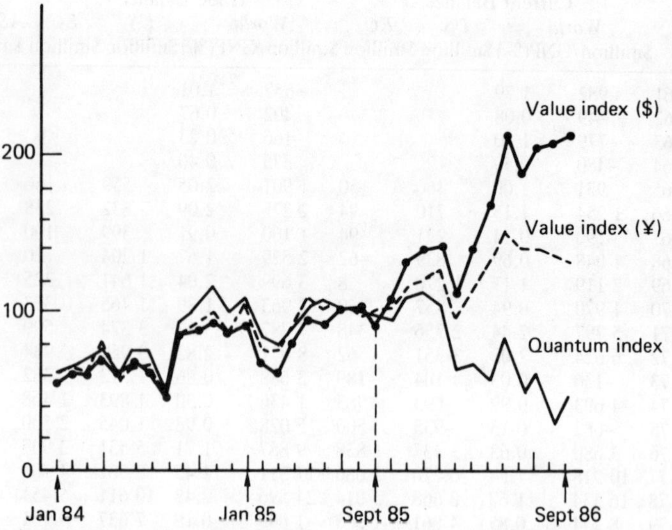

Note: The base period=July-Sept 1985. Seasonally adjusted. Excluding imports of gold for special commemorative coins for the period May-July 1986.

Source: Yoshio Suzuki 'The Trade Surplus will Decline Steadily'. *Nikkei Shinbun* (Japan Economic Journal), November 4, 1986

The Japanese yen has appreciated by about 50 percent during the twelve months since August 1985. This is the sharpest increase the Japanese economy has experienced since the 360 yen per dollar parity was established in 1952. Before 1985 the largest appreciation occurred between 1977 and 1978 at 14.77 per cent. Despite such appreciation of the yen, the Japanese current surplus seems to be expanding further. However, the Japanese current surplus should be examined more carefully.

First, the surplus is still increasing in dollar terms, but (as shown in the Figure 12.1) it has already begun decreasing in yen terms since May 1986. The quantum index of the surplus has sharply declined since December 1965.

Second, the Japanese current surplus has been heavily affected by the declining prices of crude oil and other natural resources. If crude

Table 12.3 Exchange rate appreciations, August 1985 to July 1986

		(per US dollar, %)			
Japan	(Yen)	48.56	Malaysia	(Ringgit)	–6.71
Belgium	(Francs)	27.38	Netherlands	(Guilders)	29.39
Denmark	(Kroner)	25.39	Philippines	(Pesos)	–9.04
France	(Francs)	25.06	Portugal	(Escudos)	12.05
Germany	(Mark)	29.57	Singapore	(Dollars)	1.32
Greece	(Drachmas)	–4.91	Spain	(Pesetas)	19.26
Indonesia	(Rupiah)	–1.18	Thailand	(Baht)	–2.35
Ireland	(Pound)	20.17	United Kingdom	(Pound)	8.96
Italy	(Lire)	22.12			

Source: IMF *International Financial Statistics*

oil prices increase again, the current surplus will rapidly decrease.

Third, the appreciation of other currencies has been much less than that of the yen (see Table 12.3). The currencies of ASEAN countries have appreciated little or even depreciated against the US dollar. These countries' exports are one of the major sources of Japanese imports. Thus, Japanese imports, in particular light manufactured goods, will increase substantially. At the same time, the US current deficit may not decrease so easily since the decrease in Japanese exports to the United States may be replaced merely by the increase in exports from ASEAN and other developing countries.

Fourth, the Japanese economy is facing a dilemma. On the one hand, strong pressure to reduce the current surplus is mounting. On the other hand, the reduction in current surplus will have a serious deflationary effect on the Japanese domestic economy. It is true that an increase in domestic demand will solve partially at least this dilemma. However, since Japanese economic growth has relied on export growth so long, the Japanese economy does not yet have an efficient mechanism to lead growth through the expansion of pure domestic demand.

Moreover, Japanese macroeconomic policies are not free to operate. Fiscal expansion is restricted by urgent demand to reduce accumulating government debt. The Bank of Japan has operated its monetary policies to stimulate domestic demand. But, there is a good reason for hesitating to ease monetary policies further. The Japanese financial market has revealed a puzzling phenomenon.

On the one hand, real interest rates are still very high despite the lowest nominal rates in the postwar period. This is a reflection of the declining general price level. On the other hand, Japanese firms are increasing speculative transactions (aiming at capital gains) including purchases of real estate and corporate stocks and bonds. Thus, it is not clear whether the Japanese money supply is in excess or in shortage. Some policymakers are worrying about possible inflation caused by the massive purchase of dollars by the Bank of Japan. Finally, there seems to be a growing consensus that monetary policies are able to affect exchange rates, but not to control domestic demand.

ACCESSIBILITY OF THE JAPANESE DOMESTIC MARKET

It is widely and strongly believed that the Japanese domestic market remains tightly protected. However, it is not so easy to prove or disprove whether this belief is consistent with reality. As far as 'formal' trade barriers such as tariffs and quotas are concerned, Japan has one of the most accessible markets among industrial countries, as indicated in Tables 12.4 and 12.5. It is perhaps fair criticism to say that Japan's trade policies aimed at giving better access to its domestic market have been adopted so slowly that Japanese manufacturers have improved their competitiveness beyond the level with which other countries can cope. On the other hand, it should also be noted that recent Japanese trade policies have been 'one way' toward a

Table 12.4 Number of residual import quotas in major economies

	Number of import quotas	*Agricultural products*	*Industrial products*	*Discriminatory import restrictions against Japan*
United States	7	1	6	—
Canada	5	4	1	—
United Kingdom	3	1	2	—
France	46	19	27	22
West Germany	4	3	1	3
Italy	8	3	5	35
Benelux	5	2	3	9
Japan	23	22	1	—

Source: Economic Planning Agency (Japan) *Economic Papers*, 1981. (Japanese figure is for 1986)

Table 12.5 Proportion of tariff revenue in the value of imports in major countries (percentage)

	1978	*1979*	*1980*	*1981*	*1982*	*1983*	*1984*
Japan	4.1	3.1	2.5	2.5	2.6	2.5	2.5
United States	4.1	3.9	3.1	3.2	3.6	3.5	—
EC	3.4	3.1	2.6	2.5	2.7	2.7	—
Canada	5.2	4.6	4.5	4.5	4.3	4.2	—
Australia	10.1	9.5	9.5	9.0	9.3	9.7	—

Source: OECD *Foreign Trade Statistics*, Series A; *Revenue Statistics*. IMF *International Financial Statistics*. Ministry of Finance, *Monetary and Fiscal Statistics Monthly*.

more open domestic market, while many other countries are introducing protective policies.

However, these arguments may not be so important since complaints about the accessibility of the Japanese market focus not on 'formal' trade barriers but on non-trade barriers (NTB) such as approval and settlement systems, customs practices, application of standards, government procurement policies, export subsidies, and incentives. These are things that the government can control, and hence, can be relatively negotiable. However, there are many policies which are made and implemented with no intention of restricting imports, but do actually result in discouraging imports. Moreover, some foreign suppliers have recognised that Japanese domestic trade and distribution systems and practices are so peculiar that non-Japanese sellers can never be successful.

Although detailed examination of such barriers is beyond the scope of this study, some comments are in order:

1 the Japanese government recently decided to take major steps to remove such barriers. In April 1985 the Advisory Commitee for External Economic Issues proposed a policy called 'An Action Programme to Improve Market Access'. Also, the so-called 'Maekawa Report' of April 1986 proposed longer-range policies to help overcome the conflicts between Japan and its trade partners.

2 It is often argued that the Japanese market is difficult for foreign exporters to penetrate because of 'unfair' and covert barriers to foreign sales in Japan. However, many of the 'barriers' foreign suppliers point out do not particularly discriminate against non-Japanese. Japanese domestic suppliers often face exactly the same

'barriers'. It is not easy to settle the debate between the Japanese who argue that foreigners' failure to penetrate the Japanese market is due to lack of effort and the foreign suppliers who argue that the cause of unsuccessful penetration is due to Japanese policies and practices which are covertly discriminatory. A counter example of this foreigner's argument is the excellent performance of US subsidiaries in Japan such as McDonald's, Kentucky Fried Chicken, and Japan IBM. BMW boosted its auto exports to Japan after establishing its own sales company in Tokyo. These firms have been successful because of their efforts.

3 Some argue that the proof of Japan's discrimination against foreign sales is the low level and slow increase in Japanese manufactured imports. It is true that the proportion of manufacturing imports to total Japanese imports has been at a low level compared with other industrial countries as indicated in Table 12.6. However, since 1980 the proportion has increased substantially, even after excluding crude oil imports whose prices declined in this period. During the 1970s the proportion declined, but that was heavily affected by the sharp increase in crude oil prices. Note also that the proportion for imports from ASEAN countries excluding crude oil has steadily increased over the last two decades (see Table 12.7).

4 The problems of accessibility of the Japanese market have some particular aspects with respect to ASEAN–Japan trade relations. The ASEAN countries have voiced the criticism that Japanese trade policies towards making its market more accessible have been biased against ASEAN countries in favour of developed countries, the United States in particular.

One such example is the Japanese tariff on processed chicken meat. Until 1978 a unique tariff rate of 20 per cent was imposed on every kind of chicken meat. Then, the tariff rate on chicken on the bone, which the United States is one of the main exporters of, was reduced, while the rate on boneless chicken, of which Thailand is one of the main exporters, remained unchanged. This tariff rate differential still remains, though it has narrowed (14 per cent for chicken on the bone as against 11.3 per cent for boneless chicken as of January 1986). Similar differential tariff rates are imposed on soft plywood (15 per cent), which the United States and Canada are the main suppliers of and hard plywood (17 per cent), which is supplied mainly by ASEAN countries. The Japanese government decided to reduce both tariff rates in 1987, but the tariff differential has not disappeared completely.

Table 12.6 Proportion of manufacturing products in imports: industrial countries (percentage)

	Japan	*Japan* ex. oil	*US*	*EC*	*ECX*	*OECD*
1960	22.1		45.9	46.3	34.5	
61	24.5		46.1	49.1	36.8	
62	25.9		47.6	50.9	38.2	
63	24.5		49.3	52.5	39.2	
64	25.8		52.0	52.9	38.0	
65	22.7		56.0	53.8	38.7	
66	22.8		59.8	55.4	40.2	
67	26.8		62.6	55.6	40.0	
68	27.5		65.7	57.6	42.3	
69	29.5		67.5	60.4	45.5	
70	30.3	34.4	68.0	61.6	46.8	
71	28.6	33.9	70.0	61.4	46.0	60.9
72	29.6	35.6	70.8	62.0	46.6	62.4
73	30.6	36.3	67.4	60.9	45.6	61.0
74	23.7	34.1	57.4	55.5	39.1	54.5
75	20.3	36.5	55.8	56.7	41.2	54.6
76	21.5	32.0	55.8	57.5	41.6	55.4
77	21.5	32.2	54.1	58.5	43.2	56.0
78	26.7	38.0	60.7	61.5	48.1	58.9
79	26.0	37.3	56.8	60.6	47.3	56.9
80	22.8	36.6	54.0	58.9	46.1	54.3
81	24.3	38.7	57.4	56.5	43.6	53.6
82	24.9	38.3	62.2	57.7	45.1	55.3
83	27.2	39.8	66.3	59.7	48.6	58.1
84	29.8	41.8	71.0	60.2	50.0	60.1
85	31.0	42.3				

Source: OECD, *Foreign Trade Statistics*, Series B. *Highlights of US Export and Import Trade*. Japanese Ministry of Finance, *Foreign Trade Statistics*.
ECX: EC excluding intra–EC trade.

5 Finally, it is important to note that from the viewpoint of economic theory, the accessibility of a country's markets should not be directly related to the current surplus of the balance of payments of that country. Changes in trade policies may affect the commodity composition of imports and exports. However, an overall imbalance in the current account is caused by changes in exchange rates and the relative size of domestic (governmental and private) savings and investment.

Table 12.7 Proportion of manufacturing products in Japanese imports (percentage)

Exporter	World		EC		ASEAN	
	Total	*ex. oil*	*Total*	*ex. oil*	*Total*	*ex. oil*
1970	30.32	34.39	0.97	89.97	7.69	9.29
1975	20.30	30.74	85.92	85.92	6.58	11.22
1980	22.85	36.59	86.40	86.94	7.00	12.12
1985	31.00	42.30	84.17	84.17	10.12	14.01

Source: Japanese Ministry of Finance, *Foreign Trade Statistics*.

JAPANESE DIRECT FOREIGN INVESTMENT

As Figure 12.2 shows, Japanese direct foreign investment (DFI) has increased substantially, particularly in the 1980s. Investment flow in the 1985 FY (fiscal year, April – March) was $12.2 billion. The accumulated balance was $83.6 billion at the end of March 1986. The share of accumulated balance of Japanese DFI in that of the world balance was 6.9 per cent at the end of December 1984. The Japanese share is the third largest, following those of the United States (42.5 per cent) and the United Kingdom (15.5 per cent). Table 12.8 summarises the regional distribution of Japanese DFI. Japanese DFI has shifted towards North and Latin America and Europe.

The share of the Japanese DFI in the EC countries in the total Japanese DFI to Europe has increased substantially. In the 1985 FY, 95.9 per cent of Japanese DFI in Europe was received by EC countries, while the share was 60.7 per cent in the 1975 FY. On the other hand, investment in ASEAN countries has considerably decreased its share in Japan's total DFI (from 26.0 per cent in the 1975 FY to 7.6 per cent in the 1985 FY). The main causes of the stagnation of Japanese DFI in ASEAN countries, particularly in the 1980s, are as follows:

1 The Japanese demand for energy and natural resources has slowed down in this decade due to the saving of such resources since the oil crisis in 1974, general excess supplies and declining prices of crude oil and other natural resources and slowing down of the growth rate of the Japanese economy. Since a considerable proportion of Japanese DFI in ASEAN countries had been implemented for the purpose of seeking and extracting natural resources, DFI itself has been discouraged in the 1980s.

Figure 12.2 Japanese direct foreign investment

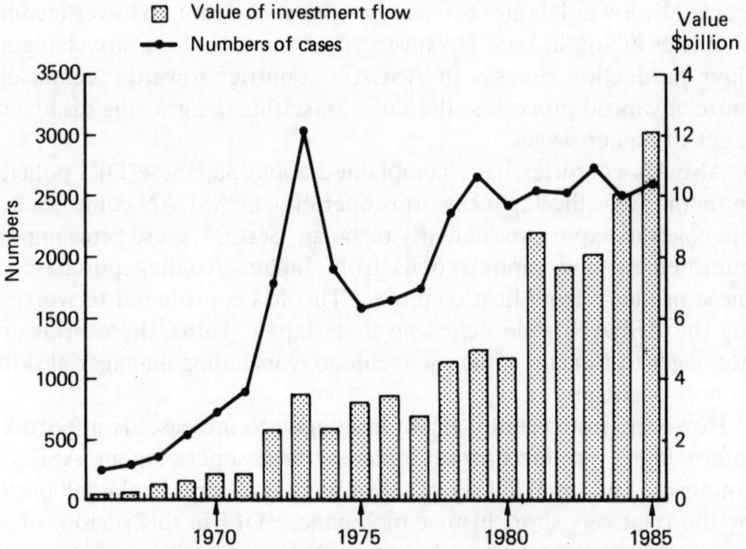

Source: MITI, *Statistical Survey of Japanese Foreign Investment*.

Table 12.8 Regional distribution of Japanese direct investment $10 million (%)

	1951–67	*1968–71*	*1972–77*	*1978–81*	*1982–85*
North America	36.8(26.4)	72.2(24.5)	401.7(23.8)	662.1(29.4)	1464.5(38.3)
Latin America	37.6(27.0)	32.5(11.0)	303.9(18.0)	355.2(15.8)	828.7(21.7)
Europe	5.6(4.0)	66.0(22.4)	227.8(13.5)	212.7(9.4)	573.3(15.0)
Asia	29.8(21.4)	66.6(22.6)	529.9(31.4)	676.1(30.0)	629.5(16.5)
Middle-East	24.0(17.2)	12.8(4.3)	58.8(3.5)	68.1(3.0)	61.7(1.6)
Africa	1.7(1.2)	9.6(3.3)	79.7(4.7)	110.4(4.9)	135.1(3.5)
Oceania	3.9(2.8)	34.9(11.9)	86.4(5.1)	168.1(7.5)	129.4(3.4)
Total	139.5(100)	294.5(100)	1688.3(100)	2252.6(100)	3822.0(100)

Source: MITI, *Statistical Survey of Japanese Foreign Investment*.

2 The ASEAN countries are finishing their import substituting phase of economic development, but much of the Japanese DFI in manufacturing industries in ASEAN countries has been attracted by such import substitution.

3 As wage rates in ASEAN countries, particularly Singapore, have risen substantially, Japanese investment, which was also attracted by lower labour costs, is changing its location to lower income countries in South Asia. However, some Japanese firms are changing their production process in ASEAN countries towards technically more advanced processes, therefore offsetting the growing disadvantages of higher wages.

ASEAN countries have complained about Japanese DFI policies in them. First, the Japanese firms operating in ASEAN countries are not eager to export, particularly to Japan. Second, these firms import intermediate and capital goods from Japan, avoiding purchase of these products from host countries. This has contributed to worsening the ASEAN trade deficit *vis-à-vis* Japan. Third, these firms are not eager to transfer Japanese technology including managerial skills to host countries.

However, just recently Japan has begun to increase its imports of intermediate products from Japanese firms operating in ASEAN countries. The small degree of technology transfer is explained partly by the relatively short history of Japanese DFI in this region, or in any region, for that matter. Japanese DFI was heavily restricted until the early 1970s but, quickly liberalised during the period 1969–1972, as part of the government's policies of coping with increasing pressure from abroad to decrease the yen appreciation in the late 1960s.

Another reason for Japanese firms' seeming unwillingness to transfer technology is the specific nature of Japanese technology. Unlike Western technology, Japanese technology tends to be transferable only through Japanese trainers. That is, Japanese technology is hard to write in manuals. Thus, a large number of Japanese managers are required to operate Japanese firms. Such practices result in delaying the transfer or making it look delayed.

However, perhaps the most serious problem for ASEAN countries is the recent stagnation of Japanese investment. Although Japanese investment has had many problems as mentioned above, it has contributed to ASEAN economic growth in substantial ways. As discussed previously, ASEAN economic growth has been supported by a favourable interaction of exports and domestic fixed investment, which is in turn supported by the supply of Japanese capital goods provided partly by Japanese DFI.

In contrast to the stagnating Japanese DFI in ASEAN countries, investment in North America and the EC has grown quite rapidly. The main causes of this development are these:

1 Japan has accumulated and improved managerial skills and technical knowledges which can be utilised to operate production profitably in advanced countries.

2 Wage differentials between Japan and other advanced countries have narrowed enough to reduce the advantage of operating in Japan.

3 Many firms have recognised the importance of close contacts with the market to obtain information about consumer preferences and to provide better services to customers.

4 Japanese exports have faced strengthening protective policies in their markets abroad. At the same time, many countries have attempted to attract Japanese DFI to their countries, expecting an increase in local employment.

This last cause needs some elaboration. It may be reasonable for a country to expect that direct investment from abroad would strengthen the competitiveness of the industry in which the investment is made. However, such investment may or may not improve the host country's balance of payments, particularly, the current account. Japanese DFI may substitute Japanese exports for production in host countries. But Japanese subsidiaries operating abroad may import intermediate and capital goods from Japan. An increase in investment income receipts may contribute to expanding the Japanese current surplus, a result which is actually occurring now. Japanese investment in Asian countries may increase exports from these host countries to the US and the EC. Japanese imports of raw materials may decrease as Japanese production shifts abroad. Japanese DFI will compete with firms in host countries and may create other frictions.

Finally, it should be noted that a country can never be simultaneously a significant foreign investor and a significant net importer of goods and services.

Table 12.9 depicts the industry distribution of Japanese DFI. The declining importance of natural resources and lower labour cost-oriented investment, which were discussed above, are apparent in the table. Another major trend of Japanese DFI, particularly in the 1980s, is the rapid expansion of investment by financial institutions and firms in service industries.

Although it is difficult to explain and evaluate the implications of such trends, several tentative comments are in order. First, this tendency may simply reflect the general trend of a highly developed economy to increase the weight of service industries. Second, the

Table 12.9 Industry distribution of Japanese direct investment $10 million (%)

	1951–67	*1968–71*	*1972–73*	*1974–77*	*1978–81*	*1982–85*
Manufactures	20.6(14.8)	72.7(24.7)	202.1(38.1)	389.7(33.7)	771.7(34.3)	952.1(24.9)
Food	2.6(1.9)	4.3(1.5)	9.7(1.8)	19.6(1.7)	36.6(1.6)	36.3(0.9)
Textile	9.1(6.5)	16.3(5.5)	48.8(9.2)	54.3(4.7)	44.3(2.0)	35.4(0.9)
Lumber, Pulp	11.3(8.1)	15.1(5.1)	9.9(1.9)	26.5(2.3)	19.9(0.9)	29.7(0.8)
Chemical	1.6(1.1)	5.0(1.7)	46.0(8.7)	84.2(7.3)	148.5(6.6)	112.8(3.8)
Metal	8.7(6.2)	10.1(3.4)	29.8(5.6)	56.6(4.9)	208.9(9.3)	205.0(5.4)
Machinery	3.8(2.7)	5.3(1.8)	12.2(2.3)	30.1(2.6)	58.8(2.6)	86.8(2.3)
Electric Machinery	2.2(1.6)	8.0(2.7)	22.5(4.2)	52.0(4.5)	120.7(5.4)	169.1(4.4)
Transport Equipment	7.4(5.3)	2.7(0.9)	12.2(2.3)	31.6(2.7)	82.1(3.6)	198.9(5.2)
Others	2.7(1.9)	5.9(2.0)	11.0(2.1)	34.9(3.0)	51.8(2.3)	77.8(2.0)
Natural Resources	47.9(34.3)	97.4(33.1)	154.8(29.2)	322.6(27.9)	475.5(21.1)	234.9(6.1)
Agriculture, Fishery	3.6(2.6)	6.6(2.3)	12.5(2.4)	33.0(2.9)	46.0(2.0)	20.1(0.5)
Mining	44.3(31.7)	90.9(30.8)	142.3(26.8)	289.7(25.0)	429.5(19.1)	214.9(5.6)
Others	42.2(30.3)	124.3(42.2)	174.1(32.8)	444.9(38.4)	1005.4(44.6)	1368.5(68.9)
Wholesale, Retail	15.9(11.3)	37.0(12.6)	66.1(12.4)	176.4(15.2)	362.8(16.1)	609.5(15.9)
Financial Inst.	13.6(9.7)	23.5(8.0)	47.5(9.0)	84.8(7.3)	157.5(7.0)	759.0(19.9)
Others	12.7(9.1)	63.9(21.6)	60.5(11.4)	183.7(15.9)	485.1(21.5)	1266.2(33.1)
Total	139.5(100)	294.5(100)	531.0(100)	1157.3(100)	2252.6(100)	3822.0(100)

Source: MITI, *Statistical Survey of Japanese Foreign Investment*.

rapid increase in international operations of the Japanese financial institutions should be heavily affected by the liberalisation of the Japanese financial market, which gained momentum after the Foreign Exchange and Trade Control Act was essentially revised in December 1980. Third, the tendency may be a precautionary measure to cope with the resistance of many developing countries and some developed countries to the liberalisation of trade in services, which was revealed in the preliminary debates on the Uruguay Round of GATT multilateral trade negotiations.

13 China–EC Economic Relations: Experience and Prospects

Edward K.Y. Chen*

This paper attempts to analyse the economic relations between China and the EC since the opening up of China in 1977 in terms of China's foreign trade and the EC's investment in China. China has in recent years undergone very drastic changes in its economic system. The reforms introduced are experimental and hence policies tend to undergo much variation at various times. Specifically, the foreign trade system has been changing back and forth from centralisation to decentralisation. In industry, the emphasis was on heavy industry at one time but on light industry at another time. In agriculture, it is sometimes grains and sometimes cash crops that are given top priority. Similarly, consumption was promoted at one time but discouraged at a later stage. China's external economic relations should be discussed in the light of China's reforms and restructuring and the stop-go policies that have accompanied such reforms and restructuring.

CHINA'S FOREIGN TRADE AFTER 1976

In the direction of trade, there is a high degree of market concentration. Hong Kong and Japan now account for about 50 per cent of China's total exports. While Hong Kong has been China's major market for a long time, the importance of Japan increased after China's adoption of the open door policy. At the same time, the relative importance of the United States and ASEAN nations has significantly increased. The decline of China's export to the United States in 1983 was due to the trade frictions between the two countries over the issue of textile quotas. To retaliate, China reduced its imports from the United States drastically in 1983 and China's imports from the United States have only been recovering very slowly since then.

The EC has not been a very important market for China. Indeed, the relative share of the EC in China's exports had been falling consistently until the beginning of 1986. The increase in exports from China to the EC in 1986 is mainly due to the drastic devaluation of the renminbi (RMB) against European currencies, resulting from the RMB's devaluation against the US dollar and the US dollar's devaluation against the Japanese yen and European currencies since the G-5 meeting in September 1985. In late 1985, the exchange rate of the RMB was lowered from 2.8 RMB to US$1 to 3.1 RMB to US$1. In July 1986, there was a further devaluation of RMB to 3.7 RMB to US$1. Comparing early September 1985 to September 1986, we find that within the space of one year, the RMB was devalued by over 80 per cent against the German mark.

It must, however, be noted that because of the vast amount of China's *entrepôt* trade handled by Hong Kong, some of China's exports to Hong Kong are re-exported to other countries. In theory, the statistics reported by China's General Administration of Customs should have separated exports and re-exports. But, in practice, this is not always possible. Moreover, there is considerable 'parallel' trade (smuggling, forged export licences, *etc.*) which is never recorded.[1] Furthermore, China's trade statistics are also distorted by the widespread practice of over-invoicing for the purpose of capital flight and under-invoicing for the purpose of avoiding tax.

With regard to China's imports, Japan has always been the major supplier. China's imports from Hong Kong have increased very drastically since the opening up of Hong Kong. Imports from the United States also increased very drastically up to 1983 in which year China–US trade relations worsened because of China's dissatisfaction with the textile quotas imposed by the United States. China retaliated by diversifying its imports (especially agricultural products) from other countries. The relative importance of ASEAN as China's source of supply has not changed much even since the opening up of China.

On the other hand, China's imports from the EC have undergone ups and downs in accordance with changes in the policy directions of China's economic reforms and development. The years immediately after the fall of the 'Gang of Four', 1977–79, were a period called 'Great Leap Westward' during which huge amounts of machinery and equipment were imported without careful analysis of real needs and the consideration of complementary inputs and measures necessary for the effective use of such imports. China was then simply

Table 13.1 China's exports and imports by selected regions and countries, 1978–86 (percentage)

Year	*1978*		*1979*		*1980*		*1981*		*1982*		*1983*		*1984*		*1985*		*1986**	
Region/Country	*X*	*M*	*X*	*M*	*X*	*M*	*X*	*M*	*X*	*M*	*X*	*M*	*X*	*M*	*X*	*M*	*X*	*M*
Japan	17.6	28.5	20.2	25.2	22.1	26.4	22.1	28.6	21.9	20.6	20.4	25.9	22.4	31.8	23.2	36.4	22.0	30.0
United States	2.8	6.6	4.3	11.8	5.4	19.5	7.0	21.6	8.0	22.7	7.7	12.9	8.1	12.0	8.5	11.9	8.8	13.2
EC	12.3	17.4	12.6	21.3	12.3	14.2	11.8	14.1	9.7	14.2	9.9	18.7	8.7	13.2	8.0	13.1	9.7	17.1
Hong Kong and Macao	25.9	0.7	23.7	1.4	23.8	2.9	24.5	5.8	23.7	6.9	26.2	8.0	25.0	10.7	25.8	11.6	29.9	10.5
ASEAN Nations	5.8	2.6	6.5	2.9	6.5	3.3	5.6	2.3	5.5	3.9	5.2	2.6	7.5	2.2	9.5	3.2	7.3	2.7
Others	35.6	44.2	32.7	37.4	29.9	33.7	29.0	27.6	31.2	31.7	30.6	31.9	28.3	30.1	25.0	23.8	22.3	26.5
Total	100	100	100	100	100	100	100	100	100	100	100	100	100	100	100	100	100	100

Source: 1. *China's Special Economic Zones*, OECD, 1986, p. 52.
2. General Administration of Customs, PRC, *China's Customs Statistics*, various issues.

* first quarter of 1986 (January to March).
X exports.
M imports.

Table 13.2 China-EC trade, 1972–86 in US$ million

	Exports to EC		*Imports from EC*	
	Value	*percentage*[1]	*Value*	*percentage*[2]
1972	475	13.8	620	21.7
1974	887	12.8	1926	25.3
1976	850	12.4	1660	25.2
1978	1198	12.3	1900	17.4
1980	2246	12.3	2772	14.2
1981	2467	11.8	2750	14.1
1982	2116	9.7	2482	14.2
1983	2199	9.9	3471	18.7
1984	2131	8.7	3354	13.2
1985	2030	8.0	5141	13.1
1986*	1718	12.9	3324	16.8

Sources: 1. State Statistical Bureau, PRC, *China Statistical Yearbook*, various years.
2. General Administration of Customs, PRC, *China's Customs Statistics*, various issues.

* first half of 1986 (January to June)
[1] as percentage of China's total exports
[2] as percentage of China's total imports

hungry for Western technology after such a long period of isolation from the Western world. Western Europe with its many specialties in the production of machinery and transport equipment and less conflicting political interests with China than the United States naturally became an important supplier of capital goods to China during that 'Great Leap Westward' period.

It did not take long for China to realise that the unplanned and indiscriminate import of capital goods was unconstructive and incurred a huge waste of foreign exchange. In late 1979, China began a period of economic readjustment and reforms. Consumption was given an even more important role in economic development. The rate of capital accumulation was lowered to no more than 25–30 per cent and light industries were assigned a higher priority than heavy industries. In consequence, we witnessed during 1980–85 a spending spree on consumer products resulting in a drastic increase in the import of consumer products especially household electrical appliances, and a slowing down in the increase of capital goods imports.

This explains the sharp increase in China's imports from Japan and Hong Kong. Hong Kong also serves as *entrepôt* for China's imports, including imports from South Korea and Taiwan *via* Hong Kong. By 1984, as much as 8 per cent of Taiwan's total exports came to Hong Kong most of which was re-exported to China. The sudden increase in imports from the EC in 1983 was a result of China switching from the United States to other sources of supply when China and the United States had differences over textile quotas.

The period of consumption fever, 1980–85, led to a huge trade deficit and outflow of foreign exchange from China. In 1985, China's imports grew by 45 per cent and exports by only 2 per cent. The trade deficit in 1985 was close to US$14 billion or 52 per cent of exports. The foreign exchange reserves were reduced to an alarming level of below US$10 billion by the end of 1985. China had therefore to take very drastic measures to clamp down on money supply and the use of foreign exchange as from early 1985. By early 1986, the situation was largely under control. In order not to affect industrial development badly, the control over the import of capital goods has been relaxed considerably since early 1986, but the control over spending on consumer goods has remained. In consequence, imports from Japan, Hong Kong and ASEAN grew much slower than those from the EC in the first half of 1986. This is because most of the imports from the EC are capital goods while a large proportion of the imports from Japan, Hong Kong and ASEAN are consumer products.

CHINA'S TRADE WITH THE EC

The major EC trading partners of China are West Germany, France, the UK, and Italy. With regard to China's export to the EC, exports to France and the UK have been on the decline. There has been little change in the relative share of the Italian market in China's exports. The German market is the most important within the EC for China, and its growth has also been the most rapid resulting in an increasing relative share in China's exports.

In the first half of 1986, we witnessed a drastic increase in China's exports to the UK and as a result the relative shares of West Germany and Italy showed a decline. When examining China-UK trade in the first half of 1986 more closely, we find that the major increase in China's exports to the UK was in beverages and armament. Further investigations and observations are necessary to ascer-

Table 13.3 China's imports from and exports to EC by country, 1972–86 (percentage)

Year		*1972*		*1974*		*1976*		*1978*		*1980*		*1981*		*1982*		*1983*		*1984*		*1985*		*1986**	
Country		*(1)*	*(2)*	*(1)*	*(2)*	*(1)*	*(2)*	*(1)*	*(2)*	*(1)*	*(2)*	*(1)*	*(2)*	*(1)*	*(2)*	*(1)*	*(2)*	*(1)*	*(2)*	*(1)*	*(2)*	*(1)*	*(2)*
France	M	21.8	4.6	56.6	9.6	28.7	7.3	13.0	2.3	11.4	1.6	13.3	1.9	9.3	1.3	15.3	2.9	9.3	1.2	13.0	1.7	10.8	1.8
	X	18.1	2.5	20.3	2.5	15.2	1.9	14.9	1.8	15.1	1.9	13.8	1.6	17.7	1.7	11.5	1.1	12.9	1.1	10.4	0.8	8.6	1.1
West	M	29.7	6.4	25.6	6.5	43.4	10.9	54.2	9.5	48.1	6.8	56.0	7.9	48.6	6.9	37.5	7.0	45.0	5.9	44.6	5.8	50.8	8.6
Germany	X	18.9	2.6	23.1	3.0	26.5	3.3	27.5	3.4	31.7	3.9	31.8	3.8	32.1	3.1	38.6	3.8	33.5	2.9	33.9	2.7	24.3	3.1
Italy	M	12.7	2.8	5.9	1.5	10.1	2.5	10.1	1.8	9.0	1.3	11.3	1.6	9.1	1.3	7.5	1.4	10.5	1.4	16.3	2.1	15.3	2.6
	X	17.7	2.4	10.3	1.3	14.1	1.8	13.8	1.7	15.6	1.9	11.6	1.4	13.6	1.3	13.2	1.3	14.8	1.3	13.3	1.1	9.1	1.2
Belgium	M	3.2	0.7	1.8	0.5	1.7	0.4	4.2	0.7	2.4	0.3	2.4	0.3	4.8	0.7	4.7	0.9	5.6	0.7	4.9	0.6	4.2	0.7
	X	2.1	0.3	3.6	0.4	3.6	0.5	3.1	0.4	4.0	0.5	3.5	0.4	4.6	0.4	4.6	0.5	4.2	0.4	7.3	0.6	5.7	0.7
Nether-	M	1.9	0.4	4.3	1.1	5.1	1.3	6.6	1.2	7.2	1.0	3.9	0.6	3.1	0.4	2.6	0.5	3.9	0.5	4.9	0.6	4.3	0.7
lands	X	12.0	1.7	8.3	1.1	6.9	0.9	7.7	0.9	6.1	0.7	8.4	1.0	8.8	0.9	8.0	0.8	10.4	0.9	14.9	1.2	11.1	1.4
Luxem-	M	0	0	0	0	0	0	4.8	0.8	0.6	N.	0.2	N.	0	0	0.4	N.	1.0	N.	0.7	N.	0.3	N.
bourg	X	0	0	0	0	0	0	0.3	N.	0.3	N.	0.3	N.	0	0	0	0	0	0	0	0	0	0
United	M	30.0	6.5	23.1	5.8	10.2	2.6	15.6	2.7	19.5	2.8	11.2	1.6	18.9	2.7	30.0	5.6	21.7	2.9	13.5	1.8	12.4	2.1
Kingdom	X	28.2	3.9	31.8	4.1	31.4	3.9	30.9	3.8	25.1	3.1	28.8	3.4	21.0	2.0	21.9	2.2	21.7	1.9	16.3	1.3	37.8	4.9
Ireland	M	0	0	0	0	0	0	0	0	0	0	0.3	N.	0.2	N.	0.3	N.	0.4	N.	0	0	0.2	N.
	X	0	0	0	0	0	0	0	0	0	0	0.3	N.	0.3	N.	0.3	N.	0.3	N.	0.3	N.	0.2	N.
Denmark	M	1.1	0.2	1.1	0.3	0.6	0.2	1.3	0.2	1.9	0.3	1.6	0.2	6.0	0.9	2.6	0.3	2.6	0.3	1.9	0.3	1.7	0.3
	X	2.5	0.3	2.4	0.3	2.0	0.2	1.7	0.2	1.8	0.2	1.5	0.2	1.7	0.2	1.9	0.2	2.2	0.2	3.3	0.3	2.9	0.4

Sources: 1. State Statistical Bureau, PRC, *China Statistical Yearbook*, various years.
2. General Administration of Customs, PRC, *China's Customs Statistics*, various issues.

* first half of 1986 (January to June).
(1) as percentage of EC's trade with China.
(2) as percentage of China's total trade.

M imports.
X exports.
N. insignificant.

Table 13.4 China – EC trade balance, selected countries, 1972–85
in US$ million

Country / *Year*	*France*	*West Germany*	*Italy*	*United Kingdom*	*EC Total*
1972	−46	−94	5	−52	−145
1974	−554	−289	−23	−162	−1039
1976	−348	−496	−47	97	−810
1978	−69	−700	−26	74	−702
1980	25	−622	102	24	−526
1981	−24	−754	−24	403	−283
1982	143	−526	62	−24	−366
1983	−279	−452	29	−559	−1272
1984	−39	−792	−37	−267	−1223
1985	−457	−1602	−568	−365	−3111

Source: General Administration of Customs, PRC, *China's Customs Statistics*, various issues.

tain whether the recent increase in China's exports to the UK will be maintained in the future.

With regard to China's imports from the EC, the relative shares of France and the UK have been on the decline and that of West Germany on the increase. The relative share of Italy was generally on the decline up to 1983. Since then, China's imports from Italy have increased rapidly.

In the balance of trade between China and the EC, China has a persistent trade deficit, largely the result of the adverse balance of trade between China and West Germany. Recently, China's trade deficit in trading with Italy has also been significant. In general, because of China's heavy demand for industrial products, particularly capital goods, supplied by industrialised countries, China's import from such countries is significant. On the other hand, what China can offer the industrialised countries are only raw materials, fuel and light manufactured goods (particularly clothing). But China's export of raw materials and fuel is limited and the export of light manufactured goods is subject to the keen competition of other developing countries, expecially the newly industrialising countries (NICs).

On the other hand, China's light manufactured goods do find markets in many developing countries, whilst China does not import that much primary products from developing countries because China's resources endowment is quite similar to many of the resource-rich developing countries. China earns a significant proportion of its foreign exchange from exporting foodstuff and light manufactured products to Hong Kong. In the import of staple food, China imports from such developed countries as the United States, Canada, and Australia. In general, the trade pattern of China reveals that it runs a huge trade deficit from trading with developed countries which it makes up by trading with developing countries.

CHINA–EC TRADE: COMMODITY PATTERN

As we can expect and as discussed above, China's major imports from the EC are semi-manufactured goods, processed raw materials, and machinery and equipment. Table 13.5 gives China's imports from the EC in the major commodities at the 1-digit level, *viz.* group 5: chemicals and related products, group 6: manufactured goods classified by materials, and group 7: machinery and transport equipment. Selected commodities at the 2-digit level are also shown to give a better idea of the commodity pattern of China-EC trade. Table 13.5 gives two percentage figures for each commodity imported in a particular year. The first percentage figure shows the relative share of that commodity in China's total imports from the EC; the second percentage figure shows the relative share in China's total imports of that commodity from the EC and other sources.

First of all, we notice that the commodity concentration of China's imports from the EC is very high. In 1985, about 90 per cent of China's imports from the EC belonged to the above-named three groups of commodities, groups 5, 6, and 7 of the Standard International Trade Classification. This is in fact true of China's imports from all sources, and the degree of concentration increased over time. The commodity concentration indexes for China's total imports at the 1-digit level are:

	Index
1981	42.6
1982	41.0
1983	42.8
1984	43.7
1985	49.7

A similar trend can also be detected in the case of China's import from the EC.

Table 13.5 China's imports from EC by commodity, 1982–86

Value in million RMB

Commodity	5			51			58			56			6		
Year	*V*	*(1)*	*(2)*	*V*	*(1)*	*(2)*	*V*	*(1)*	*(2)*	*V*	*(1)*	*(2)*	*V*	*(1)*	*(2)*
1982	1106	24.1	20.3	413	9.0	40.2	265	5.8	21.1	262	5.7	11.3	734	16.0	10.1
1983	1348	22.0	21.4	350	5.7	36.0	381	6.2	31.5	258	4.2	9.4	1811	29.6	14.6
1984	2035	30.1	21.4	490	7.2	35.7	757	11.2	29.3	324	4.8	8.6	1415	21.0	8.6
1985	2558	16.5	19.5	760	4.9	37.1	770	5.0	18.1	396	2.6	9.1	3737	24.1	10.6
1986*	1155	11.2	20.2	483	4.7	37.8	347	3.4	15.6	35	0.3	0.6	1822	17.7	11.1

Value in million RMB

Commodity	67			7			72			78 + 79			74		
Year	*V*	*(1)*	*(2)*	*V*	*(1)*	*(2)*	*V*	*(1)*	*(2)*	*V*	*(1)*	*(2)*	*V*	*(1)*	*(2)*
1982	528	11.5	15.9	1687	36.8	28.4	1091	23.8	36.0	410	8.9	64.6	104	2.3	9.5
1983	1543	25.2	22.1	1860	30.4	23.6	781	12.8	28.7	767	12.5	61.7	145	2.4	5.6
1984	1100	16.3	11.3	2243	33.2	13.3	1321	19.5	27.6	420	6.2	43.2	142	2.1	3.2
1985	2926	18.9	13.9	7711	50.0	15.7	4476	28.9	28.9	1692	10.9	54.6	374	2.4	2.7
1986*	1457	14.1	14.7	6407	62.2	24.9	4164	40.4	37.2	786	7.6	39.6	417	4.0	6.5

Sources: General Administration of Customs, PRC, *China's Customs Statistics*, various issues.

* first half of 1986 (January to June).
V value.
(1) as percentage of China's import from EC.
(2) as percentage of China's total import of that commodity.
For description of commodity codes, see Appendix.

Nonetheless over some time there have been some changes in the relative importance of China's imports from the EC. In general, the relative importance of chemicals and related products has declined, notably in organic chemicals, artificial fertilizers, and artificial resins and plastic materials and esters. The reason is that some of these products are increasingly produced by domestic firms and joint-venture firms and China has been able to find alternative sources at lower costs. For example, in the case of artificial resins and plastic materials, and esters, Singapore has increasingly become an important source of supply. Iron and steel are important imports of China from the EC and the relative importance of these imports has not been changed. Machinery and transport equipment are by far China's major imports from the EC, accounting for over 60 per cent of China's total imports from the EC and about 25 per cent of China's total import of machinery and transport equipment in the first half of 1986. The trend is clearly that over the past few years, China has been dependent on the EC for the supply of industrial machinery, both specialized and general machinery and equipment for industries. On the other hand, there is the indication that China has become less dependent on the EC for the import of road vehicles and other transport equipment.

When examining the commodity trade between China and individual EC countries, we note that West Germany is by far the major supplier in all major commodities. It is however of interest to note that Italy has very recently been rising rapidly in supplying industrial machinery to China.

With regard to China's exports to the EC, the commodities are highly concentrated in food and crude materials, and textiles (including clothing). In 1985, almost 30 per cent of China's exports to the EC was textiles. Food and raw materials accounted for another 36 per cent of China's exports to the EC in 1985. China's total amount of exports to the world is quite commodity concentrated, but somewhat less so than its imports, and the degree of concentration has not been on the increase in the past few years. The commodity concentration indices for China's total exports at the 1-digit level are:

	Index
1981	40.5
1982	39.5
1983	39.7
1984	39.5
1985	40.2

Table 13.6 China's imports from EC by selected countries and commodities, 1982–86 (as percentage of China's total import from EC)

Commodity *Country*		*5*	*51*	*58*	*56*	*6*	*67*	*7*	*72*	*78+79*	*74*
France	1982	2.7	0.7	0.7	1.0	1.0	0.6	3.3	1.9	0.9	1.0
	1983	3.3	0.4	0.7	0.5	3.6	3.5	3.4	1.8	0.8	0.8
	1984	4.4	0.5	0.6	0.5	3.5	3.2	3.5	1.7	1.1	0.3
	1985	2.6	0.3	0.5	0.5	3.9	3.5	6.1	3.0	1.7	0.7
	1986*	1.2	0.6	0.4	N.*	1.9	1.6	7.2	3.1	2.9	0.5
West Germany	1982	11.1	5.5	1.7	1.6	6.5	5.2	20.1	15.2	3.1	0.3
	1983	8.9	3.5	2.1	1.3	12.9	11.1	15.6	6.4	6.9	0.5
	1984	12.9	3.8	4.1	2.3	12.8	11.2	15.5	8.9	2.6	0.9
	1985	7.3	3.1	2.0	0.6	12.2	10.6	25.5	15.0	5.7	1.1
	1986*	5.5	3.0	1.2	N.	10.6	9.4	34.0	23.3	3.1	1.9
United Kingdom	1982	2.1	0.9	0.6	0.3	5.2	3.9	4.3	2.9	1.3	0
	1983	2.5	0.5	0.6	0.3	8.7	7.6	3.8	1.4	1.7	N
	1984	2.8	1.2	0.6	0	1.9	0.4	6.2	3.2	1.9	0.3
	1985	1.4	0.4	0.7	N.	3.9	1.8	6.8	3.3	2.0	0.4
	1986*	1.5	0.4	0.7	0	2.4	1.1	7.2	4.5	0.8	0.4
Italy	1982	4.1	1.5	0.4	2.2	1.0	0.6	2.1	1.7	0.2	0.2
	1983	3.8	0.9	0.8	1.2	2.4	2.0	1.9	1.4	0.2	0.2
	1984	3.9	1.1	2.0	1.3	1.3	0.7	5.7	4.2	0.3	0.5
	1985	2.7	0.5	0.9	0.7	2.6	2.2	9.1	6.1	1.0	N.
	1986*	1.6	0.5	0.4	0.2	2.0	1.5	10.1	7.0	0.8	1.1

Source: General Administration of Customs, PRC, *China's Customs Statistics*, various issues.

N. insignificant.
* first half of 1986 (January to June).

Table 13.7 China's exports to the EC by commodity, 1982–86

Value in million RMB

Commodity	*0*			*2*			*26*			*5*			*55*		
Year	*V*	*(1)*	*(2)*	*V*	*(1)*	*(2)*	*V*	*(1)*	*(2)*	*V*	*(1)*	*(2)*	*V*	*(1)*	*(2)*
1982	377	12.3	7.0	727	23.6	23.7	488	15.9	4.4	430	14.0	19.4	133	4.3	75.5
1983	478	11.5	8.5	818	20.0	21.9	461	11.1	34.8	556	13.3	22.5	152	3.6	74.1
1984	547	12.9	7.6	944	22.2	17.7	491	11.6	24.1	634	14.9	20.9	215	5.1	82.4
1985	680	12.3	6.0	1287	23.4	16.3	685	12.4	20.2	873	15.8	21.6	261	4.7	80.0
1986*	1054	23.8	1.7	652	14.7	13.8	258	5.8	13.5	500	11.3	20.8	158	3.6	90.0

Value in million RMB

Commodity	*6*			*65*			*8*			*84*		
Year	*V*	*(1)*	*(2)*	*V*	*(1)*	*(2)*	*V*	*(1)*	*(2)*	*V*	*(1)*	*(2)*
1982	551	17.9	6.9	467	15.2	10.1	610	19.8	8.9	350	11.4	9.7
1983	680	16.3	7.9	476	11.4	8.3	807	19.4	10.8	416	10.0	10.2
1984	844	20.0	7.5	624	14.7	7.6	1011	23.8	9.7	569	13.4	9.7
1985	1134	20.6	8.5	869	15.8	9.0	1283	23.4	12.4	705	12.8	11.5
1986*	631	14.2	8.0	456	10.3	7.8	787	17.8	12.1	437	9.9	11.3

Sources: General Administration of Customs, PRC, *China's Customs Statistics*, various issues.

* first half of 1986 (January to June).
V value.
(1) as percentage of China's export to EC.
(2) as percentage of China's total export of that commodity.
For description of commodity codes, see Appendix.

Table 13.8 China's exports to EC by selected countries and commodities, 1982–86 (as percentage of China's total export to EC)

Commodity *Country*		*0*	*2*	*26*	*5*	*55*	*6*	*65*	*8*	*84*
France	1982	2.0	1.5	1.3	1.7	0.5	3.8	2.2	3.8	1.5
	1983	1.6	1.3	0.9	1.5	0.2	2.5	1.5	3.3	1.5
	1984	2.0	1.6	1.0	1.5	0.3	3.3	2.2	3.7	1.8
	1985	2.1	1.5	0.8	1.3	0.2	3.2	2.3	3.8	1.9
	1986*	2.2	1.1	0.3	1.1	0.3	2.2	1.4	3.1	1.7
W. Germany	1982	5.7	12.5	7.0	6.7	2.0	5.9	4.8	9.4	6.3
	1983	5.4	9.7	5.2	7.3	2.4	5.4	3.7	8.4	5.5
	1984	5.6	9.1	3.6	8.1	3.0	6.4	4.5	10.9	7.7
	1985	5.0	8.3	3.4	8.4	3.6	6.8	5.0	9.8	6.3
	1986*	5.1	5.4	1.9	6.0	2.6	4.8	3.4	7.3	4.6
United Kingdom	1982	2.4	3.8	2.2	2.1	0.5	3.5	3.5	2.8	1.7
	1983	2.6	3.7	1.9	1.8	0.1	4.0	2.9	2.8	1.2
	1984	3.4	4.4	2.1	2.1	0.2	4.5	3.3	3.3	1.4
	1985	2.3	5.7	3.1	2.5	0.5	4.9	3.6	3.1	1.4
	1986*	2.1	3.4	1.4	1.8	0.3	2.8	1.8	2.4	0.9
Italy	1982	0.9	5.2	4.8	0.6	0.4	1.6	1.6	2.1	1.0
	1983	0.8	4.1	2.6	0.6	0.3	1.9	1.3	3.3	1.1
	1984	1.0	5.9	4.1	0.8	0.5	2.6	1.9	4.0	1.5
	1985	0.6	6.3	4.5	1.0	0.7	2.5	2.1	4.4	1.9
	1986*	1.4	3.5	2.0	0.5	0.3	2.2	1.9	3.5	1.8

Source: General Administration of Customs, PRC, *China's Customs Statistics*, various issues.

* first half of 1986 (January to June).

In terms of the direction of trade of China's exports to the EC, West Germany is China's largest market. But the UK has also been quite important. It is again of interest to note the rather significant increase in China's export of textiles (semi-manufactured goods and clothing) to Italy in the years 1984 to 1986.

FOREIGN DIRECT INVESTMENT BY THE EC IN CHINA

The major EC investors in China are again West Germany, France, the UK, and Italy. In this paper, foreign direct investment (FDI) undertaken by these EC countries in China will be discussed. Tables 13.9–11 summarise the salient features of the EC's FDI in China. Three features should be noted:

First, the EC's FDI in China was much more significant in the earlier period 1979–82 than the later period 1983–85. In the earlier period, the EC's FDI accounted for 41 per cent of all FDI in China, and France and Italy were the major investors. In the latter period, 1983–85, the EC's FDI only constituted 9.8 per cent of total FDI in China, and West Germany and the UK were the major investors.

Second, in terms of sectoral distribution, the EC's FDI concentrated on the exploitation and exploration of natural resources, particularly petroleum and energy plants, and only France and the UK have participated in these activities. At the same time, many EC countries have invested in China for manufacturing.

Third, in terms of the form of participation in production in China, the EC countries' participation exhibits a simple and clear-cut pattern. In energy plants and petroleum production, it is in the form of joint exploration. In manufacturing, it is in the form of equity joint-venture.

Fourth, the average size (in terms of capital investment) of the EC projects is much larger than that of all projects undertaken in China. The average size of EC projects in China is US$18.8 million while the average size of all projects in China is only US$1.4 million.

It is therefore interesting and significant to examine a little further these features of the EC's FDI in China. The reason for a large relative share of the EC in the total FDI in the earlier period 1979–82 is the signing of many of the existing oil exploration and energy projects during that period, mainly by France with China. The UK began to participate in the oil exploration projects in 1983 – this explains its relatively large FDI in China that year. But since 1983,

Table 13.9 Foreign Direct Investment (FDI) of EC in China by country, 1979–85

value in US$ million

Year	*1983*			*1984*			*1985*			*1983–85*			*1979–82*		
Country	*value*	*(1)*	*(2)*	*value*	*(1)*	*(2)*	*value*	*(1)*	*(2)*	*value*	*(1)*	*(2)*	*value*	*(1)*	*(2)*
France	31.0	8.3	1.6	2.4	1.7	N	50.0	34.0	2.6	81.3	12.3	1.2	149.1	47.3	19.4
W. Germany	0.6	0.2	N	105.2	74.5	3.7	20.2	13.5	1.0	126.0	19.2	1.9	36.4	11.4	4.7
Italy	35.6	9.6	1.9	10.1	7.1	0.4	24.4	16.5	1.2	70.1	10.6	1.0	67.4	21.3	8.8
Belgium	N	N	N	8.1	5.7	0.3	2.7	1.8	0.1	10.8	1.6	0.2	42.0	13.3	5.5
Netherlands	N	N	N	1.9	1.4	N	2.7	1.8	0.1	4.6	0.7	N	0.2	N	N
United Kingdom	304.8	82.0	15.9	12.6	8.9	0.4	44.2	29.7	2.3	361.6	54.9	5.4	16.6	5.4	2.2
Denmark	N	N	N	0.5	0.4	N	3.6	2.4	0.2	4.1	0.6	N	3.3	1.0	0.4
EC Total	372.0		19.4	140.8		4.9	147.8		7.6	658.5		9.8	315.0		41.0
China Total	1917.0			2875.0			1956.3			6748.1			769.0		

Source: *The Almanac of China's Foreign Economic Relations and Trade*, various issues.

(1) as percentage of EC's FDI in China.
(2) as percentage of total FDI in China.
N insignificant.

Table 13.10 Industrial distribution of EC's foreign direct investment in China by country, 1979–84 (in number of contracts)

Sector / *Country*	*Manufacturing Sector*	*Construction*	*Mining and Quarrying and Related Services*	*Transport, Storage and Communication*	*Financing, Insurance, Real Estate and Business Services*
France	2	0	11	0	2
W. Germany	3	1	0	0	0
United Kingdom	1	1	6	0	1
Italy	5	0	0	1	0
Denmark	2	0	0	0	0
Belgium	2	0	0	1	0
EC Number	15* (38.5)	2 (5.1)	17** (43.6)	2 (5.1)	3 (7.7)
US$million	152.2 (15.5)	1.5 (0.2)	774.7 (79.4)	40.0 (4.1)	10.2 (1.0)

Source: 1. External Services Department of *Economic Daily*, Beijing, *China Economic News*, various issues.
2. *The Almanac of China's Foreign Economic Relations and Trade*, various issues.

* These 15 manufacturing contracts engage in:
(1) wine manufacturing, (2) cosmetics manufacturing, (3) iron and steel manufacturing, (4) glass manufacturing, (5) the manufacturing of oil extraction equipment, (6) leather shoes manufacturing, (7) furniture manufacturing, (8) the production of automobiles, (9) textiles and garments manufacturing, (10) ceramic machinery manufacturing, and (11) the production of asbestos.

** These 17 contracts mainly engage in the exploration of off-shore oil together with the provision of offshore navigation and positioning services. The exploration site is mainly at the Beibu Gulf and Pearl River Mouth of South China Sea.

Table 13.11 Type and average size of EC's FDI in China by selected countries, 1979–84

	Types															*Average size*** *US$ m.*
	Equity JV			*Contractual JV*			*Joint Exploration*			*Fully Foreign owned*			*Total*			
	no.*	(1)	(2)	no.	(1)	(2)	no.	(1)	(2)	no.	(1)	(2)	no.	(1)	(2)	
France	5	19.2	0.5	0			10	76.9	32.3	0			15	38.5	0.5	12.2
W. Germany	4	15.4	0.4	0			0			0			4	10.3	N.	32.4
Italy	6	23.1	0.6	0			0			0			6	15.4	0.2	9.2
United Kingdom	6	23.1	0.6	0			3	23.1	9.7	0			9	23.1	0.3	34.8
Denmark	2	7.7	0.2	0			0			0			2	5.1	N.	2.2
Belgium	3	11.5	0.3	0			0			0			3	7.7	N.	15.9
EC	26		2.8	0			13			0			39		1.2	18.8
World	931			2212			31			74			3248			1.4

Sources: 1. External Services Department of Economic Daily, Beijing, *China Economic News*, various issues.
2. *The Almanac of China's Foreign Economic Relations and Trade*, various issues.

* number of contracts
** total amount of all five types of investment divided by the number of contracts.
(1) as percentage of EC's contracts with China.
(2) as percentage of total contracts with China.
N. Insignificant.

companies have become extremely cautious in investing further in oil exploration in China which takes place mainly in the South China Sea. This is because exploration beyond the sites already under exploration requires huge capital outlay and high risk. In fact exploration of the original sites was also very costly. Furthermore, from early 1985, oil prices have been falling rapidly and persistently. Thus, oil exploration in the South China Sea has become increasingly unprofitable. One company, the China Nanhai-Baker Drilling Corporation, a joint-venture company started by China and the United States, had to close down at the end of 1985 because of high operation costs and uncertainties about the potential oil reserves. Under these circumstances, there has been little new investment in oil exploration in China, which is so far the major investment activity of the EC in China.

It is of course not surprising that we find the EC heavily involved in China's oil exploration and energy industries because of the high level of technology and long experience EC countries have in these areas. Those firms investing in China are just exploiting their special ownership-specific advantages in China. But, there are also, at the same time, a wide range of manufacturing activities undertaken by EC countries in China. Generally speaking, the EC's FDI in China falls into two basic categories. First, there are the heavy manufacturing industries such as iron and steel, specialised machinery, and automobiles. Second, there are the light, labour-intensive manufacturing industries such as leather shoes, furniture, textile production and garment making. It is therefore evident that for the first category, that of heavy industries, the firms coming to China are doing so in order to exploit their ownership-specific advantages, and that for the second category – light industries, foreign investment is attracted by China's locational factors (such as raw material supply, low wages, and the domestic market of the host country).

Finally, we need to explain the preference of EC firms for equity joint-venture agreements in contrast to other forms of FDI in China. In oil exploration, firms have no choice but to go by the form specified by the Chinese government which is joint exploration. This is in any case the normal form of co-operation between a foreign firm which supplies the technology and capital and the host government which has sole ownership of the exploration site. But why do EC firms choose equity joint-venture in their investment in manufacturing in China? The major reason is probably the relative unfamiliarity with the economic environment in China *vis-à-vis* other investors from say Hong Kong, ASEAN, Japan or even the United States. Many investors prefer contractual joint-venture to equity joint-venture because the former is a much more flexible form of co-operation. But to take advantage of this flexibility, the investors must be very familiar with the business and economic conditions in China so that in the negotiation of contracts they are not being taken advantage of. Firms from the EC, knowing their relative unfamiliarity with China, would therefore choose the form of investment which involves a sharing of risks and profits explicitly on an equity basis. Further, the foreign investment law governing equity joint-venture offers the most detailed legal protection to the investors and the income tax law governing equity joint-ventures is more favourable to the investors than that applied to other forms of investment.

PROSPECTS

At present, the volume of trade between China and the EC is still relatively small and in fact has been generally on the decline since the opening up of China. It is only recently, in the first half of 1986, that we have begun to see some rather rapid increase in China-EC trade. With reference to the investment activities of EC countries in China, the focus has been over concentrated on oil exploration. With some setbacks (rising operation costs and falling oil prices), such activities have slowed down. Meanwhile, EC countries have not been making as much use of the increasing opportunities for investment offered by China in different sectors as have other countries such as Japan, the United States, Australia, and Hong Kong. Owing to European investors' relative unfamiliarity with the China situation, they have to play the game very cautiously and have missed many opportunities. For example, up to the present time, EC investors will only go for the equity joint-venture form of investment which is much less flexible than contractual joint-ventures and many other forms of production co-operation.

Despite all this, there is in fact a great deal of potential for the EC and China to escalate their existing level of economic contacts. Most importantly, China has in fact a preference to trade with and import technology from European countries. In his speech at the Belgian Royal Society of International Relations in 1984, Premier Zhao Ziyang said, 'there is no fundamental conflict of interest between China and Western Europe, nor are there any major obstacles against the further development of relations. In this rapidly changing world, peace and stability are our common interests. China's desire to strengthen its relations with Western European countries, and in particular to accord priority to the development of economic and technical cooperation, is not a short-term measure. Rather, it reflects the needs of the world and identifies where our common interests lie.'

It can be believed that in saying this Premier Zhao was not just being diplomatic, he really meant it. From the experience of the past few years, it was clear that China was not exactly happy with its economic relations with Japan. It was found that the Japanese flooded the Chinese market with sub-standard products, taking advantage of China's consumption fever in the 1982–85 period. It was reported that in many Japanese firms special sub-standard production lines were set up especially for the Chinese market. But, more importantly, China was not happy with Japan's reluctance to transfer technology in a form which is possible for the Chinese to assimilate and learn. Japan always prefers to sell only turn-key projects. And even in this case, in the Baoshan steel plant project, the Chinese were taken advantage of. An unsuitable and somewhat outdated technology was transferred to China. In financing China's development, Japan focusses on loans for specific purposes rather than foreign direct investment. The Japanese prefer not to share with the host country the risks of production and marketing.

Table 13.12 shows a breakdown of foreign capital in China by country and type (loan *vs*. equity). It can be seen that Japan's loans to China were more than three times the amount of Japan's FDI. The United States on the other hand has been making more FDI in China than granting loans and is much more prepared to transfer technology to China, especially after the relaxation of controls by COCOM over the export of technology to China. But the United States does not enjoy as good political relations with China as do the countries in Western Europe. The political relations between China and the United States have to remain precarious because of the Taiwan question and the balance of power that China has to maintain between the Soviet Union and the United States. In the case of Hong Kong, the amount of FDI has been huge, but it is largely confined to

Table 13.12 Sources of China's foreign capital, 1979–84
in US$ million

	Total	*Loan*	*Equity* (FDI)
Hong Kong, Macao	663 123	13 659	649 464
Japan	496 109	380 314	115 795
USA	125 810	23 311	102 499
Australia	15 340	6 223	9 117
UK	60 903	27 501	33 402
France	43 757	22 502	21 255
W Germany	41 399	27 218	14 181
Italy	22 669	11 371	11 298
Belgium	11 977	6 966	5 011

Source: *The Almanac of China's Foreign Economic Relations and Trade*, 1984, 1985.

the labour-intensive manufacturing sector or is invested in tourism and construction.

Besides the generally good political relations between China and the EC, China does recognise that Western European countries are generally more liberal about transferring technology to China, and that Western Europe is particularly advanced in many areas of production and technology which are essential to China's modernisation programmes.[2] It is recognised that Western Europe is particularly advanced in the fields of petroleum exploration, coal mining, aviation, telecommunications, iron and steel, automobiles, building materials, agriculture, chemicals and machine tools. Specifically, West Germany and France are world leaders in the field of nuclear powered energy; as are West Germany and Britain in the aviation industry; France and Britain in petroleum and telecommunications; Italy in ceramics, tanning and marble processing; Denmark in cement and diesel engines; Holland in farmland reclamation, harbour design and construction, and electrical appliances; Belgium in power generating telecommunication equipment; Spain in fruit and vegetable preservation; Portugal in softwood plantations and processing. Thus, the Chinese government does fully realise the importance of promoting economic ties with Western Europe in the course of China's modernisation.

Moreover, the current economic trend in China is towards further development in China-EC economic ties. The seventh Five-year Plan for 1986–90 places emphasis on reforms in the economic system, including price reforms, urban reforms, and major reforms in the financial sector. These reforms if successfully implemented will remove many of the bottlenecks in the current operation of the Chinese economy. It is expected that China will be able to fulfill its target growth rate of 7 per cent per annum towards the year 2000.[3] The priority development areas are energy, telecommunications, transport and industrial raw materials (iron and steel, building materials, petro-chemicals, *etc.*). Another important directive of the seventh 5-year Plan is to undertake massive technological transformation and rejuvenation of the existing large and medium enterprises. In all of these, EC countries are able to play an important part through trade, investment and technological co-operation. There are indeed vast opportunities for the EC to exploit in the future development of the Chinese economy.

So far the EC countries lack the Americans' tradition of aggressiveness and do not have as favourable a geographical position and therefore as much understanding of the China situation as the Japanese. It is therefore desirable for EC investors and traders to set up an information network and more representative offices in China to make themselves more familiar with the China market. They should try to be less conservative in choosing the form of investment and the sectors in which they operate. Moreover, EC investors and traders must have a better understanding of their competitors, especially the Japanese who almost invariably offer products, technology, or services at prices lower than the Europeans. But in actual fact, the Japanese deal might incur a higher cost in the end when other considerations such as after-sale services and personnel training are taken into consideration. The following example is a case in point. Both France and Japan bid for a contract for the supply of petrochemical equipment to China.[4] The Japanese won the contract by giving a quotation which was 25–30 per cent lower. However, a re-examination of the two offers showed that the French were actually offering favourable technical terms as provided by the preferential supply of parts and technicians' training; and the energy consumption of the French equipment was 50 per cent lower than the Japanese equipment, whilst production capacity was 30 per cent higher.

To sum up, the current economic trend in China favours Western Europe doing business with China. In fact, for some reason, the Chinese do have a priority of trading with and buying technology from Western Europe. The opportunities are there; it all depends on how traders and investors from Western Europe knock at China's door.

APPENDIX

Commodity codes

0 = food and live animals chiefly for food
2 = crude materials, inedible, except fuels
26 = textile fibres and their wastes
5 = chemicals and related products
51 = organic chemicals
55 = oils and perfume materials; toilet, polishing and cleaning preparations
56 = manufactured fertilisers
58 = artificial resins and plastic materials, and cellulose esters and esters
6 = manufactured goods classified chiefly by materials
65 = textile yarn, fabrics, made-up articles and related products
67 = iron and steel
7 = machinery and transport equipment
72 = machinery specialized for particular industries
74 = general industrial machinery and equipment, and machine parts
78 = road vehicles
79 = other transport equipment
8 = miscellaneous manufactured articles
84 = articles of apparel and clothing accessories

Notes

* The author is grateful to Ms Teresa Wang for her able research assistance.

1. For example, in the notorious case of raw silk exports, it was discovered that total exports licensed amounted to four times the annual raw silk production in China.
2. See Ling Xing, 'Western Europe is China's Treasured Partner,'' *Intertrade*, May/June 1985.
3. Chinese scientists and social scientists presented over 10 papers on the overall and sectoral projections of China towards the year 2000 at the Asia-Pacific Towards the Year 2000 Conference in Beijing in November 1986. Westerners can now have a rather clear picture of the economic and technological trends in China.
4. See D.A. Bourgery, 'France Ready to Pursue the China Market,' *Intertrade*, May/June 1985.

14 ASEAN Relations with the United States: Developments in the 1980s

Djisman S. Simandjuntak

THE OVERALL ENVIRONMENT

Approaching its 20th anniversary, ASEAN with its widely praised reputation as an oasis of political stability and as a growth centre within the troubled Third World is now facing serious challenges. Though there is no reason to worry about the political stability of the region in the near future, there are various developments within the region and its immediate surroundings that may accumulate in such a way as to undermine ASEAN's long-term stability.

Among domestic political issues, lack of institutionalised succession is likely to create tension, not only in the Philippines where President Aquino's efforts towards national reconciliation are apparently stumbling on resistance from different groups, but also in other countries such as Indonesia where discussion of political succession is somehow avoided and couched in terms of apparent support for President Suharto's re-election for another term. In the immediate environs, the Kampuchean conflict has not only persisted thereby inviting the Soviet Union and China into South-East Asia, it has also strained somewhat intra-ASEAN relations, especially those between Thailand and Indonesia. In the Pacific which prematurely has been projected as the ocean of the 21st century, various changes are in the offing some of which are likely to be unfavourable to ASEAN.

Gorbachev's speech in Vladivostok in July 1986 has clearly indicated the intention of the Soviet Union to develop the Asia-Pacific part of her vast territory as a new centre of industrial growth and the related need for securing Soviet interests in the Pacific, economically and otherwise. This may strengthen the position of those Americans who see the primary role of US Pacific policy as a containment of Soviet influence in the Pacific. Indeed, some American conservatives would like to see smaller Pacific countries including those of ASEAN sharing the US perception of the Soviet threat.[1] The reaction of ASEAN, however, is understandably less than enthusiastic. Having the Zone of Peace, Freedom and Neutrality (ZOPFAN) as a political-security design for South-East Asia which to some extent reflects the commitment of both Malaysia and Indonesia to non-alignment, ASEAN is likely to remain ambivalent towards US security initiatives in the Pacific.[2] Given this ambivalence and assuming a US Pacific policy which is centred on the containment of the Soviet influence, ASEAN is likely to become less interesting than China to the United States and, thereby, also to Japan.

One can easily extend the list of regional and global issues in which ASEAN is adhering to a position which differs from that of the United States. While some of these differences can produce unnecessary barriers to the expansion of economic exchanges between ASEAN and the United States, it is apparently in the area of economic exchanges that the two parties have the strongest convergence of interest. Exhausting any potential for mutually beneficial economic relations is not only a necessity because of the obvious limits to political-security co-operation, it is, according to ASEAN's understanding, an essential ingredient of political stability and security in the ASEAN region. This is not meant to give the impression that economic co-operation is necessarily easier to progress than political co-operation. In fact, the global economic environment is undergoing rapid changes some of which are likely to hamper rather than promote ASEAN-US economic interactions.

Unlike the 1970s which were characterised by a cry of resource scarcity and thereby presented the resource-exporting countries of ASEAN with a comfortable windfall, the 1980s started with a general decline of international commodity trade thanks to the successful adjustment in the major importing countries. The decline is not cyclical and it persists even when the growth performance in the United States, Japan and the EC has recovered. Shifted GDP structure in favour of less resource-intensive products, innovation of resource efficient methods of production and the introduction of substitutes including artificial materials have produced a combined effect of declining growth of consumption of a number of important raw materials relative to growth of production as can be seen from Table 14.1. This decoupling of production growth from that of resource consumption is among the most important changes occurring in the 1980s, and it is expected to intensify in the next decade.

Table 14.1 Annual growth rates of GDP and demand for selected raw materials

	World		*United States*		*Japan*	
	1975–80	*1980–84*	*1975–80*	*1980–84*	*1975–80*	*1980–84*
Growth Rates of GDP[1]	–	–	3.6	2.6	5.0	3.7
Growth of Resource Consumption:[2]						
Primary Aluminium	6.0	1.0	6.4	0.4	7.0	1.6
Refined Copper	0.8	1.1	5.9	2.2	7.0	4.3
Lead	2.5	0.1	–0.5	–0.1	8.5	–0.1
Nickel	4.2	1.0	1.5	0.3	7.9	3.9
Zinc	4.4	1.3	2.1	2.8	6.6	0.7
Tin	–	–	–4.8[3]		1.8	–0.7

Source: 1. *OECD Economic Outlook*.
2. From *Metallgesellschaft* as reproduced in *Pacific Regional Growth and Changing Industrial Structure: Effects on Minerals and Metals Production and Consumption*, A Report presented at the Mineral and Energy Forum of the Pacific Economic Co-operation Conference, held in Jakarta in 1986.
3. Average 1972–1982.

The decline of international commodity trade has already had severe impacts upon the ASEAN economies. First of all, the combined current account deficits of the ASEAN countries soared from a small 2271 million SDRs in 1980 to 15 251 million SDRs in 1983, though it went down to 7949 million SDRs in 1984, partly as a result of import suppression especially in Indonesia and the Philippines.[3]

Secondly, growth performance of the ASEAN economies exhibited a substantial decline in the first four years of the 1980s as compared to the last four years of the 1970s as can be seen from Table 14.2. Thirdly, as a combined result of weakening growth-performance that implies weakening incentive to import competing investment, declining international commodity trade that makes resource exploration less and less promising, and protectionism-related increase of intra-OECD direct investment, ASEAN is now suffering from declining attractiveness to foreign direct investment. Total foreign direct investment in ASEAN has in fact declined from 3292 million SDRs in 1982 to 2941 million SDRs in 1984 while foreign direct investment in the industrial countries increased from 22 582 million to 36 342 million SDRs in the same period. ASEAN's share

Table 14.2 Annual growth rates of GDP of the ASEAN countries in percentages

	1976–1980	*1980–1984*
Indonesia	8.2	4.8
Malaysia	7.9	6.4
Philippines	6.2	2.6[1]
Singapore	9.1	8.1
Thailand	7.3	5.6

Source: ESCAP, Social Statistics for Asia and the Pacific 1984.

in total foreign direct investment in all reporting countries has declined from 7.4 per cent in 1982 to 5.7 per cent in 1984 while that of the industrial countries increased from 51 per cent to 71 per cent.[4]

Thirdly, with earnings from commodity trade declining and at the same time debt services increasing, the remedy for current account deficit can only come from a forceful expansion of export of manufactured products. Yet, the major markets for these products appear to have been approaching saturation level, giving rise to a growing protectionism. In other words, the reliance of the ASEAN countries on 'cheap labour' as an ingredient of comparative advantage in trade in manufactured products is increasingly vulnerable. This is not to exclude the possibility of a continuous growth of export of manufactured products from the ASEAN countries to the industrial countries. What is at issue is that such a growth is likely to be followed by heightening tension.

It is possible to add other changes in the global environment that may further constrain the economic development of ASEAN in the years ahead. A marriage between Japan's mounting capital surplus and the Soviet resources in its Far Eastern territory, for instance, is conceivable. The above exposition, however, is sufficient to demonstrate how the ASEAN economies are likely to face serious difficulties in the near future. The rhetoric of interdependence notwithstanding, the first half of the 1980s has witnessed such dramatic changes that they led Peter Drucker to predict a decoupling of the developed economies from the developing ones.[5] Before it happens, however, efforts towards regaining interdependence need to be made. ASEAN countries have not exhausted their potential yet, and it is here that relations with the United States are becoming more and more important.

ASEAN INCREASED DEPENDENCE ON THE UNITED STATES

Trade is among the most important elements of the relations between ASEAN and the United States. Changes in its size, balance and composition have in fact somewhat strained these relations in recent years and forced the ASEAN countries to address issues which were hardly of relevance in the 1970s. One of these issues relates to the growing trade deficit of the United States *vis-à-vis* the ASEAN countries which is hardly surprising in view of the gigantic budget deficit of the United States which works like a Black Hole sucking in any floating object in its surroundings. While United States' exports to the ASEAN countries increased by only 10 per cent from 8.4 billion dollars in 1981 to 9.3 billion dollars in 1984, the combined imports of the United States from the ASEAN countries exhibited an increase of 17 per cent from 14.4 billion to 16.9 billion dollars in the same period, meaning an increase of US deficit by 27 per cent.[6]

ASEAN countries are likely, therefore, to be included in the target group of American criticism directed at the mounting trade deficit, in spite of the fact that ASEAN countries' share in total import of the United States is still very small and declining, namely from 5.3 per cent in 1981 to 5 per cent in 1984. Secondly, the first four years of the 1980s witnessed a growing importance of the United States as a major market for ASEAN countries' export, despite the cry of worsening protectionism. In this period, the United States' share in total exports of the ASEAN countries increased from 16.9 per cent in 1980 to 19.8 per cent in 1984, while those of Japan and the EC declined from 26.8 per cent to 24.4 per cent and from 13 per cent to 10.2 per cent respectively.[7]

If one confines one's attention to examining the OECD countries as major markets, the increased importance of the United States for ASEAN countries' export will be all the more apparent. While Japan's share in the OECD's total imports from ASEAN countries declined by a full 6 per cent between 1981 and 1984 and that of the EC – which is the biggest customs area in the world – experienced no change, the United States' share increased by nearly 4 per cent though it remains second after Japan. Following this increased share of the United States, the burden-sharing campaign is also likely to be targeted at imports from the ASEAN countries, though trade deficit *vis-à-vis* ASEAN was only about 6 per cent of the United States' total deficit in 1984.

Thirdly, United States' imports from the ASEAN countries have undergone significant changes in terms of their commodity composition. While the share of industrial raw materials (SITC 2, 3 and 4) and simple processed materials (SITC 6) declined from 60.5 per cent in 1981 to 42.4 per cent in 1984, the share of processed products (SITC 5,7 and 8) increased by more than 18 per cent to 48.9 per cent in 1984. This of course is somewhat defective in view of the differences that exist between the individual members of ASEAN. While machinery, transport and telecommunication equipment and miscellaneous manufactured products constituted nearly 85 per cent and 72 per cent of United States' imports from Singapore and Malaysia respectively, mineral fuels contributed about 74 per cent and 84 per cent of imports from Indonesia and Brunei respectively. Nevertheless, imports from Indonesia, too, have shifted slightly in favour of manufactured products, namely by 4 per cent between 1981 and 1984. In other words, United States imports from the ASEAN countries are no longer dominated by raw materials, unlike Japan's imports which consist almost exclusively of raw materials, namely 92.2 per cent in 1984. This changed composition of United States' imports from the ASEAN countries has various implications.

Facing a global environment as described earlier, the ASEAN countries have no choice but to force the growth of export of manufactured products. Yet, experiences in the first four years of the 1980s suggest that ASEAN's options are tightly limited as far as the export market is concerned. While an intensified effort to penetrate markets for manufactured products in Japan – the new trade giant, the EC, EFTA, the CMEA countries, or even the developing countries may lead to increased ASEAN exports, the experiences in the first four years of the 1980s show that these markets are no match for the United States' market.

Following their increased reliance on the export of manufactured products, the ASEAN countries are becoming more and more dependent on the United States' market. Accordingly, the United States' trade policy agenda is increasingly crucial to the future economic development of the ASEAN countries which in turn need to revise their policy agenda as regards trade with the United States. Yet, this revision is likely to turn out to be difficult. While the overall shift in composition of exports is strong enough in the case of Singapore, Malaysia and the Philippines to justify a concentration of attention on issues related to trade in manufactured products, it appears too weak to divert Indonesia's attention from issues related to commodity trade, however wasteful the long debates on commodity trade may have been in historical perspective. Reaching a consensus among the ASEAN countries tends, therefore, to be more difficult than in the early years after the signing of the Declaration of ASEAN Concord in 1976.

The discussion has so far been limited to trade in merchandise or the tangible part of the balance of payments. Yet, it is clearly insufficient to reflect the state of affairs between countries. The fact that ASEAN countries as a group enjoy a comfortable trade surplus with the United States does not exclude the possibility that the overall balance is in favour of the United States. While data are not available to prove whether the latter is true, it certainly is narrow-minded to design a trade policy on a basis which is confined to trade figures.

A considerable proportion of ASEAN's mounting current account deficit – the combined deficit soared from 2271 million SDRs in 1980 to 15 251 million dollars in 1983 before it halved to 7949 million SDRs in 1984 – is due to a large and chronic deficit in trade in services. Other Direct Investment Income and Other Investment Income alone on the debit side doubled from 6299 million SDRs in 1980 to 12 585 million SDRs in 1984. And the United States is among the major lenders to the ASEAN countries both directly and indirectly through multilateral agencies.[8] Similarly impressive is the United States' direct investment in ASEAN countries which, according to a US Trade Representative,[9] amounted to over 11 billion dollars in 1984. In other words, a considerable amount of investment income must have been paid by the ASEAN countries to the United States. Unfortunately, while abundant volumes of trade statistics are produced by national and international bureaux, statistics of trade in services with country disaggregation are not available. Nevertheless, it cannot be overemphasised that figures on trade in merchandise alone cannot serve as a good basis for the making of trade policy, the more so in today's world where services are gaining in importance over transborder economic exchanges. In fact, the United States' current account is much more favourable than its trade balance, though the current account deficit, too, has been soaring from 7.5 billion SDRs in 1982 to 99.4 billion SDRs in 1984.

Capital transactions constitute another important link between the ASEAN economies and the United States. It has been noted earlier that the United States is among the major sources of capital flowing to the ASEAN countries. Yet, there are indications of an unfavourable trend in this area of relations. First of all, President Reagan's strong preference for direct investment as the major element of development assistance policy is well-known. This perhaps is one of the reasons behind the declining trend of loans extended by the US government in recent years. Taking repayment of existing loans into account, United States' net loan has in fact declined from 4.4 billion SDRs in 1982 to 3.6 billion SDRs in 1984. Secondly, this decline in official credits is not compensated by an increase in US direct investment abroad. On the contrary, the latter declined from 13.3 billion SDRs in 1980 to a small 4.4 billion SDRs in 1984 while direct investment in the United States increased from nearly 13 billion SDRs in 1980 to nearly 22 billion SDRs in 1984. In other words, the United States has become a major competitor of the developing countries as far as direct investment is concerned. This is one of the major changes characterising the 1980s.

Thirdly, with overall economic performance weakening and prices of raw materials at a historical low, ASEAN countries' attractiveness to foreign investors may have suffered seriously. Though total inflow to ASEAN countries declined only slightly from 3280 million SDRs in 1983 to 2941 million SDRs in 1984, the share of the ASEAN countries in new foreign investment worldwide has declined from 7.4 per cent in 1982 to 5.7 per cent in 1984 with the rest of the decade likely to witness further deterioration.[10] Fourthly, United States' direct investment in ASEAN is concentrated in the resource sector. Of the total stock of 11.6 billion dollars investment in 1984, nearly 47 per cent is in the oil sector.[11] With prices of raw materials unlikely to rebound in the foreseeable future, new direct investment of the United States in the ASEAN countries may also have declined rapidly. Such a decline will have serious implications not only upon investment financing and foreign exchange constraints, but also upon the transfer of technology which so far has been highly dependent on the multinationals.

To summarise this section, the following changes in the pattern of economic relations between the United States and the ASEAN countries need to be restated. In the area of trade in merchandise there is a growing imbalance in favour of the ASEAN countries. The composition of United States' imports from the ASEAN countries has also undergone significant changes. Unfortunately, little is known about bilateral balances as regards trade in services, though it must be noted that the overall balance is perhaps not as unfavourable to the United States as the balance of trade in merchandise suggests. As regards capital account, the United States remains among the major sources of capital flow to the ASEAN countries. At the same time, however, it has become a serious competitor as far as foreign direct investment is concerned. All these changes are bound to have policy implications. The following section is devoted to the issues which have been dominating the trade talks between the ASEAN countries and the United States, especially in the first half of the1980s. An ASEAN-United States dialogue which fails to accommodate these changes is going to be less and less relevant.

UNITED STATES' GROWING DEMAND FOR AGGRESSIVE RECIPROCITY

No doubt, the 1980s are an extremely challenging period in the economic relations between the ASEAN countries and the United States. Both ASEAN and the United States are aware of the growing dependence of the ASEAN economies on access to the United States' market for manufactured products. While the individual ASEAN countries have launched intensified efforts to secure a fair share in the United States market, the agenda of the trade talks appears to have been dictated by the United States. Seeing the root of its mounting trade deficit in the alleged unfair trade practices of other countries, the United States has launched an aggressive fair trade campaign especially against Asia-Pacific countries, and as a bargaining chip reference is constantly made to the possibility of worsening protectionism in the United States should the Asia-Pacific countries fail to respond positively to the United States' demand for fair trade.[12] In fact, the Reagan Administration has initiated more than 40 actions against unfair foreign trading practices since January 1985 in addition to numerous investigations on subsidies and dumping.[13]

Not all the findings of President Reagan's 'Trade Strike Force' through its MOSS (Market-Oriented Sector Specific Talks) and MAFF (Market Access Fact-Finding Talks) are of immediate relevance to the ASEAN countries. This Strike Force's attention is still primarily targeted at Japan, South Korea, Taiwan, Hong Kong and Singapore. Nevertheless, given the changed composition of United States' imports from the ASEAN countries and the increased tendency of the United States to resort to selective trade measures that is more or less irrespective of overall balance, some issues are of particular importance to the ASEAN countries.

One of these issues relates to the eligibility of manufactured products of the ASEAN countries for the United States' Generalized System of Preferences (GSP). Though a linkage between GSP and the improved performance of ASEAN countries' products in the United States market is difficult to establish, both the ASEAN countries and the United States tend to see the existence of the GSP as one of the main ingredients of the success of ASEAN. Accordingly, the maintenance of the GSP is among the preoccupations of the ASEAN countries as regards their relations with the United States who in turn threatens to tighten its GSP should the ASEAN countries fail to comply with the United States' demand for more reciprocity.[14] The keyword in this regard is the graduation or the competitive-need provisions,[15] and the element of reciprocity sought by the United States is improved access to ASEAN markets.

The second group of issues relates to countervailing duties. The employment of this policy measure by the United States has increased in frequency in recent years. There were 21 cases in 1983, 14 cases in 1984 and nine cases in the first half of 1985 in which subsidy investigation initiated by the US government led to the imposition of countervailing duties. Yet, the probability is high for a subsidy investigation being initiated prematurely. The number of cases in which US investigation against subsidies proved groundless has increased from 27 in 1983, 36 in 1984 and 26 in the first half of 1985. As of August 31, 1985 as many as 70 subsidy investigations were in progress in the United States.[16] And it is in respect to this policy measure that the ASEAN countries have been put into the target group of US trade policy initiatives, together with the more advanced developing countries who suffer most.

Similarly discouraging from the exporters' viewpoint is the number of anti-dumping investigations initiated by the United States in recent years. Anti-dumping duties were imposed in 14 cases in 1983, 22 cases in 1984, and five cases in the first half of 1985, while negative findings numbered 46 in 1983, 68 in 1984 and 69 in the first half of 1985 and investigations in progress number 124 as of August 31, 1985.[17] The ASEAN countries, however, have rarely been involved in this investigation thanks to the composition of United States' imports from the ASEAN countries which is far from having been dependent on chemical and steel products on which the dumping investigations have been concentrated in recent years. Should the investigation, however, be extended to telecommunications equipment, the ASEAN countries, especially Singapore and Malaysia, can soon become as vulnerable as South Korea to anti-dumping measures.

There is another important aspect of subsidy and dumping investigations. They are highly vulnerable to blind protectionism since their initiation is based on a loosely defined concept of market disruption in respect to a specific commodity. Consider for instance the case of Indonesia whose total export of manufactured products (SITC 5, 7 and 8) to the United States was as small as 326 million dollars in 1984 or less than 0.2 per cent of the total import of the United States in this category of trade. However, as the import of apparels and accessories from Indonesia to the United States increased 'very rapidly' from a negligible 42 million dollars in 1981 to 206 million dollars in 1984 – this implies an annual growth rate of 70 per cent in the space of three years – Indonesia becomes vulnerable to countervailing measures. Furthermore, the fact that most dumping and subsidy investigations have come to negative findings does not reflect generosity on the part of the investigating country. On the contrary, initiation of an investigation can easily lead to the acceptance of voluntary export restraints, orderly marketing arrangements, minimum valuation and similar measures in the grey area of trade policy lest the investigation leads to unilateral actions that may turn out to be more severe than the actions agreed upon on a 'voluntary' basis.

Issues related to the protection of intellectual property are among the important elements of the United States campaign for aggressive reciprocity. The Annual Report on National Trade Estimates 1985 has already listed some areas in which lack of or insufficient patent protection and infringement of both copyrights and trademarks in each of the ASEAN countries were supposed to pose serious problems to some industries in the United States, though it appears impossible to quantify the effect in monetary terms. Again, to facilitate compliance by the ASEAN countries, the United States came up with the idea of linking the availability of its GSP with the response of the ASEAN countries to the United States demand for more protection for intellectual property.

For the sake of completeness, it is important to recall here that the United States campaign for reciprocity includes better treatment of American companies in the service industries, especially in insurance and banking. Furthermore, there is growing criticism of investment policy or specific elements thereof such as Malaysia's localisation programme as part of its New Economic Policy, lack of national treatment on land ownership and widespread graft in the case of Indonesia, prohibition of land ownership and rigorous joint venture requirements in the case of the Philippines, and a severe restriction of access to Thailand's banking industry.

The above description demonstrates how extensive the issue-coverage of the United States' package of demands for reciprocity is. No doubt, there are areas of these issues in which the ASEAN countries' compliance would not only lead to a more secure access to the US market, but also to improved competitiveness of ASEAN countries' products inside and outside the region. However, there are areas in which the United States' demand touches upon policies which are primarily social and political in nature such as Malaysia's New Economic Policy or Indonesia's policy requiring local equity participation in any foreign company. While a continuous deterioration of economic performance may force the respective governments to relax these 'performance criteria', it is more than questionable whether or not the ASEAN governments are willing to compromise some of their politically favoured policy instruments for the sake of access to the US market.

RESHAPING THE ASEAN-US DIALOGUE

Facing the trade offensive by the United States, the ASEAN countries can seek to protect their interests through various forms of consultations and negotiations. There is the new round of multilateral trade negotiations under the auspices of GATT which is expected to address both the pending issues which are of prime relevance to the ASEAN countries and the new issues which preoccupy the United States. Bilateral consultations and negotiations can also be pursued without necessarily undermining existing multilateral efforts. Furthermore, there are various fora within the Pacific in which consultations between the ASEAN countries and the United States can be promoted. Finally, there is the ASEAN-US dialogue which is open to improvement of various sorts. All these fora can complement each other in seeking the long-awaited restoration of the international trading environment. Nevertheless, the attention of this paper will be concentrated on the ASEAN-US dialogue which is basically as old as ASEAN's economic co-operation and has so far been held several times.

Like any other ASEAN external dialogue, the ASEAN-US dialogue has so far largely been shaped as a North-South dialogue with limited country coverage. This is hardly surprising in view of the international environment that prevailed at the time the dialogue was proposed. An ASEAN-US dialogue which indicates a departure by

ASEAN from the position of the Group of 77 was perhaps unthinkable in the mid 1970s when the unity of the Group of 77 was thought to be the sole powerful leverage of the developing world on dealing with the developed world. As a result, the similarity of the agenda of the ASEAN-US dialogue to that of UNCTAD is unsurprising. It includes the Integrated Programme for Commodities (IPC) and the related Common Fund, STABEX, the GSP, direct investment and the transfer of technology.[18]

As can be seen, the agenda is hardly of relevance to the United States which basically has never had much sympathy for the demand by the developing countries for revolutionary and dirigistic changes in the international economic order. From the outset of the dialogue, ASEAN has positioned itself as a recipient and their dialogue partners as a group of donors. And it is this recipient-donor relationship which perhaps prevents ASEAN from extending the dialogue coverage to countries such as South Korea which in terms of economic interactions with the ASEAN countries is more important by far to ASEAN than New Zealand apparently is.

The adoption by the United States of the dialogue agenda is perhaps politically rather than economically motivated. As a result, the performance of the dialogue has so far turned out to be meagre. In all of the substantial issues ASEAN has hardly got what it wants.[19] The main contribution of the dialogue lies in the inflow of technical assistance in favour of ASEAN and an improved image of ASEAN as a regional grouping.[20] The latter, however, can turn out to have a boomerang effect should the inability of the dialogue to address substantial issues including newly emerging issues as described in earlier sections persist.

It follows from the above that the ASEAN-US dialogue is in need of reshaping in order that it does not sink into oblivion. First of all, the dialogue needs to be converted from a 'recipient-donor' dialogue into a 'full' dialogue which is sensitive to the interests of the parties involved. Otherwise, ASEAN will find it more and more difficult to keep United States' enthusiasm in participating in the dialogue. Secondly, the agenda needs to be revised in such a way as to reflect the rapid changes in economic relations in the first half of the 1980s and, if possible, perspective changes in the years to come. ASEAN should finally learn the lesson that its interest is hardly convergent with that of the United States as regards commodity trade price stabilisation and many other elements of the UNCTAD agenda. This is an argument for the concentration of the dialogue on issues of mutual interest, especially issues relating to trade in manufactured products, US investment in ASEAN and the related issues of technology transfer.

This is not to underestimate the importance of tariff escalation which certainly deserves to be put as priority issue. Thirdly, ASEAN should seriously consider the way in which it can reciprocate by putting into question the protection against imports in its individual member countries. It was the generous inflow of export earnings from commodity trade, of borrowed money and of foreign direct investment that in the past helped the ASEAN countries to absorb the costs of this protection. This generous inflow, however, will no longer be there whilst investment services continue to increase. Finally, ASEAN's success or failure in dealing with its dialogue countries is crucially dependent on the seriousness with which ASEAN chooses to foster intra-ASEAN economic co-operation which in turn is unlikely to flourish unless ASEAN can agree on the integration of the small national markets into a significantly greater regional market. The emergence of an integrated regional market appears to be the strongest leverage which ASEAN has in dealing with the United States, Japan and the EC which in their turn seem to have found ASEAN less and less interesting in the making of the Asia-Pacific century.

Notes

1. See for instance Admiral William J. Crowe, Jr., 'The Security Underpinnings of US-Asia Trade', a speech delivered at the conference on the next decade in US-Asia Trade', held in Washington, D.C., on February 19–20, 1986, organised by the US-Asia Institute. See also Martin L. Lasater, 'Soviet Objectives in ASEAN Countries and Regional Political Stability', a paper presented at the Conference on US-ASEAN Relations: Prospects for the 1990s, held in Kuala Lumpur on 31 March–2 April, 1986, organised jointly by the Institute of Strategic and International Studies (ISIS) Malaysia, and the Centre for Strategic and International Studies (CSIS), Georgetown University, Washington, D.C.
2. On this ambivalence and the underlying reasons see Hans H. Indorf, 'Undercurrents of Change in US-ASEAN Relations', in K.S. Nathan and M. Pathmanathan, *Trilateralism in Asia. Problems and Prospects in US-Japan-ASEAN Relations*, pp. 1–29, Kuala Lumpur: Antara Book Company, 1986.

3. International Monetary Fund, *Balance of Payments Statistics Yearbook 1984*, Part I, Washington, D.C.
4. Ibid., Part III.
5. If so, the projection of the 21st century as the century of the Pacific is indeed premature. On the nature of the decoupling see Peter F. Drucker, 'The Changed World Economy', in *Foreign Affairs*, Spring 1986. For a parallel scenario see Richard L. Drobnick, 'The United States as World's Largest Debtor: Implications for the International Trade Environment,' in *The Global Economy. Today, Tomorrow, and the Transition*, pp. 175–90, Bethesda 1985: World Future Society.
6. OECD, *External Trade Statistics*, Series C, Paris.
7. International Monetary Fund, *Direction of Trade, Yearbook 1985*.
8. Recent data on ASEAN countries' debt to the United States are not available, unfortunately. Otherwise, it would have been possible to estimate the amount of interest paid to the United States.
9. United States Trade Representative, *Annual Report on National Trade Estimates 1985*. This report includes estimates of US direct investment in each of the countries being investigated.
10. Direct investment in the ASEAN countries exhibits a very high degree of country concentration. Of the total inflow between 1980–1984 more than 49 per cent went to Singapore and another 35 per cent to Malaysia, leaving only 16 per cent to be distributed between Indonesia, the Philippines and Thailand.
11. United States Trade Representative, op. cit.
12. This diagnosis is defective in many ways. Some observers in the United States tend to disagree with the mainstream argument according to which the deteriorating current account deficit is the result of unfair trade practices of other countries. See for instance C. Michael Aho and Jonathan David Aronson, *Trade Talks: America Better Listen!*, New York 1985: Council on Foreign Relations.
13. Congressional Statement by US Secretary of Commerce Malcolm Baldrige on September 9, 1986. This statement provides an outline of the way in which the United States is likely to pursue its fair trade campaign in the years to come.
14. The review of the GSP is the most frequently mentioned step to be taken by the United States against the ASEAN countries which discriminate against US products in ASEAN markets. See US Trade Representative, op. cit.
15. On the new GSP of the United States see US Trade Representative, *Annual Report of the President of the United States on Trade Agreements Program 1984–1985*, Twenty-Eight Issue, Transmitted to Congress February 1986, pp. 155–7.
16. Ibid., pp. 191–7.
17. Ibid., pp. 181–9.
18. In addition to the issues listed above the United States would also like to see the inclusion of issues related to trade in high-technology products in its trade talks with other countries. On this see for instance Geza Feketekuty and Lawrence B. Krause, 'Service and High Technology

Goods in the New GATT Round', a paper presented at the First Pacific Trade Policy Forum, convened by the Pacific Economic Co-operation Conference, March 20–22, 1986.

19. Various studies have come to similar conclusions. An excellent assessment can be found in M. Hadi Soesastro, 'Future ASEAN-US Economic Relations: Perspectives on Strategic Planning', in *ASEAN External Economic Relations*, Proceedings of the Fifth Conference of the Federation of ASEAN Economic Associations, pp. 33–76 Singapore, October 30–November 1, 1980: Chopmen Publishers 1982. See also by the same author, 'ASEAN-US Economic Relations: An Update', in *The Indonesian Quarterly*, vol. XIII, Jakarta, 1985, pp. 376–91: CSIS. Further see Chia Siow Yue, 'Development and Issues in US-ASEAN Economic Relations', in Karl D. Jackson and Hadi Soesastro (eds), *ASEAN Security and Economic Development*, pp. 117–140, Berkeley, California 1984: Institute of East Asian Studies.
20. As of 1985 the ASEAN-US dialogue has resulted in 22 co-operation projects in various areas, of which some have entered the stage of implementation involving funds amounted to about 33 million dollars. See *Annual Report of the ASEAN Standing Committee 1984–1985*, Jakarta: ASEAN Secretariat.

Appendix I Percentage shares of Japan, the United States and the EC in OECD's imports from ASEAN

		OECD's Imports from ASEAN (000 $)		*Japan's share*		*US share*		*EC's share*	
		1981	*1984*	*1981*	*1984*	*1981*	*1984*	*1981*	*1984*
All Commodities		45 939 915	47 909 183	51.9	45.9	31.3	35.2	16.5	16.5
SITC	0	4 369 039	4 556 366	27.6	28.5	23.8	25.3	41.7	37.1
	1	214 608	179 082	10.1	7.9	21.8	24.6	45.9	45.7
	2	6 706 499	6 021 482	54.8	60.1	14.8	16.5	22.4	22.7
	3	22 025 365	19 085 210	78.9	81.6	28.9	24.5	1.2	0.5
	4	1 227 134	1 604 715	9.8	11.8	28.0	32.2	50.9	44.8
	5	305 346	592 505	63.1	35.8	12.6	11.7	14.3	41.3
	6	3 071 127	3 233 254	22.0	29.0	32.7	29.6	35.5	30.2
	7	5 007 674	8 733 434	6.1	4.4	64.9	70.5	22.3	20.7
	8	2 638 861	3 432 587	5.0	3.7	43.0	59.0	37.1	25.5

Note: SITC stands for Standard International Trade Classification.
Source: OECD, *Statistics of Foreign Trade*, Paris, various volumes.

Appendix II Commodity composition of ASEAN countries' export to the United States (in percentage)

		Brunei		*Indonesia*		*Malaysia*		*Philippines*		*Singapore*		*Thailand*		*ASEAN*	
		1981	*1984*	*1981*	*1984*	*1981*	*1984*	*1981*	*1984*	*1981*	*1984*	*1981*	*1984*	*1981*	*1984*
All Commodities		100	100	100	100	100	100	100	100	100	100	100	100	100	100
SITC	0	0	0	4.2	5.1	1.7	2.0	20.1	15.7	2.2	1.5	24.2	22.7	7.2	6.8
	1	0	0	0.2	0.2	0	0	0.7	0.3	0	0	2.0	1.5	0.3	0.3
	2	0	0	7.0	9.6	11.0	8.4	5.8	2.2	2.7	1.1	11.0	6.8	6.9	5.9
	3	99.9	82.5	84.4	73.9	20.2	2.1	0.8	0.6	6.0	5.7	0	1.1	44.2	27.7
	4	0	0	0	0.2	4.5	7.3	11.1	11.1	0	0.1	0	0.2	2.4	3.1
	5	0	0	0.2	0.3	0.1	0.3	0.2	0.4	0.2	0.4	1.3	1.1	0.3	0.4
	6	0	0	2.4	5.2	10.7	5.7	10.3	4.2	2.7	1.5	32.3	22.3	7.0	5.7
	7	0	2.3	0.8	1.7	46.1	64.7	24.5	36.7	68.0	73.0	13.2	18.4	22.6	36.5
	8	0	0.1	0.7	3.6	3.8	7.5	25.5	27.5	14.0	12.8	14.4	24.9	7.9	12.0
	9	0	15.1	0.1	0.3	1.7	1.9	1.0	1.2	4.0	3.8	1.6	1.1	1.2	1.6

Source: See Appendix I

Appendix III ASEAN countries shares in import of the United States from world (in percentage)

		Brunei		*Indonesia*		*Malaysia*		*Philippines*		*Singapore*		*Thailand*		*ASEAN*	
		1981	*1984*	*1981*	*1984*	*1981*	*1984*	*1981*	*1984*	*1981*	*1984*	*1981*	*1984*	*1981*	*1984*
All Commodities		0.1	0	2.4	1.7	0.8	0.8	0.8	0.8	0.8	1.2	0.4	0.4	5.3	5.0
SITC	0	0	0	1.6	1.5	0.2	0.3	2.6	2.1	0.3	0.3	1.5	1.7	6.3	5.9
	1	0	0	0.3	0.3	0	0	0.4	0.2	0	0	0.6	0.5	1.4	1.1
	2	0	0	3.7	4.6	2.0	2.0	1.0	0.5	0.5	0.4	0.9	0.8	8.1	8.2
	3	0.4	0	6.4	6.9	0.5	0.1	0	0	0.2	0.4	0	0	7.5	5.4
	4	0	0	0.2	1.3	19.5	27.7	45.5	39.0	0	0.8	0	0.4	65.3	69.3
	5	0	0	0.1	0.1	0	0.1	0	0.1	0	0.1	0.1	0.1	0.4	0.5
	6	0	0	0.4	0.6	0.6	0.3	0.6	0.2	0.2	0.1	0.8	0.6	2.5	1.9
	7	0	0	0.1	0.1	1.4	1.5	0.7	0.8	2.1	2.4	0.2	0.2	4.5	5.0
	8	0	0	0.2	0.5	0.3	0.5	2.0	1.6	1.1	1.2	0.5	0.8	4.1	4.5
	9	0	0	0.1	0.2	0.8	0.8	0.4	0.5	1.8	2.3	0.3	0.2	3.4	4.0

Source: See Appendix I

Appendix IV Shares of individual commodities in total import from ASEAN (in percentage)

	Japan		*United States*		*EC*	
	1981	*1984*	*1981*	*1984*	*1981*	*1984*
All Commodities	100	100	100	100	100	100
SITC 0	5.1	5.9	7.2	6.8	24.0	21.3
1	0.1	0.1	0.3	0.3	1.3	1.0
2	15.4	16.4	6.9	5.9	19.9	17.3
3	72.8	70.7	44.2	27.7	3.4	1.2
4	0.5	0.9	2.4	3.1	8.2	9.1
5	0.8	1.0	0.3	0.4	0.6	3.1
6	2.8	4.2	7.0	5.7	14.4	12.3
7	1.3	1.8	22.6	36.5	14.7	22.8
8	0.5	0.6	7.8	12.0	12.9	11.1
2 + 3 + 4 + 6	91.5	92.2	60.5	42.4	45.9	39.9
5 + 7 + 8	2.6	3.4	30.7	48.9	28.2	37.0

Source: See Appendix I

15 EC-ASEAN Interaction and Collaboration in a Multilateral Framework: The Economic Aspects

Mohamed Ariff

1 INTRODUCTION

Inter-regional economic relations between ASEAN and the EC have been fairly cordial thanks to both historical factors and the current pattern of inter-regional division of labour. Historically, some of the countries in the ASEAN grouping were colonies of countries which now belong to the EC. Post-colonial relationships have been carried forward in one form or another into the new geopolitical matrices. Economically, ASEAN and the EC have factor endowments which are different enough to permit a meaningful commercial relationship that is mutually profitable.

ASEAN countries have a comparative advantage in a number of primary commodities and labour intensive goods for which there is a sizeable market in the EC, while EC countries likewise have a comparative advantage in capital intensive and technology intensive products for which there is demand in the ASEAN region. Trade in goods and services and movement of capital have emerged to take advantage of the opportunities created by factor endowments, although policy distortions have tended to limit their scope. A more plausible explanation for the cordial relations between ASEAN and the EC is perhaps that the EC views ASEAN as a new generation of countries following the EC footsteps in the direction of regional integration. ASEAN as a 'newcomer' could benefit from the EC experience, while the EC itself has taken a sympathetic attitude towards the new South-East Asian experiment. Perhaps the most forthright explanation for the close EC-ASEAN relationship is that a healthy ASEAN is in the interests of the EC which would like to see ASEAN as a source of stability in turbulent South-East Asia, a region of considerable economic and strategic importance to the EC member countries.

While historical heritages, current realities and political imperatives can explain why a fairly cordial bilateral relationship does exist between the EC and ASEAN, the fact remains that there has been hardly any interaction or collaboration between these two regional groups on matters of multilateral or global dimensions. This represents an area which has not been researched. The present paper therefore represents a pioneering attempt and, as such, it can only scratch the surface. There is no evidence of any collaboration between the EC and ASEAN pertaining to multilateral issues of global concern. This paper attempts to explain why this has been the case and to examine the future prospects for such inter-regional collaboration.

2 PROFILE

The EC is ASEAN's third major trading partner after Japan and the United States. The EC accounts for about 14 per cent of total ASEAN exports and imports. However, EC-ASEAN trade relations have always been asymmetrical, with ASEAN accounting for no more than 2.5 per cent of the EC's total exports and imports. Evidently, ASEAN is not as important to the EC as the EC is to ASEAN in broad economic terms. Nonetheless, in terms of specific primary commodities, ASEAN figures prominently in EC imports. For the EC relies heavily on ASEAN for such items as natural rubber, timber, palm oil, tapioca and tin.

The lopsided EC-ASEAN trade relations are reflected in the composition of the two-way trade flows. For one thing, the ASEAN exports to the EC consist mostly of primary products with a high degree of concentration in a narrow range of products, while the EC exports a wide range of manufactured goods to ASEAN. For another, there has been very little intra-industry trade between the two regional groups. Nevertheless, ASEAN countries more often than not have registered trade surpluses with the EC, although the trade balance has turned increasingly in favour of the EC in recent years.

There are also important inter-country variations in the EC-ASEAN trade flows. Brunei, Indonesia, Malaysia and Thailand import more from the EC than from the United States, whereas the

Philippines and Singapore import less from the EC than from the United States. Japan, of course, invariably ranks number one as a source of imports. On the export side, Malaysia and Thailand sell more to the EC than to the US, while in the case of other ASEAN countries the reverse is the case. Japan is the most important export market for all ASEAN countries except for the Philippines and Singapore. However, the EC is far more important as a market for ASEAN manufactures than Japan, a market which ASEAN countries have found it extremely difficult to penetrate.

As in the case of ASEAN, there are significant inter-country variations within the EC in terms of its trade with ASEAN. West Germany, the United Kingdom and the Netherlands account for nearly three-quarters of the EC's trade with ASEAN. ASEAN's trade links with other EC countries are weak. The absence of any strong trade link with France is indeed conspicuous, considering that country's prominent profile within the EC.

The EC represents the third largest investor in ASEAN, accounting for about 12 per cent of the total foreign investment in the ASEAN region, after the US (28 per cent) and Japan (16 per cent). But, then, there are again interesting inter-country variations. EC investment in ASEAN ranges from a low of less than one-tenth of the total in Indonesia to a high of nearly one-third of the total in Singapore. It is of interest to note that the United Kingdom, the Netherlands and West Germany account for nearly 90 per cent of the total EC investment in ASEAN. Britain has by far the largest EC investment stake in ASEAN, with a total of US$2.03 billion, followed by the Netherlands with US$690 million and West Germany with US$329 million. Much of the EC investment in ASEAN has gone into the petroleum sector and other primary industries, while the manufacturing sector has become increasingly important as a recipient of EC investment in recent years.

The EC is one of the important dialogue partners of ASEAN. ASEAN's external relations with third countries have been guided by bilateral dialogues that ASEAN has been engaging in actively with Japan, the US, the EC, Canada, Australia and New Zealand. This is in line with ASEAN's Declaration of Concord which called for, among other things, 'common approaches and action in dealing with regional groupings and individual economic powers.' The formation of the Joint Study Group (JSG) in 1975 marked the beginning of fruitful discussion that led to meaningful co-operation in the spheres of agriculture, industry and social development.[1] In addition, several

ASEAN-EC Conferences have been held in Brussels (1976), Jakarta (1979) and Kuala Lumpur (1983) to foster closer industrial and commercial co-operation between the two regions. These conferences have brought together bankers, businessmen and government officials of the EC and ASEAN. Other EC-ASEAN co-operative activities include exchanges of fact-finding visits between ASEAN and EC businessmen. The first ever Ministerial Meeting on economic matters between ministers from ASEAN and EC countries took place in Bangkok in October 1985.

The most significant development in EC-ASEAN relations was the signing of the Co-operation Agreement on 7 March 1980. The Agreement, which marked a milestone in EC-ASEAN relations, extended, *inter alia*, Most-Favoured-Nation (MFN) treatment to the contracting parties in their commercial dealings. The Agreement also promised extension and diversification of inter-regional commercial exchanges to the highest possible level, taking into account each other's interests and needs, and to promote closer economic links through mutually beneficial investment and through co-operation in scientific and technological fields. To accelerate the pace of economic development in the ASEAN region, the Agreement paved the way for EC assistance in undertaking projects in food production and supplies, rural development, education and training. A Joint Co-operation Committee (JCC) was also established to replace the Joint Study Group (JSG) and to facilitate the implementation of various programmes in conformity with the Agreement.

Much of the discussion at both the JSG and JSC levels has centered on the question of market access to the EC market in general and the Generalised System of Preferences (GSP) in particular. ASEAN exports encounter protectionist barriers in the EC. The EC tariff rates tend to escalate with the degree of processing. For example, MFN duty on palm oil ranges from 4 to 15 per cent while the GSP rates vary between 2.5 to 8 per cent. Tariff and non-tariff barriers (NTBs) faced by ASEAN manufactures, especially textile, clothing, footwear and wood products are formidable. Among the more prominent NTBs are quantitative restrictions, voluntary export restraints (VERs) and orderly marketing arrangements (OMAs). ASEAN has expressed grave concern over the growth of NTBs in recent years, as these involve administrative discretion rather than open rules of protection, quite unlike tariffs.

While ASEAN is appreciative of the fact that the EC was the first to implement the GSP scheme before countries like the US and

Japan followed suit, ASEAN has found the EC's GSP scheme wanting in several respects which include the restrictive rules of origin, low quotas and uncertainty about the time frame.

3 POLARITY

It may be inferred from the above sketch that EC-ASEAN interactions have been limited to issues of bilateral importance. More specifically, the joint efforts have focussed on eliminating thorns in EC-ASEAN relations. Issues of global or multilateral dimension have been conveniently sidestepped. References to issues such as multilateral trade negotiations, if any, in the EC-ASEAN dialogues were no more than scanty and peripheral. However, Article 2 of the Co-operation Agreement highlights the need for such efforts in agreeing

> 'to study ways and means of overcoming trade barriers and in particular existing non-tariff and quasi tariff barriers, *taking into account the work of international organisations*'

and

> 'to cooperate *at the international level* and between themselves in the solution of commercial problems of common interest including trade related to commodities' (emphasis supplied).

These words are yet to be translated into concrete actions.

The absence of any active interaction or collaboration between the EC and ASEAN on matters of global and multilateral interest is not hard to explain, although economic theory is somewhat deficient with respect to the treatment of international economic policy co-operation.[2] International policy co-operation may be losely defined as 'any common action aimed at improving a working system.'[3] However, common action will not be forthcoming unless there is sufficient community of interest on the part of the two regional groupings.

It is not difficult to understand why there is considerable divergence of interests between the EC and ASEAN. No doubt, both these groupings compromise market economies which subscribe to the philosophy of the free-enterprise system and which maintain a high degree of economic openness in the sense that foreign trade and investment activities are vigorously promoted. But, then, the similarity ends here and the polarity begins.

There are many disparities which reflect the polarity that characterises the EC-ASEAN stance with respect to international economic affairs. Although ASEAN is twice as large as the EC in geographical size, the former's clout in the international, political and economic arena pales in comparison with that of the latter. More striking is the disparity in terms of GNP, with ASEAN's aggregate GNP being only one-fifteenth that of the EC. It is of interest to note that the richest country within ASEAN, *i.e.*, Singapore, has a *per capita* income that is roughly comparable to that of the poorest members of the EC. The EC is far more industrially advanced than ASEAN. Besides, the EC represents a more closely knit regional integration scheme than ASEAN. For instance, intra-regional trade within the EC accounts for more than 50 per cent of total EC trade, in contrast to the 15 per cent intra-ASEAN trade.

It may be argued that such differences would only render the EC and ASEAN complementary to each other.[4] But, then, this complementarity seems to have served to limit EC-ASEAN economic relations to bilateral dealings only. As alluded to earlier, the bilateral economic relations between the two groups are lopsided or asymmetrical in the sense that the EC is much more important to ASEAN than the other way round: ASEAN accounts for only a small proportion of the EC's external trade and foreign investment. Besides, the EC's trade policies have a stronger regional orientation in contrast to ASEAN. Top priority in the EC is given to the promotion of intra-community trade, followed by the emphasis placed on the promotion of trade among the OECD countries. Understandably, developing countries are accorded a lower ranking in terms of EC trade policy orientation. Among the developing countries, 66 ACP (African, Caribbean and Pacific) countries have been singled out for special treatment under the Lomé Convention. In addition, the EC has entered into special contractual arrangements with other developing countries, such as the Maghreb countries (Algeria, Morocco and Tunisia), Mashrek countries (Egypt, Jordan and Syria), Israel and Lebanon. ASEAN represents no more than a recent addition to this list.

The points we are driving at are the following. First, EC-ASEAN economic relations are no more special than those that have been established between the EC and other groups of developing countries. Second, there is a strong North-South flavour in EC-ASEAN economic relations. Third, there is a strong preference in the EC for establishing special, rather uniform relations with the rest of the world, as such preferential treatment tends to provide more leeway in international economic policies.[5] The net upshot of all this is that inter-regional interactions between EC and ASEAN have been confined to matters of immediate bilateral interest.

The preceding analysis does not suggest that it is not in the interest of either the EC or ASEAN to address the wider global issues, but it does imply that the inclusion of such issues in the agenda for inter-regional co-operation at this juncture will not have contributed to the growth and development of close economic co-operation between the two groups, given the North-South axis present in their special relationship. The EC and ASEAN would tend to be in opposing camps when it comes to a question of sorting out the existing international economic system and institutional set-up. In this regard, the EC seems to have a lot more in common with the OECD countries which are perceived to benefit more from the existing order than the Third World to which ASEAN belongs.

There has been little or no EC-ASEAN collaboration in dismantling trade barriers, partly because the two regional groupings play by different rules. The EC, like other OECD members, has insisted on reciprocity as the basis for tariff cuts, while ASEAN countries have laid emphasis on unilateral tariff reductions by developed countries. It is basicaly this difference in approach that has rendered any collaboration between the two groupings somewhat impossible. It is therefore a small wonder that in the previous GATT rounds, including the Kennedy and Tokyo rounds, items of export interest to developed countries were the targets of tariff cuts, while developing countries like the ASEAN ones have complained that their export items had received little attention in these multilateral trade negotiations.

Another explanation for the lack of collaboration between the EC and ASEAN in multilateral endeavours is that both groupings seem to have entrenched themselves in the present régime of managed trade based on a power relationship. There seems to exist a strange preference for bilateralism. Even in its dealings with ASEAN, the EC seems to prefer to go bilateral with each of the six ASEAN countries rather than ASEAN as a block. For example, the EC chose to negotiate its multifibre arrangements with individual ASEAN countries rather than with ASEAN as an entity, as this would enable the EC to drive as hard a bargain as would have been otherwise possible.

ASEAN, too, seems to be somewhat unenthusiastic about multilateralism, partly because of its past disheartening experiences and partly because of the apparent 'gains' ASEAN has made in its bilateral dealings with its major trading partners including the EC, US, Japan and Australia. It cannot be denied that ASEAN's common external approach towards its major trading partners has paid handsome dividends, although the latter cannot always be attributed to the stronger bargaining position that ASEAN countries enjoy by sticking together than by going it alone. Upon closer scrutiny, most of the 'gains' are clearly 'concessions' given by third countries to ASEAN. These concessions on the part of the third countries should be seen not as succumbing to the ASEAN 'pressure' but rather as friendly gestures motivated by genuine concern for the viability of ASEAN as a regional grouping. In other words, ASEAN may have extracted concessions not because of its strength as a 'power block' but because of its weakness as perceived from the outside. Whichever way one looks at it, the fact remains that bilateral dealings have led to some concrete results insofar as ASEAN is concerned.

ASEAN would be reluctant to enter into full-scale multilateral trade negotiations, if it means giving up the present concessions obtained through bilateral action for the sake of gains which multilateralism might offer but which are by no means certain. In fact, ASEAN countries have complained in the past that the Tokyo Round eroded the preferential margins of GSP. To put it differently, the previous MTN rounds have not only failed to benefit ASEAN countries by excluding the so-called 'sensitive' items of export interest to ASEAN, but also reduced the preferential margins ASEAN countries had been enjoying outside the GATT framework.

Under the present régime of managed trade, there has been a lot of rent-seeking activities in exporting and importing countries. Consequently, pressure groups have emerged in these countries to preserve the present arrangements. Thus, for example, textile quotas under the MFA have given some ASEAN countries a secure market in the importing countries including the EC and US without their really having to compete with others. In the case of some manufactured exports, free competition may not be in the best interest of some ASEAN countries. Hence the reluctance to upset the *status quo*.

4 PROSPECTS

It would be quite incorrect to infer from the preceding analysis that there is little or no room for fruitful collaboration between the EC and ASEAN in the multilateral arena with respect to the UN system and various inter-governmental fora. Difference in the economic structure of the two groupings, which have given rise to a multiplicity of policy approaches under the prevailing set of circumstances, do not preclude the possibility of meaningful inter-regional interaction and collaboration in seeking alternative solutions. International specialisation and commercial transactions based on the principle of dynamic comparative advantage call for multilateral approaches. Bilateralism tends to contribute to the perpetuation of an order which deviates from the first-best. Viewed from this angle, bilateral approaches are capable only of providing short-term solutions which cannot adequately take into account the interests of the rest of the world.

This is not to deny the legitimacy of the role of bilateral approaches. No doubt, bilateral arrangements have played a useful role in providing solutions to some of the pressing problems in EC-ASEAN relations. Indeed, some of these problems can only be effectively dealt with in a bilateral manner. Now that some of these problems of immediate concern are being taken care of through bilateral talks and negotiations, the time is ripe for the EC and ASEAN to initiate an exploration of the possibility of interaction and collaboration in a multilateral framework. It is encouraging to note that at the sixth EC-ASEAN ministerial meeting in Jakarta (October 1986), references were made for the first time to the need for joint efforts in bringing down protectionist barriers and in formulating a new international economic order.

It must be acknowledged that the UN system has substantial achievements to its credit, but it cannot be denied that there has been much backsliding from the ideals of its founders. There are deficiencies in the various international institutions such as the GATT, the World Bank and the IMF. GATT, for example, is silent on matters of the utmost importance including restrictive business practices, intrafirm trade, trade in technology and services and government procurements. The principle of non-discrimination has been eroded by 'selectivity' in the application of 'safeguard' provisions, while GATT principles and its prescribed rules, especially in respect of quantitative restrictions have been blatantly abused or evaded. The World

Bank also leaves much to be desired. For instance, the existing currency-pool arrangements do not help minimise the burden of borrowing countries, and there have been suggestions of converting the profits into a currency risk equalisation fund so as to minimise the borrowing countries' debt burden resulting from exchange rate fluctuations. In the IMF, there are severe financial and other constraints which have led to some backsliding from the original ideals. These are but a few of the areas within the UN system which can be improved through international and inter-regional consultation and collaboration.

To be sure, ASEAN countries are not indifferent about global issues, as their economies remain closely linked with the rest of the world. ASEAN countries are certainly interested in contributing positively to the policy formulation of the UN through active participation in the UN system. Indonesia, Malaysia and the Philippines have served as non-permanent members at the UN Security Council. ASEAN's ties with the UN system have been strengthened by its strong links with ESCAP and the UNDP. It has also dawned on those within the UN system that joint efforts at regional level could make significant contributions to global policy-making and programme implementation.

Although ASEAN as a regional grouping has received recognition internationally, it does not have the clout or the muscle to influence the global scene. By teaming up with the EC, ASEAN may be able to stand tall and be counted on a number of global issues of common interest. It might appear, as alluded to earlier, that polarities would prevent effective EC-ASEAN collaboration on global issues. This notwithstanding, there seems to exist enough overlapping of interests for these two regional groupings to join hands in the international arena. As a first step, it is important to identify those areas where common positions can be easily established. In this context, it appears that the American and Japanese economic hegemony may provide a focal point for a start. For instance, the role played by the US dollar in the international monetary system, and its ramifications through its external value, the US budget and balance of payments deficits, external debts and international-capital flows all affect the EC and ASEAN alike. In the same vein, there are the huge trade surpluses that Japan has with her major trading partners and all the attendant problems ranging from Japanese protectionism to yen appreciation which have caused difficulties internationally.

There are several areas where the interests of the EC and ASEAN can converge. For example, trade liberalisation and structural adjustment are no zero-sum games, as they would lead to a more efficient resource allocation and international division of labour. This is not to deny that there may be short-term adjustment problems which could be solved by give-and-take measures.

ASEAN countries, like other developing countries, have some misgivings about the new MTN round. ASEAN is worried that the Uruguay Round may result in increased protectionism rather than freer trade. In particular, ASEAN countries share the concern of other developing countries that the new MTN round would sidestep 'old issues' such as tariff and non-tariff barriers on trade in tropical products, special and differential treatment, code on safeguards, *etc.* and concentrate on 'new issues' ranging from trade in services to trade in counterfeit goods. ASEAN's initial reluctance to including trade in services in the new MTN agenda was not because these issues are considered unworthy of discussion but because ASEAN, like other Third World countries, is afraid that progress on old issues will be made conditional upon progress on new issues. There is also the thorny problem of the definition of services. If the term 'services' is defined broadly to stretch beyond banking, insurance and telecommunications, in which Americans are interested, to areas in which Less Developed Countries (LDCs) do have comparative advantage, the Uruguay Round will be more welcome and meaningful.

Interaction and collaboration between the EC and ASEAN on matters such as these may help put the UN system in general and the Uruguay Round in particular on an even keel. ASEAN has always been known for its moderation in its approach in international fora. It is remarkable that at the meetings of the Group of 77 (G77), ASEAN has always conducted itself in a down-to-earth, pragmatic fashion without giving in too much to Third World rhetoric. ASEAN has always been a moderate. It is this factor, more than anything else, that would make collaboration and interaction between the EC and ASEAN in a multilateral framework both feasible and fruitful. However, the EC's internal weaknesses, which have been compounded by the enlargement of the grouping, and ASEAN's sluggishness in integrating the economies of the region into a cohesive economic entity may reduce the impetus for a closer rapport between the two groupings in dealings with the rest of the world.

Notes

1. Examples of such co-operation include the setting up of Regional Grain Post-Harvest Research and Training Centre and the launching of the study of commercialisation of ASEAN timber resources. In addition, several projects in scientific and cultural fields have also been mounted.
2. For an elaborate theoretical discussion, see J. Pelkmans, 'Economic Co-operation Among Western Countries', in *Challenge to Inter-dependent Economies*, New York: Council on Foreign relations, 1979.
3. Ibid, at p. 97.
4. See: Narongchai Akrasanee, 'ASEAN-EEC Trade Relations: An Overview', in N. Akrasanee and H.C. Rieger (eds.) *ASEAN-EEC Economic Relations*, Institute of Southeast Asian Studies, Singapore, 1982.
5. See: Detlef Lorenz, 'International Division of Labour or Closer Co-operation? A look at ASEAN-EEC economic relations', *ASEAN Economic Bulletin*, Vol. 2, No. 3, March 1986, p. 174.

16 Interaction and Collaboration of the EC and ASEAN in the UN System and International Conferences

Kusuma Snitwongse

THE GROWING POLITICAL CONTENT

Initial regular contact between the EC and ASEAN was initiated by ASEAN and was motivated by economic concern resulting from the loss of Commonwealth preference trade for Malaysia and Singapore due to British accession to the EC in 1972. Nevertheless ASEAN soon saw the need for a politico-diplomatic contact as the Joint Study Group (JSG), established in 1974 to deal with trade co-operation, made little progress. ASEAN therefore pressed for meetings between the ambassadors of ASEAN countries in Brussels (the ASEAN Brussels Committee or ABC) and the ministers of the EC countries.

While economic reason had been the initial motivating force, political concerns were also present in the background to ASEAN reaching out to the EC as well as other groupings. The changing international environment in and around the South-east Asian region with the growing conflict between the United States and the Soviet Union as détente was fast waning, the Sino-US rapprochement and the communist victory in Indo-China caused ASEAN countries to look for alternative options in search of their security.

It was no accident, therefore, that ASEAN as an organisation came out of its lethargy and its relationship with the EC gained momentum following the Bali Summit in 1976. In Bali, the ASEAN countries reached an understanding that contact should be widened with the West. In November 1977, ASEAN clearly asked for a ministerial meeting with the EC and the first EC-ASEAN Ministerial Meeting was held in Brussels on 20–21 November 1978. Although a major part of the Joint Declaration made at the end of the meeting dealt with economic co-operation (24 out of 39 paragraphs), ASEAN achieved its overriding objective by being recognised as 'a factor of stability and balance which contributes to the maintenance of peace in South-East Asia.'[1] In return, ASEAN recognised 'the role played by the Europe of the Nine as a factor of economic stability and as an element of balance in international relations.' The issue of Indo-Chinese refugees was introduced, with the two groupings expressing serious concern over the unabated flow of refugees to the ASEAN countries and urging international consideration and efforts on this issue. The refugee question has since appeared in all Joint Statements issued at subsequent EC-ASEAN Ministerial Meetings (EAMM). Nevertheless, the developing political relations appeared to be intended as a base for expanding economic co-operation. It was at this meeting that the idea of signing an EC-ASEAN Co-operation Agreement was first agreed upon.

By the time the Second EAMM met in Kuala Lumpur, on 7–8 March 1980, at which the EC-ASEAN Agreement was to be signed, Vietnam had invaded Kampuchea in December 1978 and the Soviet Union had invaded Afghanistan exactly one year later. These two events provided an occasion for closer EC-ASEAN political collaboration. The EAMM released a common declaration on political questions on 8 March 1980 signed by all the foreign ministers of the two groupings, deploring the armed interventions – against small independent states – in flagrant violation of international law.[2] The EC also came out strongly in the same document in support of ASEAN's proposal to turn South-East Asia into a 'Zone of Peace, Freedom and Neutrality' (ZOPFAN). At the United Nations General Assembly (UNGA) session that year, EC and ASEAN members took a common position in supporting resolutions on the issues of Kampuchea and Afghanistan which made them implicit allies.

The Third EAMM in London, on 13–14 October 1981, was again essentially political in character. ASEAN's initiative on the holding of the International Conference on Kampuchea (ICK) was endorsed along with its proposed solution to the Kampuchean conflict. The by now twin issue of Afghanistan was raised and the ASEAN ministers reiterated their support of the European Council's proposal for an international conference on Afghanistan.

At the Fourth EAMM in Bangkok, on 24–25 March 1983, a Joint Declaration was worked out in such a way as to show concession on ASEAN's part to a great extent despite initial French reservations on certain points regarding the Kampuchean question. It was agreed that 'no assistance should be given to Vietnam of such a nature as to sustain and enhance the Vietnamese occupation of Kampuchea' which reflected ASEAN's concern about France's assistance to Vietnam. Despite the fact that a number of EC members, most notably France, refused to recognise the ASEAN-backed Coalition Government of Democratic Kampuchea (CGDK) because of the presence of the Khmer Rouge faction, the Joint Declaration nevertheless noted that the formation of the coalition 'constitutes a significant step in the search for a comprehensive settlement.' Again, in return, the ASEAN ministers declared their support for the 1981 EC proposal for an International Conference on Afghanistan. The issue of the Middle East was introduced at the Meeting by the EC for discussion and the Joint Statement urged for progress towards settlement of the conflict in the region.

Besides repeating very much what was said in Bangkok on Kampuchea, Afghanistan, the Middle East and refugees, the Fifth EAMM in Dublin, on 15–16 November 1984, added the issues of East-West relations, Lebanon and the Iraq-Iran war to its agenda for consultation.

At the Sixth EAMM in Jakarta, on 20–21 October 1986, the EC continued to show its support of ASEAN's position on Kampuchea by its endorsement of the Eight Points Programme put forth by Prince Norodom Sihanouk as President of the CGDK, describing it as 'containing constructive elements for a peaceful settlement.' Again, the Afghanistan issue was given due attention. New issues were further added to the agenda, namely South Africa, international terrorism, narcotics and the UN financial crisis.

MODE OF INTERACTION AND COLLABORATION

It can be gathered from the above that the EC-ASEAN Ministerial Meetings have provided the most important forum for interaction and collaboration between the two regional groupings on political as well as economic matters. It is noteworthy that the EC is the only dialogue partner which has regular ministerial meetings with ASEAN, at an interval of approximately 18 months. And although the EAMM is not officially institutionalised, it appears to have become a permanent fixture, with both ASEAN and the EC sharing the view that it is useful and therefore should continue. The EAMM is basically a forum for exchanges of views rather than for negotiation. The meetings have been described by a senior Thai official as 'informal, open and frank' and as an effective means of providing broad directives at the working level.

Out of these exchanges, common positions on particular issues are forged, when possible. Thus the EAMM has proved its value as an important means of co-ordination, notably in the United Nations and international conferences. It has become normal practice, for example, for the President of the EC Council to make a statement that includes the common position adopted at the previous EAMM at the beginning of the annual session of the UNGA. Another example of the EAMM's value for co-ordination can be seen during the first meeting which was held at the same time as UNCTAD VI in Belgrade. The developing countries were disappointed and concerned with the lack of a concrete result of the UNCTAD meeting and requested Thailand to raise the problem in the EAMM. The result was the so-called ASEAN-EC Impetus, with respective representatives of the EC and ASEAN at UNCTAD being given instruction to work together to try to salvage the meeting as best they could.[3]

In cases where special issues come up without prior consultation, efforts will be made to lobby the other group's members individually. As certain ASEAN countries are members of a number of groupings, such as the Non-Aligned Movement, Group of 77, OPEC and the Islamic Conference, the EC has looked to those ASEAN countries to help lobby in those groups not only for a common position taken by the EC and ASEAN in the EAMM, but also because in general ASEAN countries are considered to advocate relatively moderate opinions.

HOW CLOSE A COLLABORATION? A SAMPLING OF THE EC AND ASEAN VOTINGS IN THE UNGA

Reading the Joint Declarations of the EAMM would give one an impression of harmony and optimism about growing collaboration between the two groups. This impression should be further reinforced by the fact that the meetings have been taking place regularly over a number of years and consequently a habit of consultation, compromise, and harmonisation of interests should have taken some root. The first part of this paper has also established the fact that the issues brought in for consultation have grown in number.

A random sampling of the voting by the EC and ASEAN member countries in the UNGA reveals an interesting pattern that could be taken to mirror the extent of the common ground within each group and between the two groups. These could also be taken as an indicator of the extent of collaboration that can be expected between the two groups.

On the Kampuchean question, ASEAN and the EC member countries have been solidly unified from 1979 in supporting resolutions calling for Vietnamese troops' withdrawal and self-determination by the Kampuchean people. (See Table 16.1). However, the EC members took different stands on the recognition of the CGDK. France and Ireland abstained all along until the report of the Credential Committee was adopted without voting in 1983. On the twin issue of Afghanistan, ASEAN and the EC have been voting *en bloc* in support of the call for Soviet troops' withdrawal. (Table 16.2)

On the question of Namibia and South Africa, ASEAN countries have always taken a common position, reflecting their identification with the Third World countries. On the other hand, votes by the EC members vary from resolution to resolution, either in favour or against or abstention on the question of Namibia. As to the question of South Africa and apartheid, all EC members, with the exception of Greece who abstained, voted against the resolution calling for comprehensive sanctions against South Africa. The voting on other resolutions on South Africa differed from case to case. (Tables 16.4–16.10)

On the question of the Middle East, ASEAN members' votes split along a religious line on a resolution calling for members to suspend all relations with Israel. The Philippines, Singapore and Thailand who have diplomatic relations with Israel, not being constrained on religious grounds, abstained. The other three Muslim members, Brunei, Indonesia and Malaysia voted in favour. On two other resolutions that focussed on opposition to Israel's takeover of Arab territories, ASEAN voted as a bloc. All three resolutions under study were opposed by the EC members almost solidly, the exception being Greece who voted in favour and Spain who abstained on all three. (Table 16.3)

A conclusion that one can draw from these limited samples is that EC-ASEAN convergence of positions is issue-specific. Moreover, members of each regional grouping do not always vote as a bloc. Each country seems to vote as it sees fit.

DIAGNOSIS AND PROGNOSIS

From the above, it is evident that a degree of collaboration between the EC and ASEAN exists. Nevertheless, certain constraints to greater collaboration can be detected as well. One such constraint can be found in the nature of political co-operation among members of each of the two regional groupings.

In the case of the EC, co-operation in the sphere of foreign policy is done within the framework of the European Political Co-operation (EPC) which was started in 1970 'in order to achieve a capacity for joint action' on entry into the final phase of the Common Market and before its first enlargement.

Special emphasis should be placed here on the fact that the EPC is outside the framework of the EC, though some overlap does exist. The key word of the EPC is *co-operation*. Operationally, the EPC is based on continuous co-operation among the foreign ministers and relevant sections in the respective foreign services. The foreign ministers are committed to 'consult partners before adopting final positions or launching national initiatives on all important questions of foreign policy which are of concern to the Ten as a whole.'[4] It is clear that EPC members maintain their sovereignty on matters of foreign policy and the EPC's nature is far from being supra-national. While consultation is customary, individual states are still at liberty to pursue their own policies should co-ordination fail to materialise.

The EPC members have been successful in co-ordinating their positions on a large number of issues such as the Conference on Security and Co-operation in Europe (CSCE), the Euro-Arab Dialogue, and Afghanistan. Nevertheless, the foreign policy content of the member countries that can be fully co-ordinated remains relatively limited, and the growth in the number of member countries could add to the complication. An indication of this can be seen in Portugal's refusal to attend the Sixth EAMM in Jakarta because of its stand on East Timor despite the long-standing precedent that bilateral issues should not interfere with meetings with other regional groupings.

Unlike the EC which conceives of political integration as its eventual goal, ASEAN from its beginning disavowed becoming a supra-

Table 16.1 Recorded vote on Kampuchea issue UNGA 34 – UNGA 39

Country	*I CGDK Credentials*						*II Resolutions*					
	GA34	GA35	GA36	GA37	GA38	GA39	GA34	GA35	GA36	GA37	GA38	GA39
ASEAN					------ ADOPTED WITHOUT A VOTE ------	------ ADOPTED WITHOUT A VOTE ------						
Brunei	–	–	–	–			–	–	–	–	–	Y*
Indonesia	Y	Y	Y	Y			Y*	Y*	Y*	Y*	Y*	Y*
Malaysia	Y	Y	Y	Y			Y*	Y*	Y*	Y*	Y*	Y*
Philippines	Y	Y	Y	Y			Y*	Y*	Y*	Y*	Y*	Y*
Singapore	Y	Y	Y	Y			Y*	Y*	Y*	Y*	Y*	Y*
Thailand	Y	Y	Y	Y			Y*	Y*	Y*	Y*	Y*	Y*
EC												
Belgium	Y	Y	Y	Y			Y*	Y*	Y*	Y*	Y*	Y*
Denmark	Y	Y	Y	Y			Y	Y	Y	Y	Y*	Y*
France	A	A	A	A			Y	Y*	Y	Y	Y	Y
FRG	Y	Y	Y	Y			Y*	Y*	Y*	Y*	Y*	Y*
Greece	Y	Y	Y	Y			Y	Y	Y	Y	Y	Y
Ireland	A	A	A	A			Y	Y	Y	Y	Y	Y
Italy	Y	Y	Y	Y			Y	Y	Y*	Y*	Y*	Y*
Luxembourg	Y	Y	Y	Y			Y*	Y*	Y*	Y*	Y*	Y*
Netherlands	A	A	A	Y			Y*	Y*	Y*	Y*	Y*	Y*
Portugal	Y	Y	Y	Y			Y	Y	Y	Y	Y	Y
Spain	A	A	Y	Y			Y	Y	Y	Y	Y	Y
UK	Y	Y	Y	Y			Y	Y	Y*	Y*	Y*	Y*

Y = YES N = NO
A = Abstention
– = Non-Participation
* = Co-Sponsor

Table 16.2

Resolution 39/13: The Situation in Afghanistan and Its Implications for International Peace and Security. Adopted in November 1984.					*Resolution 40/12: The Situation in Afghanistan and Its Implications for International Peace and Security. Adopted in November 1985.*				
Voting	In Favour	Against	Abstaining	Absent	Voting	In Favour	Against	Abstaining	Absent
ASEAN					ASEAN				
Brunei	/				Brunei	/			
Indonesia	/				Indonesia	/			
Malaysia	/				Malaysia	/			
Philippines	/				Philippines	/			
Singapore	/				Singapore	/			
Thailand	/				Thailand	/			

EC				
Belgium	/			
Denmark	/			
France	/			
FRG	/			
Greece	/			
Ireland	/			
Italy	/			
Luxembourg	/			
Netherlands	/			
Portugal	/			
Spain	/			
UK	/			

EC				
Belgium	/			
Denmark	/			
France	/			
FRG	/			
Greece	/			
Ireland	/			
Italy	/			
Luxembourg	/			
Netherlands	/			
Portugal	/			
Spain	/			
UK	/			

Table 16.3

	Resolution 40/168A: The Situation in the Middle East. Adopted in December 1985.				*Resolution 40/168B: The Situation in the Middle East. Adopted in December 1985.*				*Resolution 40/168C: The Situation in the Middle East. Adopted in December 1985.*			
Voting	Y	N	Abst.	Abs.	Y	N	Abst.	Abs.	Y	N	Abst.	Abs.
ASEAN												
Brunei	/				/				/			
Indonesia	/				/				/			
Malaysia	/				/				/			
Philippines	/						/		/			
Singapore	/						/		/			
Thailand	/						/		/			

EC												
Belgium		/				/				/		
Denmark		/				/				/		
France		/				/				/		
FRG		/				/				/		
Greece	/				/				/			
Ireland		/				/				/		
Italy		/				/				/		
Luxembourg		/				/				/		
Netherlands		/				/				/		
Portugal		/				/				/		
Spain			/				/				/	
UK		/				/				/		

Y = In Favour
N = Against
Abst. = Abstaining
Abs. = Absent

Table 16.4

	Resolution 39/72A: Situation in Namibia Resulting from the Illegal Occupation of the Territory by South Africa. Adopted in November 1984.				*Resolution 39/72B: Implementation of the Security Council Resolution. Adopted in November 1984.*				*Resolution 39/72C: Programme of Work of the UN Council for Namibia. Adopted in November 1984.*			
Voting	Y	N	Abst.	Abs.	Y	N	Abst.	Abs.	Y	N	Abst.	Abs.
ASEAN												
Brunei	/				/				/			
Indonesia	/				/				/			
Malaysia	/				/				/			
Philippines	/				/				/			
Singapore	/				/				/			
Thailand	/				/				/			

EC												
Belgium		/			/					/		
Denmark		/			/					/		
France		/			/					/		
FRG		/			/					/		
Greece			/		/				/			
Ireland		/			/					/		
Italy		/			/					/		
Luxembourg		/			/					/		
Netherlands		/			/					/		
Portugal		/			/						/	
Spain			/		/						/	
UK		/				/				/		

Y = In Favour
N = Against
Abst. = Abstaining
Abs. = Absent

Table 16.5

	Resolution 39/72D: Dissemination of Information and Mobilization of International Public Opinion in Support of Namibia. Adopted in November 1984.				*Resolution 39/72E: UN Fund for Namibia. Adopted in November 1984.*				*Resolution 39/72G: Special Session of the General Assembly on the Question of Namibia. Adopted in November 1984.*			
Voting	Y	N	Abst.	Abs.	Y	N	Abst.	Abs.	Y	N	Abst.	Abs.
ASEAN												
Brunei	/				/				/			
Indonesia	/				/				/			
Malaysia	/				/				/			
Philippines	/				/				/			
Singapore	/				/				/			
Thailand	/				/				/			

EC												
Belgium	/				/						/	
Denmark			/		/				/			
France	/				/						/	
FRG			/		/						/	
Greece	/				/				/			
Ireland	/				/				/			
Italy	/				/						/	
Luxembourg	/				/						/	
Netherlands			/		/				/			
Portugal	/				/				/			
Spain	/		.		/				/			
UK			/				/			/		

Y = In Favour
N = Against
Abst. = Abstaining
Abs. = Absent

Table 16.6

	Resolution 40/97A: Situation in Namibia Resulting from the Illegal Occupation of the Territory by South Africa. Adopted in November 1985.				*Resolution 40/97B: Implementation of Security Council 435 (1978). Adopted in November 1985.*				*Resolution 40/97C: Programme of work of the UN Council for Namibia. Adopted in November 1985.*			
Voting	Y	N	Abst.	Abs.	Y	N	Abst.	Abs.	Y	N	Abst.	Abs.
ASEAN												
Brunei	/				/				/			
Indonesia	/				/				/			
Malaysia	/				/				/			
Philippines	/				/				/			
Singapore	/				/				/			
Thailand	/				/				/			

EC												
Belgium			/				/		/			
Denmark			/				/		/			
France			/				/				/	
FRG			/				/				/	
Greece			/				/		/			
Ireland			/				/		/			
Italy			/				/		/			
Luxembourg			/				/		/			
Netherlands			/				/		/			
Portugal			/				/		/			
Spain			/				/		/			
UK			/				/				/	

Y = In Favour
N = Against
Abst. = Abstaining
Abs. = Absent

Table 16.7

	Resolution 40/97D: Dissemination of Information and Mobilisation of International Public Opinion in Support of Namibia. Adopted in November 1985.				*Resolution 40/97E: UN Fund for Namibia. Adopted in November 1985.*				*Resolution 40/97F: Special Session of the General Assembly on the Question of Namibia. Adopted in November 1985.*			
Voting	Y	N	Abst.	Abs.	Y	N	Abst.	Abs.	Y	N	Abst.	Abs.
ASEAN												
Brunei	/				/				/			
Indonesia	/				/				/			
Malaysia	/				/				/			
Philippines	/				/				/			
Singapore	/				/				/			
Thailand	/				/				/			

EC												
Belgium			/		/				/			
Denmark			/		/				/			
France			/				/				/	
FRG			/				/				/	
Greece			/		/				/			
Ireland			/		/				/			
Italy			/		/				/			
Luxembourg			/		/				/			
Netherlands			/		/				/			
Portugal			/		/				/			
Spain			/		/				/			
UK			/				/				/	

Y = In Favour
N = Against
Abst. = Abstaining
Abs. = Absent

Table 16.8

	Resolution 40/64A: Comprehensive Sanctions Against the Racist Regime of South Africa. Adopted in November 1985.				*Resolution 40/64B: Situation in South Africa and Assistance to the Liberation Movements. Adopted in November 1985.*				*Resolution 40/64C: World Conferences on Sanctions against Racism in South Africa. Adopted in November 1985.*			
Voting	Y	N	Abst.	Abs.	Y	N	Abst.	Abs.	Y	N	Abst.	Abs.
ASEAN												
Brunei	/				/				/			
Indonesia	/				/				/			
Malaysia	/				/				/			
Philippines	/				/				/			
Singapore	/				/				/			
Thailand	/				/				/			

EC												
Belgium		/				/				/		
Denmark		/					/		/			
France		/				/					/	
FRG		/				/				/		
Greece			/		/				/			
Ireland		/					/		/			
Italy		/				/				/		
Luxembourg		/				/					/	
Netherlands		/					/				/	
Portugal		/				/				/		
Spain		/					/				/	
UK		/				/				/		

Y = In Favour
N = Against
Abst. = Abstaining
Abs. = Absent

Table 16.9

	Resolution 40/64D: Public Information and Public Action against Apartheid. Adopted in November 1985.				*Resolution 40/64F: Programme of Work of the Special Committee against Apartheid. Adopted in November 1985.*				*Resolution 40/64G: International Convention against Apartheid in Sports. Adopted in November 1985.*			
Voting	Y	N	Abst.	Abs.	Y	N	Abst.	Abs.	Y	N	Abst.	Abs.
ASEAN												
Brunei	/				/				/			
Indonesia	/				/				/			
Malaysia	/				/				/			
Philippines	/				/				/			
Singapore	/				/				/			
Thailand	/				/				/			

EC												
Belgium	/						/				/	
Denmark	/				/						/	
France	/						/				/	
FRG	/						/				/	
Greece	/				/						/	
Ireland	/				/						/	
Italy	/						/				/	
Luxembourg	/						/				/	
Netherlands	/						/				/	
Portugal	/						/				/	
Spain	/						/				/	
UK			/			/					/	

Y = In Favour
N = Against
Abst. = Abstaining
Abs. = Absent

Table 16.10 *Resolution 40/64 I: Concerted International Action for the Elimination of Apartheid. Adopted in November 1985.*

Voting	Y	N	Abst.	Abs.
ASEAN				
Brunei	/			
Indonesia	/			
Malaysia	/			
Philippines	/			
Singapore	/			
Thailand	/			
EC				
Belgium	/			
Denmark	/			
France	/			
FRG			/	
Greece	/			
Ireland	/			
Italy	/			
Luxembourg	/			
Netherlands	/			
Portugal	/			
Spain	/			
UK		/		

Y = In Favour
N = Against
Abst. = Abstaining
Abs. = Absent

national organisation. The Bangkok Declaration of 1967 reaffirmed each individual member's right to retain its separate identity and political sovereignty. Its political programme of action in the Declaration of ASEAN Concord of 1976 spelled out a framework for co-operation: 'Strengthening the political solidarity by promoting harmonisation of views, co-ordinating position and where *possible and desirable* [emphasis added] taking common actions.' Such co-operation within the formal institutional structure at the highest level is carried out at the annual ASEAN Ministerial Meeting, with each foreign minister representing the sovereign position of the member countries.

Co-operation among sovereign entities always poses a dilemma between the common interest of the group and particular national interests when the two do not coincide. Decisions have to be taken on a basis of consensus, giving each member a veto power. ASEAN has so far shown impressive solidarity, particularly on the Kampuchean problem. Its principle of consultation and consensus has so far served it well and this includes its dealings with the dialogue partners. Normally at the meeting of its foreign ministers, ASEAN will work out a common strategy for use in the discussion with the dialogue partners, the EC included. Nevertheless, differences do exist among member countries and a number of signs of assertiveness by individual member countries can be discerned that have to do, for example, with the approach to the Kampuchean problem or the Pacific co-operation issue.

Constraints on political collaboration between the EC and ASEAN can be expected to arise also out of the fact that the present day international system has grown more complex. Consequently, there are inevitably cross-cutting links among nations and groups of nations and there will be areas where the interests of the EC and ASEAN converge and diverge.

On the issues of Kampuchea and Afghanistan, the two groupings are linked along ideological and security lines and can thus fully collaborate. Their coincidence of interests can be seen in the Joint Statement issued at the Second EAMM in Kuala Lumpur in 1980. The two separate invasions were linked together by an explanation that they 'have as a common denominator the imposition of will on small independent states by foreign powers through the use of force in open violation of international law, thereby threatening international peace and security.' Both sides' security concerns were mutually served by the common position taken.

Certain other statements in joint declarations are of a more general nature, revealing attempts to gloss over the differences that exist. On the issue of South Africa, for example, the EC and ASEAN declared that

> 'they were in complete agreement in expressing grave concern at the increasing tense and repressive situation in South Africa – and called for strong international pressure to bring about the total abolition of apartheid.'

However when it comes to voting on the UNGA resolution calling for comprehensive sanctions against South Africa, ASEAN and the EC appeared to be on different axes, reflecting different political, strategic and economic perspectives. ASEAN, with limited economic and strategic interests involved on this issue, identified itself politically with the Third World countries.

Collaboration between the EC and ASEAN is constrained also by the lack of symmetrical interests and concerns about particular issues between them. While there is no denying that in a politically and strategically interdependent world, the EC cannot help but be interested in the stability of South-East Asia, nevertheless, ever since the decolonisation of South-East Asia, the EC countries as a whole and individually cannot be said to have vital interests or significant political or military influence in the region. Moreover, it is towards the United States that the EC countries look for the protection of the region against threats from Vietnam and the Soviet Union (which is also true in the case of ASEAN). This is reflected in a 1982 article by the West German Foreign Minister, Hans-Dietrich Genscher,[5] who was known to be an ASEAN enthusiast. In the article he described the emergence of a pentarchy in the South-East Asian region, consisting of the United States, the Soviet Union, China, Japan and ASEAN. The EC was conspicuously absent from the scene which perhaps reflects the fact that political influence generally lags behind the economic one.

That South-East Asia stands lower in the EC's order of priorities can be detected from the 1980 EAMM when it was reported that the EC showed more concern for Afghanistan and tried to have the problem precede the Kampuchean conflict in the joint declaration.[6] The strong condemnation of the Soviet Union and Vietnam in the Joint Declaration on Political Issues that came out of the meeting was the result of ASEAN's linking the two issues together in a global security framework. Similarly, the report to the European Parliament by Lord Carrington in December 1981 on political co-operation[7] reflects the differing weight given to other regions and South-East Asia. While an extensive mention was made of Afghanistan, the Middle East and Eastern Europe, for example, ASEAN was accorded one sentence in the text.

On the ASEAN side, its orientation is primarily towards Asia and the Pacific, thus its reaction cannot be termed enthusiastic when at the 1983 EAMM in Bangkok, the Europeans suggested that the meeting widen its scope of discussions, 'taking it out of purely local or economic context and towards a more global appreciation of the world situation.'[8] This initiative by the EC tended to be regarded more as a peripheral diversion, as one ASEAN senior official was reported to have commented: 'We don't mind talking on the international political situation. But the issues are very remote from the region and the valuable time for the meeting is so limited.'[9]

It would appear that the solidly unified position of the EC and ASEAN on the Kampuchean and Afghanistan questions is based more on expediency than serious conviction about the security linkage between them. At the 1980 EAMM, the EC members had wanted ASEAN states to help lobby Non-aligned nations to support the EC Plan for the withdrawal of Soviet troops and the neutralisation of Afghanistan. ASEAN similarly wanted EC support for its position on Kampuchea.[10] By linking the two together, both sides' interests were served.

Not only do the interests of the EC and ASEAN appear to be asymmetrical in the geopolitical context, there are indications also that ASEAN puts greater stress on economic issues in the relationship and is concerned that the EC might be putting undue weight on political issues. This is to be explained by the fact that the ASEAN countries' major security concern is still basically domestic stability which is seen to be closely linked with successful economic development. This concern can be detected from a statement made by Indonesian President Suharto at the opening of the Sixth EAMM on 20 October 1986 in which he called on the EC to increase its investment in an economic co-operation with ASEAN, stressing that the advancement of the economic progress will contribute significantly to the stability of South-East Asia as well as the stability of Asia and the world in general.[11] It may be recalled that in reaching out and strengthening its ties with the EC, ASEAN was motivated by economic concern and saw political ties more as providing support to economic ones.

Looking at the overall trend in EC-ASEAN economic relations can lead to differing prognostications. With the decline, percentage-wise, in EC-ASEAN trade and investment, one possible prognosis is that the emphasis on future relations may very well be on politics.[12] However, if political relations had been intended to strengthen economic relations, the downward trend in EC economic presence in the region may not augur well for greater political relations.

Relations between nations are not determined by concrete interests alone but can be affected by more subjective factors such as values and perceptions. ASEAN countries, because of their historical experiences and less advantageous position, may be particularly sensitive about what the EC countries consider trivial such as representation at the EAMM. Non-appearance by their EC counterparts can touch the sensitivity of ASEAN regarding equality. When Belgian Foreign Minister Leo Tindemans, the then President of the EC Council, informed ASEAN that he was not coming for the dialogue with them in 1982 and was sending a lower-level delegation instead, ASEAN's reaction was unexpectedly indignant. The EC was told that the lower-level delegation would be rejected and the dialogue for that year was regretfully cancelled.

ASEAN also regards dialogues with the Third Country partners as a 'growing recognition of institutional viability' and as an 'assurance of its significant role' in international affairs.[13] Thus when only five out of the twelve EC foreign ministers turned up at the Jakarta EAMM, both the Singapore and Indonesian foreign ministers expressed unhappiness. This also led the *Indonesian Times* to raise questions as to whether the EC felt its relations with ASEAN had not yet become warm enough and whether the shrinking role of the EC in ASEAN economic activities could be interpreted as lack of enthusiasm on the part of the EC.

ASEAN countries' sensitivities are likely to be affected also by questions like human rights and freedom of the press raised in the European Parliament. Although the Dutch Foreign Minister stressed that the subjects were not elements which belong to multilateral discussion and apparently were not raised in the EAMM at Jakarta despite some concern on the part of ASEAN, such open criticism of ASEAN is apt to give the impression of Europe's feeling of moral superiority.

Overall, a considerable degree of sensitivity to each other's feeling and interests, ability to compromise, and a give-and-take spirit on a large number of issues provide observers of EC-ASEAN political relations with cause for optimism. The refugee problem is a good example of this. Initially there was tension between the two on this matter. ASEAN countries, being faced with the vast outflow of refugees, tried to push them off and brought upon themselves criticism from the Europeans. ASEAN, on the other hand, was disturbed by the fact that European nations were not resettling the refugees fast enough. The refugee problem was the first topic on which the EC and ASEAN interacted politically at the First EAMM and successfully collaborated. A common ground was established to push for an international conference on refugees, which was held in Geneva, in July 1979. ASEAN and the EC collaborated to get Vietnam to establish control over the movement of the refugees and for the rest of the world to share the burden of resettling them. The EC has since supplied about 40 per cent of the total international aid for refugees.

Neither has the EC support for ASEAN's policy on Kampuchea been without any problems. Tensions existed regarding the EC's reluctance to support the CGDK because of the Khmer Rouge faction in it. ASEAN, on the other hand, was disturbed by the EC's decision to give emergency medical supplies to Vietnam in December of 1981 and 1982. Both sides did reach a compromise in the 1983 Joint Declaration, with the EC committed to considering the formation of the CGDK as 'a significant step' in the search for solution to the crisis, short of recognising it as the legitimate government of Kampuchea. At the same time, the EC also agreed that no assistance should be given to Vietnam of such a nature as would sustain and enhance the Vietnamese occupation of Kampuchea which gave France a leeway in continuing her aid to that country. On the basic issue of opposition to Vietnamese invasion and occupation, ASEAN receives the full support of the EC.

Considering the constraints on EC-ASEAN collaboration discussed above, the overall output of the two groupings has been 'remarkable,' as one close observer described it.[15] It is evident that despite the constraints, there are enough agreements between the EC and ASEAN over a broad range of political issues for the two to find continuing the transactions between them worthwhile.

Notes

1. For excerpts of the Joint Statement, see *European Political Co-operation (EPC)* (Bonn: Press and Information Office of the Federal Government, 1982), pp. 149–152.
2. Quoted by Eric Teo, 'ASEAN-EEC Diplomatic Consultations', *Contemporary South-east Asia*, vol. 7, no. 2, September 1985, p. 119.
3. An interview given by Ambassador Manaspas Xuto on 'ASEAN's Role in North-South Negotiation', in Vinita Sukarasep, editor, *ASEAN in World Politics* (Bangkok: Institute of Security and International Studies, 1985), pp. 100–101. (In Thai).
4. 'Report on European Political Co-operation issued by the Foreign Ministers of the Ten on 13 October 1981 (London Report)', *European Political Co-operation (EPC)*, op. cit., p. 273.
5. Hans-Dietrich Genscher, 'The European Community and ASEAN Partners in Building a World of Peaceful Co-operation', *Europa*, July – August, 1982, p. 8.
6. Sompong Kittinaradorn, 'Behind-the-scenes talks begin for ASEAN-EEC meet', *The Nation Review*, Bangkok, 18 March 1983, p. 5.
7. Speech by Lord Carrington to the European Parliament on the development of Political Co-operation (Strasbourg, 17 December 1981, excerpts), *European Political Co-operation (EPC)*, op. cit., pp. 298–302.
8. Teo, op. cit., p. 121.
9. Kittinaradorn, op. cit.
10. Stuart Harris and Brian Bridges, *European Interests in ASEAN*, (London: Routledge & Kegan Paul, 1983), p. 53.
11. *The Jakarta Post*, 21 October 1986.
12. Hans H. Indorf, 'Political Dimensions of Inter-Regional Co-operation: ASEAN and the EEC', *Asia Pacific Community*, No. 19, Winter, 1983, p. 91.
13. Ibid.
14. *Indonesian Times*, 21 October 1986.
15. Indorf, op. cit., p. 105. Indorf deems transaction between ASEAN and the EC 'remarkable' in that it produced a convergence of political interests without either side having a joint foreign policy and it brought about co-operation with either side having at best only a secondary concern for the other.

17 The Soviet Union in Asia: Conflict and Co-operation

Luigi Vittorio Ferraris

For any judgment on Soviet political initiatives and trends in Asia in the last decades, we have to pay special attention to seven elements, which exert a deep influence on the position of the USSR (also as the heir of Tsarist Russia) in Asia:

(i) Russia in its historical dimension was formed by fighting against an Asiatic invasion and from the European portion Russia started the conquest of Siberia (in 1639 the Pacific Ocean had been reached) and later on of Central Asia. The Russian colonialism is completely different from the colonialism of other European powers. The push to conquer was fostered by the State, which was moved by the search for security to overcome the weaknesses of uncertain borders. The conquest was entrusted to military units and not to peasants or to colonisers. A further peculiarity was, in contrast to other overseas Empires, the contiguity of the territories to be conquered and colonised.[1] The Asiatic and colonial dimension of the only remaining colonial Empire has not been overrun by the decolonisation process, because the colonised territories in Asia were and are an integral part of the Russian state in its globality and they could not be separated from it. Siberia is not an appendix, but an essential part of Russia as a whole,[2] and to Siberia should be added Central Asia, which is an independent factor in itself, above all in the political context of Russian domination.

(ii) The USSR is a multinational state. Leaving aside any appreciation of Soviet policy on nationalities – beginning with the well-known article by Stalin in 1913 – and of the content of socialist internationalism, it is a clear fact that, in 1979, 46 per cent of the population belonged to non-Russian stock (embracing the White Russians into the Russian population) and that half of this 46 per cent is of non-European and culturally of non-Christian origin: such a proportion unfavourable to the Russians is due to aggravate itself because of the demographic upsurge of the Asiatic racial groups. We should speak rather of the Russian peoples and not of a Russian people.[3] The expectations for larger autonomies or for a different policy to the benefit of the nationalities are to be put in context with the proclaimed right to secession,[4] a potentially dynamic element, which has always been present, although well concealed, since the birth of the federal structure of the Soviet Union.

(iii) The USSR, the fatherland of real socialism and the first country in the world on the path towards communism, has met in Asia (and not in Europe, as Lenin was hoping and pleading) other people that won their struggle for socialism through their own endeavours without the help of the Red Army. China succeeded in being the second great socialist country and developed itself in full autonomy into an ideological competitor or adversary. Its weight has been magnified by a military-political hostility deepening the ideological conflict. The ensuing polycentrism turned out to be a disavowal of the Soviet claim of being the centre of socialism and/or communism.

(iv) In Asia, the Soviet Union has an open feud on territorial issues with Japan as a former enemy from the Second World War. The controversy over the Kurile Islands hinders a peace treaty not because of the balance of power (as is the case for Germany) but because of a bilateral dispute and even worse with the second strongest Asiatic power – if China is really the first one – which on the basis of a very successful capitalistic system exerts a large influence in Asia. With Japan any kind of 'bipolar' agreement is highly improbable.

(v) In Asia the Soviet Union has an array of relations with socialist countries, which are all very different from each other. Therefore, the USSR has not succeeded, as in Eastern Europe, in forging with them relations founded on mutual confidence, political affinities or parallel political choices. We mean by that Vietnam, North Korea and in a different framework Afghanistan, not forgetting Mongolia, whose dependence on the USSR is total.

(vi) In Asia the USSR keeps in direct contact with the group of the Non-Aligned countries. This does not happen with supposedly Non-Aligned countries elsewhere (for instance Cuba), but with mighty and resourceful countries such as India. Such a situation makes even more clear the ambiguous and often contradictory posture of the Soviet Union towards the Non-Aligned countries. Notwithstanding the frequent reference to the advantages for the Soviet Union of the changes in correlation of forces and to the trilogy of anti-imperialism, laicism and socialism, the image of the Soviets no longer has a great appeal for the Non-Aligned countries,[5] because it no longer reflects a power in the forefront of the fight against Western imperialism, but rather a power with national or at least opportunistic interests of the same nature as that of other world powers.[6]

(vii) In Asia the Soviet Union must reckon with new structures, which are ideologically anti-imperialistic and anti-Western, but not friendly to the Soviets, because, as in Iran, they have a great religious appeal, eventually also inside the Soviet Union.

Even if we do not take the Near East into consideration, because its Arabian nature does not belong to the Asiatic dimension, we cannot avoid reaching the conclusion that the Soviet Union is very much an Asiatic power. However this fact is often rejected: for Lenin the word Asiatic had a negative meaning linked with Russian backwardness.

When we evoke the idea of the 'common European house', we should ask ourselves whether the Soviet Union avails itself of the European component in order to better balance the Asiatic component or whether it wants to guarantee stability in Europe in order to better devote itself to Asia and the future conflicts in that area. In Asia the sources of conflict and the ensuing instability depend in large measure upon the communists: from Cambodia to Afghanistan and to the Sino-Vietnamese clashes. Maybe because of that the Soviet Union acquiesced in Asia to genocide such as that of the communists in Indonesia or was a passive spectator of the change in the régime in the Philippines, where the USSR supported Marcos until the last minute.[7]

In such a framework the Soviet objectives in Asia have to take into consideration a set of different factors: the scheme of a bipolar agreement is not as conceivable in Asia as it is in Europe. These objectives can be summarised as follows:

- to contain China, with the aim of reaching an agreement or better a *modus vivendi*, without impairing the substantial military build-up facing China in the region;[8]
- to curb the American influence in Asia;
- to prevent the establishment of a common course of action between the United States, China and Japan.

The dramatic break with China represented, for the second time in Soviet history, a great failure in its Asiatic policy, which after the defeat of Japan and after the decolonisation process could have been hoped to impose upon Asia a sort of condominium, within which China would have had the role of the junior partner. The ideological conflict and the clashes in 1969 along the Sino-Soviet border were followed instead by the fear, widespread in Soviet public opinion, of an irrational, dangerous and threatening China. A defence against the yellow danger was felt to be necessary and a fourth of the land-based Soviet forces were drawn up against China. We should also not forget the importance of the Chinese influence on Eastern Europe as an alternative model to the Soviet Union, for instance in the rural sector.[9] After the Cultural Revolution, China did not hesitate to draw closer to the United States. For the Soviet Union the danger has changed in nature and presents itself as a possible encircling from the East and/or more stringent competition with the United States, which could implement such an encirclement with Chinese co-operation.

Therefore the Soviet Union pursued towards China a double-track-policy: military containment (the SS20s targeted on China) and the search for political agreements – renouncement of the use of force or a treaty of non-aggression – and commercial and cultural agreements. The opening up towards China has its most significant starting point in the Brezhnev speech in Tashkent on March 24, 1982, although some points in that speech were surely not acceptable for Beijing.[10] However, thanks also to periodical consultations, the axis of Soviet-Chinese relations has moved from the collision course as in the 1970s to the perspectives of a partial and gradual détente, although everything induces to exclude the possibility to go back to the alliances of the 1950s.[11]

These attempts were welcomed by China, which at the same time could not but take notice of the fact that the USSR was persevering in its old policy of suspicion: military dislocation along the border (despite some hints of a withdrawal of troops from Mongolia), intervention in Afghanistan and support of Vietnam in Cambodia.

With Japan the problem of the Kurile Islands is still a stumbling block. Since 1979 the Soviet Union has been reinforcing its military presence on the islands and other initiatives followed: strengthening of the Soviet fleet in the Pacific Ocean, limitations to the fishing rights of the Japanese, increasing air activity along the Japanese borders and finally the shooting down of the Korean airliner. All that has deepened Japanese mistrust above all within the public opinion.

However, the dangers of Soviet aggression are very much less for Japan than those theoretically conceivable in Central Europe.[12]

The Vietnamese victory against the United States was a success for the USSR even if it had to take over a very heavy financial burden (from \$3 to 5.5 billion per day). The entry as a full member of Vietnam into Comecon in June 1978 and the signature of a Friendship Treaty were the preconditions which made the Vietnamese invasion of Cambodia possible and gave the USSR naval bases in Cam Ranh Bay and Danang. The militarisation of the Sino-Vietnamese conflict in February 1979 was quite useful for the USSR because it opened a new front against China without any direct Soviet involvement. In the same spirit the incidents around the Spratley Islands in March 1988 were very helpful, inasmuch as they maintained a climate of distrust between China and Vietnam.

Such positive Soviet results had two negative aspects. First: the United States after its humiliation in Vietnam was forced to do whatever possible to take up again the mantle of a Great Power in the Pacific and therefore in Asia. Second: the members of ASEAN were adding to the previous fear of the Chinese expansion, a more actual fear of a new momentum of Soviet expansion in the region. It could be an irony of fate, that Soviet difficulties in Afghanistan started just when a communist government took power in Kabul: at that moment a popular and religious opposition rose up.[13] The reasons for the invasion are still obscure and it is useless to speculate on them. Let us only take notice of the fact that it revealed itself as a great failure.

More encouraging were the relations with India after the Friendship Treaty of 1971. For the Soviet Union India is its most important contact with the movement of the Non-Aligned countries and India has the great advantage of not belonging to the group of states with a socialist orientation. The Soviet Union has not yet succeeded in the attempt to make India its best ally in South-East Asia as a pivot of a whole system. On the contrary there are elements for possible future friction inasmuch as India pretends to play in the region the role of the Great Power able to protect everybody (its intervention in Sri Lanka is a very eloquent example). The USSR therefore does all in its power to avoid India indulging in too strict relations with other states, from China to the United States.

The attitude towards Iran and towards the crisis in the Persian Gulf would require lengthy examination. It could be that the Soviet Union has for long been nurturing the project of advancing through Iran to the Persian Gulf, but any such initiative has now to confront itself with Islamic fundamentalism.

Since March 1985 when the Soviet Union came under the leadership of Gorbachev, it has given the impression in Asia as well as elsewhere that it is willing to pursue its objectives in a more articulate manner. The heart of this new dynamism is the trend towards considering the Asian-Pacific area instrumental in the modernisation of the Soviet economy. In this light should be interpreted the Soviet wish to become a member of the Pacific Economic Co-operation Conference (PECC) and to give hospitality to the next meeting in Vladivostok in 1990. Gorbachev recalls not only the 'common European house' but also the fact that the Soviet Union is an important Asiatic power (*Pravda*, 16 January 1986) or that most of the Soviet Union lies East from the Urals (*Pravda*, 29 July 1986). At the 27th Congress of the CPSU, Gorbachev quoted the Asiatic policy as the most important course of action along with the European policy.

The operational proposal for a 'Panasiatic Forum' (put forward during Indian Premier Rajiv Gandhi's visit to Moscow in May 1985) recalls a previous proposal of Brezhnev for a system of collective security in Asia (7 June 1969): at that time the aim was the isolation of China and a reinforcement of the American withdrawal from continental Asia, while now the main aim is the inclusion of China within the system.

Anyway the most important statement of the renewed Soviet dynamism is Gorbachev's speech in Vladivostok on 26 July 1986. In that speech Gorbachev brings forward a realistic recognition of the United States as a Great Power in the Pacific with legitimate interests in Asia as well: he no longer spoke of a Panasiatic Forum, but of a Conference on the Pacific, to be held in Hiroshima, as he would like to renovate the miracle of Helsinki. According to Western translation the invited countries would be those bordering the Pacific Ocean, whilst the Russian text uses a different word (*Tjagotejushchie*) which means gravitating towards the Pacific Ocean. However, the identification of the United States with the nuclear danger is a part of the general campaign for an Asiatic security system: an idea which should be further analysed to discover how much it could match the concept of the European security. Let us not forget that such a parallelism was mentioned by Brezhnev himself back in 1969 and that the project for a denuclearised Pacific has found support.

The reactions to the Vladivostok speech have been cautious. Japan expressed itself against it as long as the territorial problem was not overcome; China rejects such ideas as long as nuclear disarmament is not spoken about and as long as the Afghanistan and Cambodia crises are not settled; the United States has taken an attitude of great reservation; India remains aloof as it does each time that a potential understanding between China, the United States and the USSR appears on the horizon.

In any case, even under Gorbachev, at least so far, relations with China remain the central point for the Soviet Union. The Soviet Union must operate on two different levels: the relations between the two Communist Parties and the relations between the two states. The offers to China in the Vladivostok speech (a settlement of the border along the Amur river, the building of a railroad from Kazakhstan to Sinkiang, the withdrawal of a symbolic 8000 men from Afghanistan) were not enough for Beijing. The same disappointment was clear in China in connection with the negotiations on the dismantlement of the INF in Europe, but in the first phase not of those targeted on China. Quite vague Soviet offers for a balanced reduction of conventional forces in Asia (an Asiatic MBFR?) were not sufficient to settle Chinese uneasiness.

The recent developments are opening new perspectives. The withdrawal from Afghanistan will not bring peace to that country, but will bring hope in China. The possible withdrawal from Cambodia is another positive element for a concrete amelioration of Sino-Soviet relations. It would not be appropriate to consider that these two moves, however significant and partially surprising they may be, will settle in a short time all possible disagreements between two major powers, which are still competitors in Asia ideologically and politically. The uncertain situation in Afghanistan, because of the danger of a civil war, and the difficult settlement in Cambodia and in the area as a whole cast doubts on the future.[14]

With Japan, Gorbachev has been courageous: visits at high level have broken the ice, but they were not able to make steps towards a settlement of the territorial controversy. It could be considered a positive fact that the USSR declares itself ready to discuss the matter, but any hope for an early solution would not be realistic, even if improved commercial relations (after the Tenth Session of the Mixed Commission in April 1986) can help create a better atmosphere.

Foreign Minister Shevardnadze's visits to Vietnam, Thailand, Indonesia and Australia in May 1987 have been very interesting. The aims were several: from commercial co-operation to the search for a way out on Cambodia, which remains a reason for the mistrust of the ASEAN countries. We should also mention the Soviet Union's intention of asking for fishing and anchorage rights. Also to be mentioned are the now elapsed agreement of August 1985 with Kiribati and of January 1987 with Vanuatu, and the signing of Protocols 2 and 3 of the South Pacific Nuclear-Free-Zone Treaty, even if only China among the nuclear states followed the example.

On a different level, we should mention the awkward relationship between the Soviet Union and North Korea, including the Soviet decision to participate in the Olympic Games in Seoul.

The most recent developments confirm, albeit with many contradictions and lingering uncertainties, this Soviet course of action and Gorbachev's visits to India underline the importance which Moscow intends to place on Asia.

The points of political attrition could be summarised as follows:

The danger of a national or nationalistic flare up from ethnical or religious sources persists in Central Asia. The case of Alma Ata and even more of Armenia involves the multinational dimension of the USSR and jeopardises the internal borders and many fundamental concepts of Soviet beliefs as a socialist and multinational country. It is not easy to interpret correctly some omissions, as for instance in the speech on the occasion of the 70th Anniversary of the October Revolution, in which the peoples of Central Asia were not mentioned as participants in the common struggle for socialism.[15]

The bipolar relationship, which is apparently successful with the United States, does not work elsewhere; we should not forget that two nuclear powers are present in Asia and that they do not intend yet to enter at short notice into a nuclear disarmament process. Therefore the content of the future relations between China and the USSR has to be clarified.[16]

The necessity of modernising the system impels the USSR to entertain a closer relationship with the highly industrialised countries of the world and therefore propels it in the direction of a development, which finds its inspiration in capitalist ideas of economic management. This means a fading out of the traditional Soviet vision of fundamentally anti-Western international relations.

The future situation in Afghanistan after the withdrawal of the Soviet troops could presage a period of great instability due to Islamic fundamentalism and to a way of life which is far away from the Soviet *Weltanschauung*, which could have been represented in Afghanistan in a more modern vision of the structure of society.

The future relations with Iran and the Persian Gulf as a whole are a great question mark, inasmuch as they will exert directly or indirectly an influence on the destinies of Soviet Central Asia.

We could support the idea – as it was said in the past referring to the Eurasian heartland[17] – that Central Asia is the unconquerable and hard core of the USSR as a European and Asiatic power. Therefore the Soviet Union goes on with its efforts to contain future crises: in Afghanistan, in Central Asia, with China, with Iran, with South-East Asia. However imaginative and flexible the 'new thinking' of the Soviet leadership could be, the Soviet threat will still exist in the near future in Asia, because the antagonisms are still there: perhaps more a political than a military threat. We have to consider as a main point the Asiatic dimension of the Soviet Union, because in the last resort Asia and its problems will represent the objective limitations of the Soviet Union as an effective and real super-power.

Notes

1. S. Fagiolo, *La Russia di Gorbaciov*, Rome, 1988, p. 122 ff; C.E. Black in I.J. Lederer (ed.), *Russian Foreign Policy*, New Haven and London, 1962, p. 3–37 *passim*.
2. C. Keeble (ed.), *The Soviet State*, London, 1985, p. 157.
3. H. Carrère d'Encausse, *L'Empire éclaté*, Paris, 1978, *passim*; G. Simon, *Nationalismus und Nationalitätenpolitik in der Sowjetunion*, Baden-Baden, 1986, *passim*; R. Pipes, *The Formation of the Soviet Union*, Cambridge, 1964, *passim*; A.L. Weeks in *Journal of Defense Diplomacy*, 5, n. 7, 1987, p. 28–32.
4. R. Medvedev, *La democrazia socialista*, Firenze, 1977, p. 330.
5. K. Fritsch in *Osteuropa*, 33, 2, Feb. 1983, p. 125–140.
6. Zaki Laidi in *Le Monde*, Feb.24, 1988.
7. R. Holbrook in *Foreign Affairs*, 64, 4, p. 744.
8. Gelman in *Adelphi Papers*, 217, Spring 1987.

9. L. Valsalice (Ferraris) in *Civitas*, n. 1, gennaio 1972
10. G. Segal, *Sino-Soviet relations after Mao*, Adelphi Papers 202; Griffith in *Problems of Communism*, 32, March–April 1983, p. 20.
11. M. Dassu', *La frontiera difficile*, Roma 1986, p. 237.
12. T. Kataoka in *Problems of Communism*, 33, March–April 1984, p. 1–16.
13. H. Vogel (Hrsg), *Die sowjetische Intervention in Afghanistan*, Baden-Baden, 1980; Z.Khalizad in *Problems of Communism*, 35, Jan–Feb. 1986, p. 1–20.
14. Statement of Mr. Gulguddin Hekmayer in *Le Monde*, March 16, 1988; Haller in *Die Zeit*, March 11, 1988.
15. U. Halbach, 'Perestrojka und Nationalitätenproblematik' in *Berichte des Bundesinstituts für ostwissenschaftliche und internationale Studien*, n. 38, 1987.
16. P.J. Opitz, *Die chinesische Außenpolitik in den achtziger Jahren*, Akademie für politische Bildung Tutzing, 1, Nov.1984.
17. H.J. Mackinder, *Democratic Ideals and Reality*, London, 1904.

Index